Child Abuse

The educational perspective

Edited by Peter Maher

BASIL BLACKWELL

© National Association for Pastoral Care in Education
First published 1987

Published by Basil Blackwell Limited
108 Cowley Road
Oxford OX4 3JF
England

British Library Cataloguing in Publication Data

Child abuse: the educational perspective.
  1. Child abuse – Prevention
  I. Maher, Peter
  362.7'044   HV715

  ISBN 0-631-15071-4
  ISBN 0-631-15072-2 Pbk

Typeset in 10 on 12pt Sabon
by Columns of Reading
Printed in Great Britain by
T.J. Press Ltd, Cornwall

To Rachel

Acknowledgements

I should like to record my gratitude to some individuals and organisations without whose help this project could never have been started. To Marge Mayes who has been a constant source of support and encouragement throughout and has acted as unpaid secretary, personal assistant, seminar administrator, receptionist, counsellor and in many other roles. The design of the logo, which appears on the front cover, was hers, and to her and John Bailey who did the original artwork for that logo, my grateful thanks. To Michael Marland for his support at a personal and professional level, for his work at the Seminar and for his thoughtful Preface to this book. To Olive Abbey for her hard work at the Seminar and her support throughout. To Susan Creighton and Eileen Vizard whose help and direction in the early days encouraged me to go on.

To Richard Whitfield who, while at Save the Children, recognised the importance of the project and persuaded that organisation and others to offer financial support. To Philip Noyes of the NSPCC and Dennis Lampard of Dr Barnardo's who had the task of representing their organisation throughout the project. Of course my thanks go to Save the Children, the NSPCC, Dr Barnardo's and to the Economic and Social Research Council who offered funding and support.

I cannot find the words to thank enough the authors of the chapters of this book. Their effort and their willingness to contribute to the seminar have helped beyond measure. My thanks to Rick Rogers for his efforts during the seminar and afterwards in making coherent sense of what was said. To James Nash and other staff at Basil Blackwell; their support and help, despite some 'kicking and screaming' in the face of my 'impossible' demands, has made this publication a reality.

To NAPCE: I received constant support and encouragement from the National Committee. Subsequently I have spoken with many NAPCE members, and other teachers, whose interest, concern and encouragement has reinforced my conviction in the issues contained here. NAPCE continues to speak for teachers who believe that care is an important aspect of their role. Oh for the day when all teachers will feel as we do and NAPCE will have completed its task! When all concerned with education place the intellectual, personal, social and moral education of pupils as the focus of their work.

Contents

Preface

Among the many aspects of the pastoral role of teachers, one which worries us all is our responsibility in relation to all forms of child abuse. Although it is a subject which from time to time captures the public indignation, and there has in recent years been very genuine concern from all sections of society, very little support has been given to teachers to help us with our contribution. What do teachers need to know about the psychiatry of child abuse? How should we be more sensitive to the signs? How should we respond to suspicions or to confidences given? What should we do?

The National Association for Pastoral Care, which has as one of its main aims the support of all teachers in the pastoral aspects of their role and especially pastoral team leaders, was therefore very grateful when Peter Maher, then its Secretary, developed the idea of the seminar that has led to this symposium. He brought together a knowledgeable and experienced group of contributors from the relevant specialisms and briefed them carefully to prepare papers which drew upon their wide clinical knowledge while also focusing closely on the school and the responsibilities of teachers. All present found the conference itself very successful; the unusual bringing together of the various specialisms with teachers and educational welfare officers proved a fruitful opportunity for mutual learning.

Peter Maher has drawn upon that seminar and subsequent work to produce this collection – the first study of the educational perspective of child abuse and the first book specially designed for teachers in schools and those who are educating teachers for the future. It will be invaluble for those who want to translate public indignation and sadness and professional worry into positive and realistic action. The National Association for Pastoral Care and all of us in education are grateful to the sponsoring organisations (*Save the Children Fund, Dr Barnardo's,* the *National Society for the Prevention of Cruelty to Children,* and the *Economic and Social Research Council*) and to Peter Maher for his far-seeing, determined, and thorough work to help us all.

> Michael Marland CBE MA
> Headteacher, North Westminster
> Community School; Honorary
> Professor of Education, Warwick
> University

Introduction

In 1984, when I came face to face with the sexual abuse of a young child for the first time, I felt absolutely helpless. This was just one of many emotions; the most difficult to deal with was anger. I felt angry for a number of reasons: angry because a young girl's innocence had been taken from her, harshly and brutally; angry because the man concerned had, it transpired, sexually abused a whole number of young girls. They in turn had dealt with it in different ways – some had kept 'the secret', others had tried to talk to adults about what had happened to them, but had not been believed. I felt angry because I had failed to read the signals that I had been offered. As a teacher and a parent, why had I been so blind? I felt angry because this man needed help; he even went as far as to re-offend after he had been charged with offences against four children. He did not get the help he needed and was eventually the subject of a brief supervision order. I was angry with the inadequacy of the law; charges relating to the two younger girls (both under ten years old) were dropped because there was little likelihood that in open court the girls' account of events would be accepted against the word of an adult.

I had to make something positive out of my anger. As a way of making my anger work constructively for me, I began to explore the issues through reading. What started off as an exploration of an area of work that was unfamiliar to me, developed into a deep concern that, as a profession, teachers generally were miserably ill-informed and largely ignorant. The information that *was* available to them was hopelessly inadequate and usually an adaptation of materials used by other professional groups. I could find little evidence of any attempt to consider what were the educational issues involved. Mostly, the material concentrated on detection and reporting of abuse; yet surely there were curricular issues to consider?

From the very start, I was aware of my motives; they may not have been the best, in seeking to start a project from a sense of anger, but at least they were honest. Over the coming months I was to learn the importance of motivation. In such a difficult and delicate area, one where your actions can have a dramatic effect on a child's life, you need to discover just what your motivation is. I was to see some work where the primary need being expressed was not the safety of the child but the need to work through some adult's psychological hang-up. Before you start to read this book my advice would be to analyse your own motivation carefully. You will be in no position at all to help a child until you know and understand how you feel about child abuse. Only when this is done should you begin to explore the problem.

My exploration was like a journey of discovery. I began, for obvious reasons, with the main focus of my attention on the issue of child sexual abuse. I soon discovered that to approach the work with that emphasis was like undertaking my journey with blinkers on. There were other forms of abuse, equally important, equally cruel, and equally likely to confront the teacher in school. What concerned me then, and still does today, was the number of fellow travellers I met on my journey who also wore those blinkers. For many of them, this particular form of abuse had become a crusade. Sexual abuse seemed to be turning into a *cause célèbre*, particularly for those radical feminists who pinpointed *power* as the abuse, not sexuality; its proponents tended to be dismissive of those who did not share their mission.

I have tried to understand why so many well educated and intelligent people could be so blind to the broader issues. In retrospect, I believe there to be a number of reasons for this. First, I think it is the very nature of sexual abuse which prompts such passionate emotions. It is often seen as a situation where men demonstrate their dominance over the other sex; a dominance which is misplaced and yet pervades so many aspects of our society still. As a cause, it has clear attractions. Such an approach does of course ignore the substantial number of boys who suffer sexual abuse. That too is symptomatic of a strange double-standard in operation: if a girl of, say, fourteen is sexually assaulted by a much older man, we protest loudly. What happens if a boy of fourteen is sexually assaulted by a much older woman? This is seen by some as socially acceptable; the boy has not been 'defiled', rather he has 'gained his spurs', 'grown into manhood' and so on. Such assault is rarely reported; it is only homosexual assault that merits our disapproval and which is the subject of the significant proportion of professional work with sexually-abused boys. For the sexually-abused boy, though, despite what may seem to be the 'tacit approval' of our society, the experience can be equally as horrific as for a girl; it is just as likely to affect his normal sexual development, and influence the way that he is able to cope with relationships in adulthood.

The second possible explanation for an over-emphasis on sexual abuse, as opposed to other forms of abuse, is again related to the nature of the assault. In physical abuse, we can understand, though not excuse, a parent who suffers such a range of stress that they lash out and injure their child. In cases of neglect, we can find excuses about the inadequacy of the parents that causes them to abandon the proper care of their children. In emotional abuse, we too can probably find examples of children we have known who have been difficult to like or love. In such circumstances it is easy to lash out with the tongue, rather than the fist, to inflict injury without there being any physical signs; emotional abuse is understandable. In these three forms of abuse we could almost say, 'there but for the grace of God . . .'

What of sexual abuse? How do we rationalise that? Some of the horrors and travesties that are carried out in the name of sexual abuse are so perverted, so abnormal, so inexcusable. Whilst we could think ourselves through a set of circumstances that might lead us to commit any other form of abuse, sexual abuse is a negation of everything we stand for in a civilised society. Sexual abuse makes us angry.

Since sexual abuse is so horrific, I do not intend to undervalue the work of those who work exclusively in this field. I have tried to maintain a balanced view. If we are going to understand child abuse, we need to understand it in all its forms. If we are going to be alert to signals that children offer us, which they may well do, when they need help, we need to have a broad understanding of the range of ways in which they suffer. If we are going to search for educational responses to child abuse, we need to look for appropriate responses to *all* forms of abuse and not develop a morbid pre-occupation with abuse in just one form.

The route that my journey took was important. I took my direction from some early reading, particularly of the works of Kempe, and from some of those I met along the way. The journey that I took was important in terms of developing my broad understanding of the problem. The culmination of that journey was at Stoke Rochford where I tried to bring together some of the people and the issues, to focus upon the educational implications of what we knew. An account of the Stoke Rochford experience is included on page 233 as an appendix to this book.

This book tries to trace at least part of that journey, so that you, the reader, can share the experience and hopefully learn, as I did, from the journey itself. It is my sincere hope that you will read this book from cover to cover. By walking that path you will begin to understand the enormity of the problem of child abuse. However, this is also intended to be a reference book. The aspects of child abuse that are covered, and the issues that are raised about the possible educational responses to child abuse, can and should be referred to when you need to know about any particular aspect of the problem.

The chapters of this book, taken in turn, mark the direction of the journey. The first, and in some ways the most important, step was to understand the historical and cultural setting within which child abuse takes place. This understanding can give us the clearest understanding of what actions we, as a society, need to take if we are to try to reduce levels of child abuse in future generations. Attitudes and historically-determined assumptions about the way that we operate as a society and about the way that we deal with children combine to create a climate in which abuse of children takes place.

The second phase was to come to terms with the extent of the problem. It soon became clear that nobody had an overall picture of the levels of abuse. The NSPCC take action on, and keep records of, the cases that are notified directly to them, but local authorities all over the country keep separate records of other cases dealt with by the local Social Services Department. All local authorities keep records of cases of child abuse notified to their local child abuse register, but some are held by the NSPCC on their behalf. Although that register is held by the NSPCC the majority of children on it will be helped by social workers from the local Social Services Department. The areas where the NSPCC holds the register cover some 10% of the child population of England and Wales. The research on these registers, which forms the background to Chapter 2 by Susan Creighton, constitutes the largest, continuous epidemiological study of child abuse to be conducted in the UK.

Child abuse registers however, reflect the *reported* cases of abuse; there is no way of knowing how many other children are subject to abuse. All that is possible was to draw statistical inference from the figures that the NSPCC hold, or to rely upon retrospective studies, using adults to recount their childhood experiences of abuse. As a consequence, we have no real idea of the nature and extent of the global problem; despite this, some of the conclusions that can be drawn about the potential levels of abuse in our society are frightening.

An understanding of the statistical background is important. It is too easy to assume that the problem is only marginal and therefore of only limited importance to us. In fact, all the indications are that we are dealing with an issue which is likely to affect the lives of a significant minority of children and families. It is this understanding that makes our consideration of the ways of detecting, reporting and reducing abuse such an urgent one.

The third signpost on the journey concerns the context within which abuse takes place. For many years we have talked to children about the dangers of 'going with strangers'; yet the statistics now help us to understand that a considerable proportion of abuse, in all its forms, takes place within the family or whilst the child is with some other trusted relative or adult. Disturbingly, abuse occurs relatively frequently when the child is in the charge of a professional carer, teacher, youth worker and so on.

Such an understanding naturally leads us to the fourth and next important area of work: that is, to examine the ways in which abusing families operate. What is it in the ways that some families function that makes them work? Can we conclude anything about families that are disfunctioning? Has this study anything to teach us about the way that we help such families and how we work with them? Are there any clues here about the parenting skills which need, generally, to be taught?

By this stage we begin to have a broad understanding of the issues relating to child abuse and are in a better position to understand the different forms of maltreatment of children. We need then to study different forms of abuse and this detail is contained in the three chapters that follow. Chapter 5 looks at physical abuse, how to recognise it, and how to respond; Chapter 6 focuses on emotional abuse and neglect, an area of work that we are only just beginning to come to terms with; Chapter 7 concerns sexual abuse, the starting point for my journey.

What comes through in each of these sections, is the need for teachers and other professional groups to work together in a multi-disciplinary team, if the problems of abuse are to be dealt with appropriately. Chapter 8 describes the procedures that have been developed over time for such an interdisciplinary working arrangement. It sets out clearly the role of those involved, where their responsibilities lie and where they might conflict. As we identify later, there is an urgent need for teachers to come to terms with this area of work, before they actually venture into the field of abuse cases.

The more you study the problems associated with child abuse, the more you begin to appreciate some of the areas where schools can play a very positive educative role. One of these is in parenthood-related education. If you intend to do work in this area you will need to understand how parenthood has been changed by trends in society; by divorce, separation and remarriage. Structures in society have undergone significant changes, and this change process is still operating. The breakdown of the extended family creates different problems that are a reality for many children. Again we find clues here as to how we might approach the question of what might constitute an appropiate 'preparation for parenthood' curriculum. There has already been a substantial amount of research in this area and the ideas put forward in Chapter 9 are particularly well developed.

The final two chapters concentrate specifically upon the role of the teacher and the school. These two sections have been illuminated by, among other things, the discussions at Stoke Rochford. It is well worth reading the Appendix on page 233 which contains a brief outline of that weekend in the Spring of 1986. What was so unusual about it was that, for the first time, groups from different areas of interest were brought together. They included clinicians, psychologists, psychotherapists, psychiatrists and paediatricians, social workers, a police officer, parents, health visitors, researchers – all, for the most part, working directly with abused children and their families – and people with a direct interest in education; a Chief Education Officer, HMI, teacher trainers, Education Welfare Officers and a range of teachers at different levels in the profession from schools throughout the country.

The specific task set that group was to raise the issues about the different constituent elements that go to make up the problem of child abuse, and to consider educational responses. The starting point for these discussions were the ten papers that I commissioned for that seminar; most of which appear, some in an amended form, as chapters in this book. One chapter, by Dr Kevin Browne, who was present at the seminar, and his colleague, Dr Sarah Saqi, is a report of work that they were carrying out at the time. Many of the ideas that I have drawn upon in compiling these last two chapters are those which emerged through the discussion at that weekend. Having said that, the views and conclusions that I have drawn must be considered my own since they may not reflect the views of all those present. Neither should the following chapters be considered other than as free-standing, authoritative accounts, written by experts in the field. Those authors may not necessarily want to be tied to the conclusions that I have reached.

The first of the final two chapters looks at the area that I have described as *reactive*; that is the role of the school in detecting and reporting cases of child abuse and in supporting those children in a school setting. The second of the two chapters was much more difficult to write; it focuses upon the *proactive*, the role that schools might play in helping to reduce levels of abuse in future generations. It is a truism to say that the adults who will be abusing their children in the next generation, are students, sitting in our classrooms today. If we could find ways of altering their attitudes we might be a most potent force in reducing levels of abuse when these students grow up and become parents in the future. Inevitably, the arguments are highly complex and pervade everything we do in schools. I suggest that it is not simply a matter of, 'what do we teach?' but is more properly an analysis of the different factors which contribute to an abusing environment and the ways in which schools might affect these. The stress then is on emphasis and orientation rather than solely on particular curricular materials.

All that I can hope for, through this book, is to raise the issue. If only one teacher in every school were to accept the importance of the problem and press, with determination and persistence, for its urgent attention, we might find an effective way to bring about change. We need, as a professional group, and in consort with other professions, to consider a whole range of matters of mutual interest.

What drives me on is the certainty that every day we delay, that we fail to consider the problem properly, that we miss the signals that children offer us, that we engage in inter- and intra-professional argument about where the responsibility lies or whose job it is, more children are being damaged, assaulted, abused and killed. For the sake of those children and the thousands more who will die or suffer in future generations, we need to accept responsibility and to take action; and we need that action *NOW!*

Chapter 1

The historical and cultural context of child abuse

Eileen Vizard

The recent emergence of 'the child', from an historical context, as a person with qualitatively different needs from the adult, has thrown into relief our difficulties in defining child abuse.

Historical context

Historical studies of childhood are surprisingly rare. Although references to ordinary children and their lives do crop up in ancient Greek and Roman literature, mediaeval art and many religious writings on child rearing throughout the centuries, it is striking how few of these describe *happy* children.

Attempts have been made to rationalise many grossly inhumane child rearing practices (such practices include customs of female infanticide, severe whipping and beating of babies and toddlers, swaddling, sexual usage of children etc.) as being 'normal' within a particular context. For example, in a study reviewing 600 years of letters from 26 fathers to their sons Valentine[1] was unable to find one father who was not insensitive, moralistic and self-centred. Nevertheless, the author concludes that 'the happiest fathers leave no history, and it is the men who are not at their best with their children who are likely to write the heart-rending letters which survive.' In a review of 250 biographies of childhood, Burr also notes that there are no happy memories recorded.[2] No conclusions about the nature of childhood are drawn by this historian. Lloyd de Mause, in a comprehensive review of the historical literature on childhood, notes that in many such studies

masses of evidence (of child abuse and unhappiness) are hidden, distorted, softened or ignored. The child's early years are played down, formal educational content is endlessly examined, and emotional content is avoided by stressing child legislation and avoiding the home.[3]

De Mause's thesis is that childhood in antiquity, and until very recently, was a time of misery, exploitation and abuse. By contrast, the historian, Phillipe Aries, seems to present an idealised picture of childhood in his work *Centuries of Childhood*.[4] Two main points support his argument:

1   That a separate concept of childhood was unknown in the early Middle Ages, and was 'invented' in the early modern period (ie the 18th century).
2   That the modern family restricts the child's freedom in a tyrannical way, destroying friendship and sociability, and inflicting upon the child the birch and the prison cell.

However, as mentioned earlier, plenty of historical evidence exists (particularly in the fields of art and religion) to disprove the notion that childhood is a recent invention – children were always perceived as 'different' from adults. Sometimes, indeed, this perspective operated in a very primitive way involving projective processes whereby the child became the container for split-off good or (more usually) evil adult feelings. St Augustine describes children who 'suffer from a demon . . . they are under the power of the devil . . . some infants die in this vexation.' This use of the child as a sort of psychic 'dustbin' for adult projections, is closely linked to the phenomena of 'changelings', who were killed, and of swaddling, used as a method of containing and repressing the evil instinctual urges assumed to be rife in the newborn baby.

Although these historical views of the child are, by our standards, distorted and primitive, nevertheless these, and many other accounts of early attitudes towards childhood, make it clear that children were indeed seen as separate beings.

Aries' second notion, that modern children are tyrannised and abused within society, more than at any previous time, seems, from a longer historical perspective, to be totally untrue. Although more cases of child abuse are currently being reported, this does not mean that more children are being abused. In fact, there is evidence that deaths from child abuse, and serious types of child abuse, decrease in frequency after the introduction of prevention programmes in a particular area.[5]

This leads us on to attempt a definition of the child, bearing in mind this historical perspective on childhood. Interestingly, the Oxford English Dictionary[6] after pointing out the derivation of 'child', as from *cild-kilpam* – *inkilpo-pregnant* (quasi-fruit of the womb), goes on to give early references to the sometimes ambiguous gender ascribed to 'child' – eg 'a boy or a childe I wonder?' – *A Winter's Tale*III-iii 71; 'a female infant' (– 1611).

Here, child and female seem to be equated. Other usages of the term include references to 'origin, extraction, dependence, attachment,' etc. From this it seems that the two qualities typifying the historical use of the word 'child' are (*i*) uncertain gender, possibly feminine, and (*ii*) dependency upon an adult.

It follows that if the origins of the concept 'child' are rooted in femininity and dependence, then child rearing and childhood itself, may also relate to current attitudes about these matters. However, current anthropological thinking about the concept 'child', puts the meaning into two distinct frames of reference, as described by Jean La Fontaine:[7]

(a) 'Child', referring to a stage of development, and the biological, intellectual and social characteristics associated with it;
(b) 'Child' – as a set of terms indicating a particular structure of (social) relations, one element in what anthropologists term a kinship system.

In an anthropological sense, the boundaries between childhood and adulthood seem to depend, cross-culturally, upon the child's social status rather than upon his or her biological development. La Fontaine says 'Adulthood is always a matter of social definition, rather than physical maturity'. Modern anthropologists, therefore, put the child and childhood firmly into a social and institutional context, where the development of individual personality or behaviour patterns is only explicable in terms of societal norms and traditions.

This contrasts with earlier studies of child development and family life in 'primitive' societies typified by the work of Margaret Mead, where the assumption is of a simplistic, causal relationship between personality and its expression in behaviour. Margaret Mead's work has been heavily criticised on methodological grounds but a more important conceptual criticism seems to be her tendency to 'virtually ignore all Social Life outside the domestic sphere', ie the wider cultural and social issues.

In a praiseworthy attempt to overview the whole 'psychohistory' of childhood, from a predominantly psychoanalytical perspective, de Mause outlines a probable evolution in child rearing modes over the last 2000 years or so (Figure 1.1).

De Mause identifies six child rearing modes:

1 *Infanticidal mode* (Antiquity to 4th century AD)
In this period, female children were totally expendable, with the result that daughters were rarely reared in ancient Greece – 'of 600 families, from the 2nd Century Inscriptions at Delphi, one per cent raised two daughters.' In Henri Vallois's study of prehistoric fossils, he found a sex ratio of 148 : 100 in favour of men. The magical practice of sealing children in the walls of foundations of buildings and bridges, to strengthen them, dates from the wall of Jericho; it is today commemorated in the children's game 'London Bridge is Falling Down', when the catching of the child at the end of the game symbolises sacrifice of a child to the River Goddess.

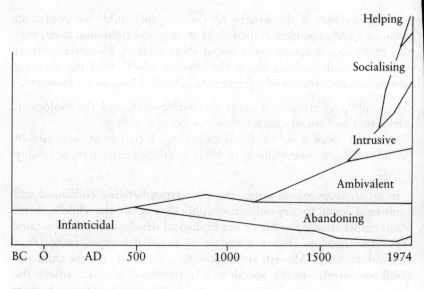

Figure 1.1

2   *Abandonment mode* (4th to 13th century)
In mediaeval religion, children were just about perceived as having souls, but primitive processes at work in their parents (described earlier) meant that children were feared and hated. Physical abandonment to nunneries and foster families; swapping of children between households so that they could be used as servants; and neglect of children's emotional needs, seemed to characterise this period. Regular beating of the child was still seen to be necessary, because of his, or her, inherent wickedness.

3   *Ambivalent mode* (14th to 17th century)
This period seems to show early attempts to develop what we might call 'relationships' between children and parents. According to de Mause, there was a proliferation of child instruction manuals, where the predominant notion in child development was of 'moulding' the child, both physically and emotionally, into a parental likeness. Ambivalence accompanied this attempt to mould the child, probably because of the concurrent perception that the child's needs were different from those of the adult.

4   *The intrusive mode* (18th century)
De Mause describes this as a period of further parental encroachment into the child – into its anger, its needs, its mind, its masturbation habits, its will. Those children directly raised by their own parents were

'prayed with, but not played with', hit, but not whipped, and punished (for masturbating) with threats and with guilt. Because the child was seen as less of a threat, empathy was possible, and so, de Mause explains, paediatrics and child health care were born.

5 *Socialisation mode* (19th to 20th century)
Included in this model of guiding children towards patterns of socially acceptable behaviour would be Freud's structural theory of superego and ego guiding id impulses; Skinner's behaviourism; and also presumably, the whole plethora of psychodynamic, cognitive and family therapies which have sprung up during this period. Even today, the socialisation mode of child rearing is probably the most commonly-held model in Western society.

6 *Helping mode* (mid-20th century)
This is described on the basis that the 'child knows best', that parents should be available to respond to the child's wishes, to empathise with the child, never disciplining the child, etc. Much of this 'helping mode', which is described in only four references, seems to put the parent in the role of therapist to the child. This approach could deprive the child of an appropriate parenting experience, and also, runs the risk of putting the child (I would suggest) in the new role of 'patient'. Nevertheless, de Mause's clear intention is to show that a co-operative approach between parent and child is possible in child rearing, and this in itself makes hopeful reading after the preceding catalogue of child abuse.

Overall, therefore, the suggestion is that an evolution in child rearing patterns in history has highlighted modes of child care which can be perceived within individual families today, and which may indicate their level of psychological functioning.

How far is it possible to apply the same criticisms to this historical view of mankind development as were applied to the model used by Margaret Mead and colleagues (see above), in tracking individual child and family behaviour? Individually-orientated psychodynamic models of personal development, valuable though they certainly are, omit cultural and social contexts which very strongly influence personal development. While de Mause's schema of child rearing modes through history is both ingenious and clarifying, there is a somewhat patronising assumption that earlier societal structures, such as those developed in antiquity and mediaeval times, were somehow less complex and less 'developed' than our current Western society. Anthropologists might dispute this point, saying that we are judging 'primitive' societies by our own inappropriate and value-laden norms.

Cultural context

Moving now from the historical context, it should be possible to discuss child abuse within a cultural backdrop. Again, we need to define our terms; before defining child abuse, perhaps we should look at those factors which affect our perception of the meaning of behaviour. These may be both internal (intrapsychic) and external (cultural), allowing a limited variation in how individuals within a society view events.

With child abuse, for instance, seeing is *not* necessarily believing. Sadly, the best form of this cognitive dissonance is to be found in the early medical literature on child abuse. Margaret Lynch has documented presentations of child abuse before Kempe.[8] She cites descriptions of recognisable child abuse, made by the 2nd century Greek physician, Soranus, as well as examples from 17th, 18th and 19th century medical writings on the same subject.

As Lynch points out, in 1860, Ambrose Tardieu, a French professor of legal medicine, described a series of 32 abused children, in great detail. Tardieu had described all the forensic, clinical and psychiatric features of the battered child, 100 years before Kempe wrote his classic paper. Why was there no response from the medical profession?

Jeffrey Masson, in his painstaking researches through the Freud Archives[9] (initially with the approval of Anna Freud, and also after study of the Freud/Fliess correspondence) discovered that Freud himself had decided to see, but not believe patients who continued to bring him childhood histories of sexual abuse. In doing this, Freud was obliged to deny his own initial clear perception that his patients were telling the truth, and, as a complex rationalisation for this denial, Freud's Oedipal Theory and theory of Infantile Sexuality was born.

Why should a respected and experienced doctor like Freud decide to go back on a theory linking cause and effect (ie childhood sexual abuse and adult neurosis), which seemed well borne out in clinical practice? Was it because Freud himself was ignorant of incest and child sexual abuse? Not according to Masson's researches, since at that time, post-mortem demonstrations in the Paris morgue, well attended by ambitious doctors in training, included the display of dead children, beaten to death and sexually abused by their caretakers. Freud was one of those doctors, and we know that he also had access to current medical literature (ie Tardieu's work) linking child abuse with parent figures.

Perhaps Freud's reasons for reneging on his (mostly female) patients, throw some light on *current* professional denial of child abuse. His reasons for refuting the 'seduction theory' could fall into two categories:

1 *Political / cultural* At a time when Jews were perceived as developing an alarming influence in Viennese political, business and academic spheres, Freud would not have wanted to point an accusing finger at the majority Gentile population, as child molesters. Conversely, Freud's discovery of childhood assault by fathers and male authority figures, would have posed an unacceptable threat to the Jewish patriarchy.

2 *Political / career* 19th century medical humanitarian reformers, such as Pinel, were removing the moral stigma of mental illness, and were emphasising 'illness' and 'recovery' as a model of the mind. The re-introduction of a moral component (as in 'mad/bad'), to explain assaultive behaviour, might not have been seen as acceptable, and would certainly not have been regarded as a 'progressive' medical/scientific view.

Following on from this point, is the traditional, yet probably quite current, medical preference for using theories about illness to play down the role of external events, which may be beyond the control even of doctors, and to play up theories of, say, bodily or psychological aetiology, giving doctors a prominent role in treatment.

Certainly, if the stunned and outraged reactions of Freud's colleagues to his delivery of the original paper *Studies on Hysteria*, linking childhood sexual assault and adult development of symptoms, was a reflection of current professional attitudes towards sexuality, then it is easy to see why Freud's career would have been very badly affected had he stuck to his guns. Kraft-Ebbing, at this meeting, said that Freud's work was a 'scientific fairytale'; the rest of the group sat in stony silence, and a synopsis of the papers itself was missing from the relevant scientific journal. Career-wise, Freud made the right decision not to believe his ears.

On a personal note, as Masson has indicated, Freud was in emotional turmoil throughout this time. His personal analysis had started, and this led towards unwelcome memories of his own sexual feelings and experiences in childhood '... carnal feelings towards mater' and the memory of being sexually assaulted by a nurse in childhood.

At the same time, Freud was engaged in a voluminous correspondence with his colleague, Fliess, updating him about the developments in his thinking, and seeking advice about theory and practice. It is clear that Freud was dependent on Fliess in a way which suggests his need for a supportive father figure, and it is also likely that Freud's high opinion of Fliess's psychological sophistry was inflated by this dependent attitude. Perhaps, like most of us, Freud could only be courageous in company. Lacking either external or internal support for his views, he abandoned them.

These criticisms are all very well, of course, but in focusing too closely on Freud's personal difficulties vis-a-vis child abuse, do we run the risk of taking too narrow a view, and omitting the wider 19th century cultural context? This cultural context is of great importance, since we know that sexual and physical abuse of children and women was not necessarily considered abusive. It might almost be seen as an extension of the rights of the father or husband, enabling him to express his 'ownership' of his dependants, by demonstrating his power over them.

An example of the really quite casual attitude towards usage of children and dependants, prevalent until as late as the 19th century, was the commonly-held view that intercourse with a child was a cure for venereal disease. Presumably the child's participation in the sexual act then needed to be rationalised as provocation or wantonness, in order to free the Victorian perpetrator from any sense of responsiblity or impropriety.

Such rationalisations were helpfully supplied by medical men of the time, such as Paul Brouardel, Dean of the Faculty of Medicine in Paris in 1880. He observed that 'Girls accuse their fathers of imaginary assaults on them or on other children, in order to obtain their freedom to give themselves over to debauchery.'[10] This statement was made on the basis of quite extensive medical contact with child victims of rape and battering, both living and in post mortem.

This cultural attitude towards abuse was upheld by the legal system which described a man's dependants as his property. It should be remembered that not until the late 19th century were most married women in England allowed to own property. The concept of ownership of one's body, for instance, would certainly have seemed a strange one to Victorian woman.

If we do not understand a society's value system, how can we make judgemental statements about the behaviour of its members? This is the problem of cultural relativity, so familiar to anthropologists in the field. Cultural relativity makes it difficult for us to be objective about child rearing practices in other cultures; at first glance, it might make the task of defining child abuse cross-culturally, seem an impossible one.

In her introduction to *Child Abuse and Neglect – Cross Cultural Perspectives*,[11] Jill Korbin addresses some of these issues. She describes three levels on which cultural considerations may affect our attempt to define child abuse and neglect:

1   Practices viewed as acceptable by one culture, but as abusive or neglectful by another. Such practices might include harsh initiation rites involving, for example, genital operations, seen as an essential 'entry' into a culture as an adult; or, in Western society, practices such as leaving children to cry, unattended, until the correct time for feeding arrives.

2   Behaviours which are defined as abusive by that particular society –

such as idiosyncratic abuse or neglect, signalling a departure from normally tolerated cultural behaviours.
3 Societal abuse and neglect of children – poverty, inadequate housing, inadequate nutrition etc.

These three definitional levels of child abuse provide a useful frame of reference for thinking about departures from the norm. Even so, can we make any clear statements about what constitutes 'normal' child rearing in the 20th century?

The same difficulties of cultural relativism which we have discussed in relation to abusing behaviours also affect our perceptions of 'normal' behaviour. We might say, with a philosophical shrug, 'So what?', as long as we can define departures from the norm. However, the lack of a normative data base about child rearing practices throughout the world, has direct implications, for instance, in funding public health programmes, and clinical research. How can we know which child abuse prevention programmes should be funded, when we may not be absolutely certain which child abusing behaviours should be prevented within certain cultural contexts? Naturally, although striving for scientific objectivity, clinical researchers are likely to ask questions which are influenced by their own cultural values, and analysis of results is likely to relate to controls who embody the normative characteristics which the researcher is trying to measure. Of course, these methodological and philosophical considerations are by no means confined to child abuse research.

Clinical context

If we assume that within our society, Korbin's second level of idiosyncratic abuse or neglect is the type of abuse which concerns us as clinicians, it might be helpful to look briefly at those factors which seem to perpetuate this cycle of abuse, from one generation to another. We might think of these as intra-familial cultural factors, and it is interesting to note that a substantial body of literature is now emerging, linking both social and cultural characteristics and a past family history of child abuse in the parents, with a risk of subsequent abuse of their own children.

The sorts of social and cultural factors associated with child abuse across the generations have been described by Oliver in a recent study,[12] and by many other researchers.[13] It seems as if young parental age, a criminal record of violence (in the father in particular), prematurity and neonatal problems in the child, physical handicap or illness in the child, coupled with social isolation, overcrowding and low income, are all cultural factors which increase the likelihood of child abuse. Arguably, unemployment may also be associated with child abuse.[14]

Physically- and sexually-abused children are abused by parents who are themselves victims. If we look at the staggeringly high levels of incest and sexual abuse among prostitutes and adult male sex offenders (at a conservative estimate 50-60% and 74% respectively),[15] and when we remember that 54% of adolescent boy sex offenders against young children have a history of phsyical and sexual child abuse themselves as children, and also that teenage runaways from home commonly appear to be running away from abusing and incestuous home situations, straight into danger and exploitation in the inner cities, we begin to get a sense of the way in which this problem is inexorably carried on across the generations.

Clinical experience in working with abusing families indicates that shame and worry about legal consequences helps maintain a conspiracy of silence about the actual prevalence of this problem. However, it would be simplistic to imagine that child abuse is perpetrated merely on the basis of learnt patterns of family behaviour. Work with victims and their families makes it clear how much these deviant patterns are internalised into the mind of the victim. When that victim grows up, a process of identification with the aggressor may occur, allowing, in different ways for boys and girls, a recreation in adult life of the initial abusing situation. Analysts might say, extraordinary though this appears, that an unconscious drive to have the abuse repeated may represent, in part, reparative wishes on behalf of adult victims.

Whatever the psychic motivation for perpetuating child abuse, it is clear that these experiences etch a never-to-be-forgotten line on the minds of victims, leaving them with a chronic sense of damage and inner destruction.[16] A 65-year-old grandmother has said that every day of her life, she has thought about the sexual assault she suffered at the hands of a close relative when she was six years old. Many victims say 'You never forget'; there are unhappy echoes here, of those accounts of childhood which we earlier looked at in an historical context. Even today, a very substantial minority of children may be growing up and spending their childhoods in pain, fear and misery.

This seems an absolutely appalling situation today – how can it happen? We also need to examine whether in fact the same levels of child abuse occur worldwide in every country today. Looking at the wider cultural context, it seems as if the value of children, as persons, may in some way relate to their treatment by adults. A really striking instance of this is described by Jill Korbin in her chapter 'Very Few Cases: child abuse and neglect in the People's Republic of China', in *Child Abuse and Neglect: Cross-Cultural Perspectives*. According to Korbin, before the liberation in China, although no specific studies had been done on child abuse, the reported experiences of anthropologists and other Western travellers in the country confirmed a very high rate of almost mediaeval exploitation and abuse of young children. Child labour, female infanticide, feet binding, prostitution of children etc were commonplace, and children could apparently be killed or sold at their parents' discretion.

By contrast, accounts of child rearing coming out of China since the 1960s, indicate a drastically changed situation. Because of the ideological basis of Chinese society, the State has the ultimate responsibility for feeding, clothing, housing and educating children. Importantly, since children are seen as 'the future of our nation', the well-being of Chinese children is now in the hands of the whole of the local community, and not left solely to parents, who may not be able to cope.

The following statement by a Chinese worker, quoted by Korbin, illustrates this point.

'Physical punishment is strictly forbidden in all schools. If a child is illtreated by his parents, the neighbours usually interfere. Sometimes the neighbourhood committee (the grassroots level) comes and criticises the parents; sometimes they are educated by the leadership of their working places. But if the case is a serious one, or the child is badly hurt, then it is brought to the community committee or even the local Public Security Bureau (the local police headquarters as called here), where the parents are questioned or detained. – Legal procedures – depends on the gravity of the offence and the attitude of the offenders. – There is a feeling among the people that child mistreatment is something intolerable. So anyone who does harm to children is condemned by public opinion and is punished by law'.

This Chinese experience is in direct contrast to the clinical examples, quoted above, of cycles of abuse being repeated again and again over generations, with little hope of change. It seems as if society *can* cause change in such patterns of behaviour, but it is also clear that this needs to be a co-ordinated attempt at change, supported by individual citizens, and by the legal system. Where there is external disapproval of child abuse, and sanctions against it, abusing parental behaviour can apparently be reduced. More information from this particular cultural context would be helpful.

In a curious way, however, the effectiveness of an integrated social response to child abuse, in China, is reflected in our own limited clinical experience with a co-ordinated multidisciplinary approach to the management of child abuse in England.[17] One hypothesis is that abusing families have never internalised a clear set of rules about boundaries and behaviour, and that this needs to be imposed first of all from the outside before internal change in members of the families can be expected.

The politics of child abuse

What do we know about the value of children in a wider cultural context? And how does this relate to the politics of child abuse? Feminists have been helpful in giving us indications of possible answers to this question.[18] From a feminist viewpoint, the politics of abuse relate to the mis-use of power within relationships, where adult women and (predominantly female) children, are subjugated and abused within a patriarchal society. Looking at the family dynamics in child abuse,[19] it is clear that a skew in power relationships is indeed present in these families, and we might ask ourselves how much abusing parents are actually reflecting wider societal attitudes. David Gil[20] has described three levels of abuse in society:

1 the abuse of children domestically;
2 institutional abuse of children;
3 societal abuse of children.

If we look at the third level of child abuse within society, it may be possible to find certain attitudes in society which condone or allow abusing behaviours towards children, such as their use in child prostitution (now very greatly on the increase worldwide) and 'kiddy porn'. Again, a feminist view would be that since women and children are still linked in the male mind as dependants and chattels, their abuse in a domestic situation is merely an extension of sexual power politics into the home.

This argument somewhat weakens when we look at the situation of men and boys as victims of abuse, usually by other men. Sexual abuse of young boys is much more common than is usually imagined.[21] While abuse of power may play some role here, it is also likely that internal factors in the perpetrator, discussed above, affect the choice of victim.

In her paper, *Incest, Intimacy and Inequality*, Jean La Fontaine[22] makes the point that '. . . the kinship relationship (between father and daughter) is characterised by a double inequality: of generation and gender'. She argues that 'the incest taboo is symbolic of a moral quality in a pair of roles.' This picks up many of the themes from feminist writings, where the abuse of a child is seen as an immoral act as well as a power-political statement.

In clinical terms we would say that the dynamics of abusing families are skewed; this may put, for instance, the sexually abused child in a spuriously powerful position in relation to her father. This position undermines her mother's authority in the home, while at the same time providing a distraction, for both parents, from their poor marital relationship. The responsibility, in a legal and moral sense, must always lie with the adult perpetrator of abuse, but in many ways, we can see that all family members become 'victims' of this dysfunctional system.

Is it possible to look in a wider sense, at power and aggression in society? There is a general feeling that 'streetwise' Western society is becoming more aggressive, with muggings and violent attacks on individuals, inner city riots and football hooliganism becoming commonplace in certain countries. The psychiatric and psychoanalytical literature[23] shows a lively current debate about the possible effects of the nuclear arms race, including the 'Star Wars' policy. From these sources, the suggestion is being made that large and powerful nations, by participating in this escalation of the arms race, are tacitly condoning violence and aggression. In turn, this may be seen as normal, if not desirable, by individuals, and particularly by children growing up within these societies. The theory goes that we are developing paranoid national characteristics which encourage primitive mental processes such as splitting and projection, to operate among the members of the societies. Analogies have been drawn with the modes of thinking prevalent in pre-war Nazi Germany, where Germanic nationalism, splitting and projection allowed that society to perceive all its problems as being located in another group.

Such primitive mental processes can certainly be seen at work in those within our society who support racist attitudes. These scapegoating mechanisms always seem to include a strong element of envy of the scapegoat. The scapegoat may be the ambitious and successful Jewish person, the industrious and law-abiding Pakistani family, or the abused child, perceived as being free from adult responsibilities and conflicts and having all his or her basic needs met.

There are few legitimate outlets for aggression in our society in peacetime. We know that in times of war, other types of aggression such as self-injury and suicide decrease rapidly, as do neighbourhood disputes and civil unrest. Projection of one's aggressive drives outwards, on to a hated enemy, therefore, would seem to reduce inner conflict.

In a societal sense, the question may be whether destructive or constructive models currently predominate. On the constructive side, there is plenty to be said, with very low infant mortality rates, greater longevity, much better public health, and an increased emphasis on prevention of illness and social problems. However on the destructive side, there is a worrying accumulation of evidence, some of which is cited above, to suggest that as a society we are becoming more preoccupied with violence and exploitation, and destructive modes of behaviour.

There is a worldwide condoning of war as the ultimate solution, and although peace movements are gradually gaining impetus, they have less support among men than they have among women. On a national level, war is still accepted. On a domestic level, the perpetuation of civil conflict and the glamorisation of violence on television do seem to be feeding into patterns of aggressive and destructive child development. Recently a group of psychiatrists were asked to comment on the effect of video violence on child development.[24] They came back with an overwhelming impression of the encouragement of violence in those children exposed to such videos.

This sort of theorising relates to de Mause's model of modes of child rearing over the centuries. It is interesting that, using a predominantly psychoanalytical approach originally derived from work with individual patients, de Mause and others now looking at the effect of nuclear war on societies and indeed on world thinking, seem to be able to make some useful comments. However, a great danger here is that of reductionism, which attempts to try to explain worldwide and historical phenomena such as child abuse, in simplistic individual based terms. Obviously, the aetiology of this problem is multifactorial, and very complex.

Protective factors

What do we know about possible protective factors in child abuse? Little has been written specifically about this issue, but a strong impression emerges from Jill Korbin's book, that the presence of an extended family, with support for young parents, may well offer one form of protection against the temptation to abuse. The corollary of this relates to a known risk factor in the sexual abuse of children, ie the *reconstituted* family, with weakened taboos against abuse, and, often, divorce from family of origin supports, as well as marital divorce.

Again, cross-culturally, children living in societies which actively value them as a future investment, such as China, may be protected both literally, and figuratively, by this higher authority. It is interesting to speculate whether the decline in *female* infanticide, since the Industrial Revolution, relates as much to changing work patterns (less emphasis on heavy manual (male) labour, and more emphasis on lighter, machine-assisted (female) labour) as it does to the development of humanitarian ideals.

The abused child in future

It is difficult to make predictions about future child rearing practices, when our definitions of child abuse are still so tentative, and when the origins of the problem seem so complex. It would be reassuring to say that greater awareness of the problem, both public and professional, should lead to a decrease in child abuse. However, history has shown us that knowledge and perception are not synonymous. Seeing is not necessarily believing.

A hopeful sign may be the emergence of a 'children's rights' movement, with children seen as the oppressed minority in society. This approach could push society into listening to children and their problems, but a danger here could be the inappropriate perception of children as mini-adults, able to decide their own futures. This may be going too far by ignoring the child's developmental needs and natural dependence on caring adults.

In the much longer term, we must hope that if children are treated with respect, they will grow up with self respect, and in turn learn to respect their own children. 'The right to freedom from neglect, abuse and deprivation'[25] should be the birthright of every child, in every context, both historical and cultural.

Notes and references

1 Valentine, A (ed) *Fathers to Sons – Advice without Consent* (Norman, Oklahoma, 1963)

2 Robeson Burr, A *The Autobiography: A Critical and Comparative Study* (Boston, 1909)

3 De Mause, L (ed) 'The Evolution of Childhood' chapter in *The History of Childhood: the Evolution of Parent-Child Relationships as a Factor in History* (Souvenir Press, 1976)

4 Aries, P *Centuries of Childhood: A Social History of Family Life* (New York, 1962)

5 Kempe, C H and Kempe, R S 'The Dimensions of the Problem' in Bruner *et al* (ed) *Child Abuse; the Developing Child*

6 *The Shorter Oxford English Dictionary (on Historical Principles)* C T Onions (ed) (Oxford University Press, 1977) 3rd ed, Vol 1 p 324

7 La Fontaine, J 'An Anthropological Perspective on Children in Social Worlds' in M Richard and P Light (eds) *Children of Social Worlds* (Polity Press, Oxford, 1986)

8 Lynch, M 'Child Abuse before Kempe: an Historical Literature Review' in *Child Abuse and Neglect – The International Journal* 1985, Vol 9, pp 7-15.

9 Moussaieff Masson, J *Freud – The Assault on Truth – Freud's Suppression of the Seduction Theory* (Faber and Faber Ltd, 1984)

10 Paul Brouardel quoted by his friend Alfred Fournier, in an address to the Parisian Academy of Medicine, 1880. See also: a) Paul Brouardel 'Les causes d'erreur dans les expertises relatives aux attentats a la pudeur' (The causes of error in expert opinion, with respect to sexual assaults) 11 June 1983, in *Annales de la Societe de Medecine Legale de France* (3rd Ser, 10, pp60-71, 148-179) and b) Paul Brouardel 'Les Attentats aux Moeurs' pp 52-72, on simulation (of sexual assaults on children)

11 Korbin, J (ed) 'Introduction: Etiology of Child Abuse and Neglect' in *Child*

Abuse and Neglect: Cross Cultural Perspectives (University of California Press, London, 1981)

12 Oliver, J E 'Successive Generations of Child Maltreatment: Social and Medical Disorders in the Parents' in *British Journal of Psychiatry*, 1985, 147, pp484-490

13 Lynch, M and Roberts, J *Consequences of Child Abuse* (Academic Press, 1982)

14 Creighton, S J *Trends in Child Abuse* (1984) NSPCC Publication, 67 Saffron Hill, London EC1N 8RS

15 Goodwin, J *Sexual Abuse – Incest Victims and their Families* (John Wright, PSA Inc, 1982)

16 Eileen Vizard, personal communication (1985)

17 Eileen Vizard, personal communication from The Child Sexual Abuse Treatment Project, Great Ormond Street Hospital, London WC1

18 Coveney, L, Jackson, M *et al The Sexuality Papers – Male Sexuality and the Social Control of Women* (Hutchinson, 1984)

19 Rush, F *The Best Kept Secret – Sexual Abuse of Children* (McGraw-Hill, reprinted by Prentice-Hall Inc, 1980)

20 David, G *Violence against children; physical child abuse in the United States* (Harvard University Press, Cambridge, Ma, 1970)

21 Finkleher, D 'Boys as Victims' in *Child Sexual Abuse – New Theory and Research* (The Free Press, Macmillan Inc, USA, 1984)

22 La Fontaine, J *Incest, Intimacy and Inequality* (in preparation) also, personal communication to Eileen Vizard

23 Dyer, T 'The Psychotherapy of Nuclear War' *Bulletin of the Royal College of Psychiatrists* Jan 1986, Vol 10, No 1, pp 2-5

24 Sims, A and Melville-Thomas, G 'Survey of the Opinion of Child and Adolescent Psychiatrists on the viewing of violent videos by children' *Bulletin of the Royal College of Psychiatrists* Dec 1985, Vol 9, No 12, pp 238-240

25 United Nations Declaration of the Rights of the Child 20 November, 1959

Chapter 2
Quantitative assessment of child abuse

Susan J Creighton

Introduction

'It was like holding a bird in one's hand and being frightened to hold it too tight in case one squeezed the life out of it.'

Of all the caring agencies involved with the Colwell family it was her teacher, Mrs Turner, who picked Maria up to comfort her, and noticed how light and thin she was. It was the teacher whom Maria felt able to confide in.[1]

Maria was seven when she died. She was not one of Kempe's 'battered babies'.[2] After the death of Maria Colwell the physical abuse of children could no longer be considered as mainly the province of paediatricians and health visitors. The tragic death of Maria Colwell and the subsequent Inquiry Report initiated the present complex procedures and guidelines for the management of child abuse. The DHSS issued a circular on Non-Accidental Injury to children[3] to local authorities in April 1974 the month that the Inquiry Report was published. This recommended the establishment of Area Review Committees (ARCS) in each part of the country. These Committees were to formulate policy for the management of child abuse in their area. They were to consist of senior representatives of all the agencies concerned with children.

The Report on Maria Colwell and subsequent reports on Lester Chapman[4] and Stephen Menheniott[5] emphasise the importance of teachers in recognising the physical abuse of children. The growing concern about other types of abuse, particularly sexual and emotional abuse, further reinforces the unique role of teachers in recognising, and helping to prevent, child abuse.

Registers

Child Abuse Registers and their predecessors, Registers of Suspected Non-Accidental Injury to Children, form a focal point in the management of child abuse in an area. The 1974 DHSS circular advised that 'a central record of information in each area is essential to good communication between the many disciplines involved in the management of these cases'. Children are placed on registers by the decision of a case conference. This case conference includes representatives of all the agencies associated with the child and its family. They share all the information they have on the family and the possible abuse and decide what should be done to help the child and its family.

Most registers are held by local Social Services Departments but some are held by the National Society for the Prevention of Cruelty to Children (NSPCC) on behalf of their local ARC. The placing of a child's name on a register held by the NSPCC ensures the child and its family priority in the allocation of available resources. Although the register is held by the NSPCC the majority of the children on it will be helped by social workers from the local Social Services Department. The co-operation of all the different agencies involved with the child and its family (multi-disciplinary co-operation) is an essential part of the management of child abuse. The areas where the NSPCC holds the register include some 10% of the child population of England and Wales. The research on these registers constitutes the largest continuous epidemiological study of child abuse to be conducted in this country. This paper is a summary of the main findings of this research over the eight years from 1977 to 1984.

Definitions

Between 1977 and 1980 the registers were called Registers of Suspected Non-Accidental Injury and included children who had been physically abused or who were suffering from non-organic failure to thrive. In 1980, in response to a DHSS circular[6] the criteria for registration were widened to include other types of abuse such as neglect and emotional abuse and the registers became known as Child Abuse Registers. Many authorities also included cases of sexual abuse at this time although it was not included in the circular. The criteria for registration were defined as follows:

a Physical injury:
All physically-injured children under the age of 17 years where the nature of the injury is not consistent with the account of how it

occurred or where there is definite knowledge, or a reasonable suspicion, that the injury was inflicted (or knowingly not prevented) by any person having custody, charge, or care of the child. This includes children to whom it is suspected poisonous substances have been administered. Diagnosis of child abuse will normally require both medical examination of the child and social assessment of the family background.

b Physical neglect:
Children under the age of 17 years who have been persistently or severely neglected physically, for example, by exposure to dangers of different kinds, including cold and starvation.

c Failure to thrive and emotional abuse:
Children under the age of 17 years
- who have been medically diagnosed as suffering from severe non-organic failure to thrive;
  or
- whose behaviour and emotional development have been severely affected;

where medical and social assessments find evidence of either persistent or severe neglect or rejection.

d Children in the same household as a person previously involved in child abuse:
Children under the age of 17 years who are in a household with, or which is visited by, a parent or another person who has abused a child and are considered at risk of abuse.

e Sexual abuse:
Children under the age of 17 years who have been involved in sexual activity with the parent or caregiver, to which they are unable to give informed consent because of their dependence or developmental immaturity.

The physically injured children were also categorised by the severity of their injuries. These categories were defined as:
- Fatal: all cases which resulted in death
- Serious: all fractures, head injuries, internal injuries, severe burns and ingestion of toxic substances
- Moderate: all soft tissue injuries of a superficial nature.

Findings

There were 8760 children placed on Child Abuse Registers maintained by the NSPCC between 1977 and 1984. These figures include children in the same household, children thought to be at serious risk of abuse and children whose injuries were subsequently judged to have been caused accidentally. Figure 2.1 shows the number registered each year by the reason for registration. The majority (65%) of the registered children were physically injured. If we exclude the 'at risk' cases from the main analysis, 95% of the children abused in 1980 were physically injured. This was the year prior to the widening of the register criteria to include other forms of abuse in addition to physical injury. By 1984 only 78% of the abused children were physically injured. Among the other types of abuse, cases of sexual abuse have shown the greatest increase. They represented 2% of the abused children in 1980, increasing to 11% in 1984.

The rate of physical abuse to children has shown a gradual increase since 1979. This is shown in Figure 2.2. In 1977 and 1979 the rate was 0.43 per thousand children under 15. This rose to 0.73 by 1984, a 70% increase. The graph also shows that this increase was in both pre-school and school age children up to 1982, but only in school age children in 1983 and 1984. These rates can provide an estimate of the number of children physically abused in England and Wales in a year. The estimates have risen from 4700 children aged 0-14 years in 1977 to 7040 in 1984.

Figure 2.1 Number of registered children by year and type of abuse

Year	Physical Injury	Failure to thrive	Sexual abuse	Neglect	Emotional abuse	Other	Total
1977	689	27	7	na	na	277	1000
1978	715	26	8	na	na	323	1072
1979	683	17	8	3	na	366	1077
1980	774	15	11	15	na	301	1116
1981	807	30	27	30	4	291	1189
1982	661	21	40	44	17	295	1078
1983	672	15	51	62	31	281	1112
1984	707	34	98	50	18	209	1116
Total	5708	185	250	204	70	2343	8760
%	65	2	3	2	1	27	100

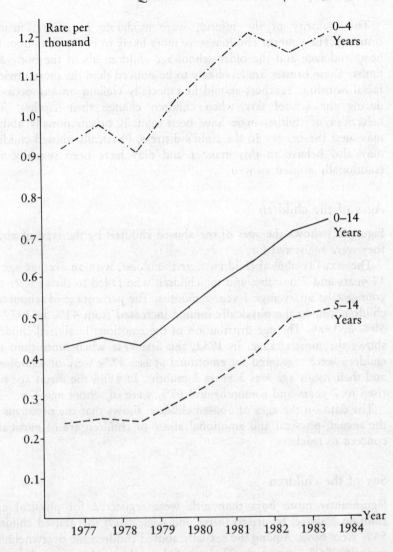

Figure 2.2 Rate of physically injured children per thousand by year 1977-1984

In contrast to the overall rise in physical abuse, the percentage of physically injured children who were fatally or seriously injured has fallen over the years. They represented 17% of the physically injured children in 1977, falling to 12% in 1979, 10% in 1982 and 8% in 1984. The youngest children were most vulnerable to fatal and serious injuries. Of the 249 cases of skull fractures or brain damage reported over the eight years 234 occurred to pre-school children, particularly infants.

The majority of the injuries were moderate in nature, usually bruising. The younger children were more likely to be bruised about the head and face and the older school-age children about the body and limbs. These bruises are less likely to be noticed than the more obvious facial bruising. Teachers should be especially vigilant on any occasion during the school day when children change their clothes. The behaviour of children who have been sexually or emotionally abused may alert the teacher to the child's distress. Physically abused children may also behave in this manner and may have been sexually and emotionally abused as well.

Ages of the children

Figure 2.3 shows the ages of the abused children by the type of abuse they were registered for.

The sexually abused children were the oldest, with an average age of 11 years and 7 months; and the children who failed to thrive were the youngest, at an average 1 year 7 months. The percentage of school age children among the physically injured increased from 41% in 1977 to 50% in 1984. The age distribution of the emotionally abused children shows the most change. In 1982, the first year when more than ten children were registered for emotional abuse, 47% were of school age and their mean age was 5 years 2 months. In 1984 the mean age had risen to 7 years and 6 months and 67% were of school age.

The data on the ages of abused children shows that the problems of the sexual, physical and emotional abuse of children are of particular concern to teachers.

Sex of the children

Significantly more boys than girls were registered for physical and emotional abuse, failure to thrive and neglect. Of the abused children 54% were boys. Among the sexually abused children the overwhelming majority (85%) were girls. The age of the children also affected the sex distribution, particularly for the physically abused children. Boys aged between 5 and 9 years and girls aged 14 or over were more vulnerable. Of the physically abused 5- 9-year-olds, 61% were boys and 67% of the children aged 15 or more were girls.

The parents

Less than half the abused children were living with both natural parents at the time of the abuse. There are no national statistics on the parental situation of the country's children. In spite of the constant stream of media articles detailing the breakdown of the nuclear family the vast

Figure 2.3 Ages of children with different types of abuse (1977-1984)

Age	Physically injured	Failure to thrive	Sexual abuse	Neglect	Emotional abuse	National* distribution
0-4 years	3147 (55)	177 (96)	10 (4)	142 (70)	30 (43)	(28)
5-9 years	1325 (23)	6 (3)	67 (27)	41 (20)	23 (33)	(26)
10-14 years	1030 (18)	1 (0.5)	130 (52)	19 (9)	14 (20)	(32)
15-17 years	206 (4)	1 (0.5)	43 (17)	2 (1)	3 (4)	(14)
Total	5708 (100)	185 (100)	250 (100)	204 (100)	70 (100)	(100)
Mean age	5 years & 8 months	1 year & 7 months	11 years & 7 months	4 years & 1 months	6 years & 10 months	

* (Population estimates, 1984)

majority of children live with both their natural parents. Figure 2.4 shows the parental situation of the abused children, by the type of abuse. More of the sexually abused children were living with their mother and a father substitute than with both natural parents. The emotionally abused children were also more likely to be living with a parent substitute than with both their natural parents.

This does not mean that every child living with a parent substitute is more likely to be emotionally or sexually abused or neglected than a child living with two natural parents. Nevertheless, as one would expect, the emotional, material and financial changes involved in the break-up or reconstitution of a family, create stress. It is hardly surprising that such family structures should be over-represented amongst the abused children.

Perpetrators

The person suspected of abusing the child was recorded for over 80% of the cases. Neglect and non-organic failure to thrive are abuse by omission rather than commission and a perpetrator was rarely recorded. When it was, the natural mother, as principal caretaker, was usually implicated. Natural mothers were also implicated most often in the physical and emotional abuse cases. In the cases of sexual abuse, father substitutes were suspected most frequently. However many more children were living with their natural mother than with their natural father or a parent substitute. Controlling for this, the natural father was implicated in 57% of the injured and 60% of the sexual abuse cases

Figure 2.4 Parental situation by type of abuse (1977-1984)

Parental situation	Physically injured	Failure to thrive	Sexual abuse	Neglect	Emotional abuse
2 NPs	2665 (47)	127 (69)	91 (36)	100 (49)	24 (34)
NMA	1030 (18)	36 (19)	31 (12)	71 (35)	12 (17)
NM & FS	1505 (26)	21 (11)	96 (38)	25 (12)	22 (31)
NFA	178 (3)	1 (1)	17 (7)	4 (2)	2 (3)
NF & MS	231 (4)		6 (2)		8 (11)
Other	102 (2)		9 (4)	4 (2)	2 (3)
Total	5711 (100)	185 (100)	250 (100)	204 (100)	70 (100)

Key:	2 NPs	Two natural parents
	NMA	Natural mother alone
	NM & FS	Natural mother & father substitute
	NFA	Natural father alone
	NF & MS	Natural father and mother substitute

where the child was living with him. For children living with their natural mother she was implicated in 35% of the injuries and 2% of the sexual abuse. The father substitute was implicated in 88% of the sexual abuse and 60% of the physical injury cases where the child was living with him.

Among the emotionally abused children, mothers and mother substitutes were more likely to be suspected even when the parental situation was allowed for. Natural mothers were implicated in 64% and mother substitutes in 62% of the cases where the child was living with them. Natural fathers were suspected in 42% and father substitutes in 23% of the emotional abuse cases.

Stress factors

A variety of stress factors; material, personal and parent-child, are listed on the register form. Workers are asked to list those which they feel may have precipitated the abuse or which are having a severe effect on the family. The same three factors have been quoted most frequently from 1977 to 1984. These were marital discord, unemployment and debts. Marital discord was seriously affecting 52% of the abused children's families, unemployment 43% and debts 34%.

The percentage of families stressed by marital disorders and debts remained fairly stable over the eight years. Unemployment as a stress factor showed a sharp increase from 1980 onwards. Figure 2.5 shows the employment characteristics of the abused children's parents from 1977 to 1984. Very few of the mothers were in paid employment, compared with a national figure of 50% for mothers of dependent children.[8] Less than 60% of the fathers were employed at any time during the eight years, but the percentage dropped from 57% in 1979 to 30% in 1984.

In 1983 the register form was changed to include additional, more detailed stress factors concerned with the parent-child relationship. 'Inability to respond to the maturational needs of the child' and 'inability to deal with "normal" child behaviour' plus 'authoritarian control' were added. Workers were also asked to rank the stress factors in the order of the severity of their effects. 'Negative feelings towards the child' was ranked as having the severest effect, followed by 'unrealistic expectations of the child', 'inability to respond to the maturational needs of the child' and 'marital discord'.

Management

The register form includes details of how the abuse was discovered, parental explanations offered, medical treatment, where the child was placed and the legal sanctions taken in the adult and juvenile courts.

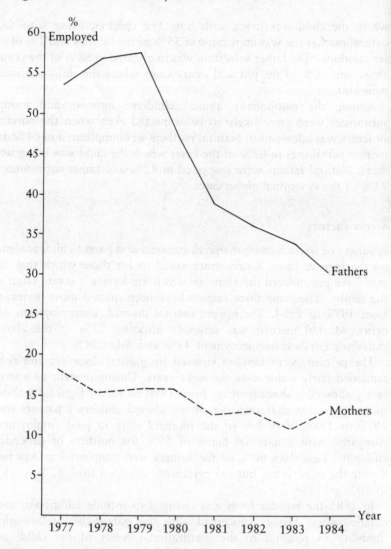

Figure 2.5 **Employment characteristics of abused children's parents by year 1977-1984**

Once the child is put on the register he or she will be monitored regularly. Any subsequent abuse or changes in legal status discovered by this monitoring are provided as update information and included in the research.

The main role of teachers in the management of child abuse will be in the discovery of information about the child at the registering case conference and the subsequent sharing of information with the keyworker appointed to the case. The register research had information on the first of these. The history of the injury or abuse included information on how it was discovered for 66% of the abused children. Additionally the referral history traces the chain of notifications made by concerned individuals and agencies between the discovery of the abuse and the registration of the child. Schools and pre-school facilities played significant roles in both of these.

In 35% of the cases with information the abuse was discovered by the school or pre-school that the child was attending. This compares with the 34% where the parents brought the child's injuries or abuse to the attention of medical personnel. Turning to the referral history, the initial referral came from parents in 25% and schools and pre-schools in 22% of the cases. Other agencies or individuals (eg neighbours, relatives) were responsible for no more than 9% of the initial referrals.

Conclusions

This paper has been based on the data from the NSPCC's register research, the largest continuous study of child abuse being conducted in this country. During the eight years from 1977 to 1984 over 8700 children were placed on these registers. The research has shown an increase in the rate of physical abuse since 1979, but a decrease in the percentage of the children who were fatally or seriously injured. The types of injury and abuse received by the children, their age and sex distributions are described. The relationship of the children's caretakers to them and the suspected perpetrator of the abuse are also depicted. Over the study period the same three external and internal stresses have been thought to have the severest effect on the families. Those aspects of the management of child abuse that are particularly relevant to teachers have been detailed.

Notes and References

1 Department of Health and Social Security *Report of the Committee of Inquiry into the Care and Supervision Provided in Relation to Maria Colwell* (HMSO, 1974)

2 Kempe, C.H. 'Paediatric Implications of the Battered Baby Syndrome' in *Archives of Disease in Childhood*, (1971) 46, 28-37

3 Department of Health and Social Security *Non-Accidental Injury to Children* LASSL (74) 13, 1974

4 Hall, J. (Chairman) *Lester Chapman Inquiry Report* (Berkshire County Council, 1979)

5 Department of Health and Social Security *Report of the Social Work Service of DHSS into Certain Aspects of the Management of the Case of Stephen Menheniott* (HMSO, 1978)

6 Department of Health and Social Security *Child Abuse: Central Register Systems*, LASSL (80) 4: HN (80) 20, 1980
7 Office of Population Censuses and Surveys, 'Population Estimates 1984', Monitor PPI
8 General Household Survey, London: HMSO, 1984

Chapter 3
The recognition of child abuse

Colin Stern

The perspective

The spectrum of child abuse

The popular idea of a 'battered' child conjures up an image of a pathetic infant, dirty and covered in bruises, gazing in an apprehensive way at the photographer. The true picture reveals that children suffer from an endless variety of abuses, usually at the hands of their parents, frequently without obvious injury and often without complaint.

Child abuse includes a spectrum of insults, ranging from the extremes of infant rape and murder to the more subtle and insidious denial of love. A child who is brought up to expect nothing other than a hostile environment will learn to live within these constraints and adapt his or her behaviour, so as to attract the minimum of aggressive attention. Such children learn early to seek to please any adult with whom they may come into contact, as a form of self-protection.

The ability to recognise that a child has been abused depends, therefore, upon an awareness on the part of each observer, not only of the physical state of a child, but also of normal childhood behaviour. It is not enough to note any change in an individual child's social interactions, because the persistently insulted child may have suffered since babyhood. Consequently, when a child seems to behave in an unusual fashion, the possibility that child abuse is the cause should be considered.

The recognition of this spectrum of child abuse depends upon two factors: training in typical patterns of presentation, and experience. In order to develop a 'nose' for the abused child each individual needs to have acquired a significant personal library of cases. Training must, obviously, come first. Only when we have a group of observers, strategically placed in the community, can we hope to achieve early detection.

The rights and needs of children

Children are looked upon by society as the possessions of their parents. This attitude is reflected in the tolerance we show of different qualities of parenting. We are, however, slowly beginning to acknowledge that each child is an individual with individual rights, although we have continuing difficulty over the definition of the age at which individuality begins: is it at birth or at conception?

On 20 November, 1959, the General Assembly of the United Nations ratified without dissent their Declaration of the Rights of the Child. These are:

1   The right to equality, regardless of race, colour, religion, sex or nationality.
2   The right to healthy mental and physical development.
3   The right to a name and a nationality.
4   The right to sufficient food, housing and medical care.
5   The right to special care, if handicapped.
6   The right to love, understanding and care.
7   The right to free education, play and recreation.
8   The right to medical aid in the event of disasters and emergencies.
9   The right to protection from cruelty, neglect and exploitation.
10 The right to protection from persecution and to an up-bringing in the spirit of world-wide brotherhood and peace.

This Declaration includes protection for the abused child, elements of which are described in statements 2, 4, 6, 7, 9 and 10. Nowhere is the role of the parent or carer defined and there is no description of the need for a family environment for the ideal prosecution of a child's healthy upbringing. These omissions stem from the stimulus for the Declaration, which was the plight of children orphaned and deprived as a consequence of war. This perspective is reflected in a certain self-consciousness – for example, in statement 10 – but it should not detract from the Declaration's value as an accepted yardstick against which the rights afforded any child may be measured.

I believe that children should be treated according to the rights laid down in the United Nations Declaration and that, in addition, they have a right to a family environment, within which they may be nurtured as individuals and develop self-reliance and self-respect.

Differences in child care

Those whose professions place them in daily contact with children swiftly become aware of the considerable variation that exists in the way in which children are brought up. Some of these differences are marked. Within some Middle Eastern family cultures girls are often treated as second-class children, in comparison with their brothers. Discipline in other families can mean the regular application of a strap, kept hanging in the hall. Some wealthy parents employ nannies to rear their children and restrict contact with their children to a minimum. In a Britain in which both parents often need to work, care is delegated to child-minders rather than grandparents, as the nuclear family loses contact with its relations. The increase in divorce and the fall in legalised marriage has led to a rise in the number of single parents.

It may be said that this variation in child rearing is valuable in that it reflects a high degree of civil liberty and adds colour and diversity to British life. However true that may be, it is also the case that, as a direct consequence of these differing methods of child-rearing, it is hard to define the point at which the pattern of child care within a family becomes intolerable.

Often, the inexperienced child care worker will see or hear about the way a child lives and, because this differs so markedly from their own experiences and values, feel an instinctive antipathy. This is wrong. The only standard of reasonable care requires one to look at the child first and the family second. If the child is happy, psychologically normal and is growing and developing within well-defined limits, then it is unreasonable to assume that the standard of care is unacceptable, although it may be deficient. In these circumstances, the appropriate management strategy is to offer help, but if this help is refused, we should accept the right of the family to continue in its own way.

The identity and place of observers

Monitoring child care has become increasingly difficult as society has become more open and government less paternal. There are those whose work allows them to act as child observers: for example teachers, social workers and health visitors, along with a variety of professionals who specialise in child care within the wider ambit of their concerns. These people are capable of assessing children: their behaviour, physical state and development, and of placing these characteristics within a known context of normality. However, unless their attention is directed specifically to an individual child, their sensitivity to the ill-used child is random and instinctive.

Statutory bodies – the local Department of Social Services and the erstwhile Juvenile Bureau of the local police – take responsibility for the investigation and management of known cases of child abuse and they enlist help from the health visitor, general practitioner, teacher and paediatrician in planning their actions.

Many studies have underlined the 'iceberg' nature of the problem – for each child known to have been abused, there are several who suffer unknown. The weakness in our ability to detect child abuse lies in our failure to establish reliable ways of monitoring *all* children. The National Society for the Prevention of Cruelty to Children (NSPCC) was formed to deal with this problem, but its officers have the same handicaps as everyone else, as has been demonstrated by recent, well-publicised events.

Teachers as observers

The teaching profession is given a special responsibility to nurture the whole child, within an educational environment, so as to encourage development into a mature, informed adult. The detection of child abuse is one of their pastoral duties and this paper has been written with this in mind.

Many teachers are concerned about their lack of training in the detection of child abuse and want guidance. However, it is important that any information provided to help them to recognise a child who is being abused, should reflect the sensitivity of the observer's eye. Consequently, I made a conscious decision to base descriptions in this paper on my personal experience of over 400 children, whose physical and emotional damage resulted from cruel treatment. A digest of the excellent research of different experts in this field would, I believe, lack the combination of clarity and intimacy of this approach. There are, as a result, no references within the text, but I have included a reading list at the end, which is meant to complement, rather than validate, my descriptions.

Classification

Arbitrary divisions

Definitions can be disadvantageous, because the desire to codify often overrides the need for instinctive assessment and this may obscure the real nature of a problem. However, definitions of child abuse are important, not least because sometimes the type of abuse lies at the root of our failure to help a child.

Conventionally, child abuse is divided into physical, sexual and emotional. The reasons for these distinctions are practical rather than having any strong clinical base. Physically abused children have physical injuries; children who are sexually abused, although injured, require a specially designed management structure. All abused children could be said to be emotionally abused, but, when emotional abuse occurs in isolation, it presents the greatest difficulty in unambiguous diagnosis and this, in turn, renders legal action complex and contentious.

For my purposes, the following arbitrary definitions will be used:

a *Physical abuse* Any child suffering from non-accidental physical injury, without evidence of sexual abuse, but including neglect.

b *Sexual abuse* Any child who is the subject of a sexual advance from a significantly older person, usually an adult, with or without evidence of physical or sexual injury.

c *Emotional abuse* A child in whom there is evidence of poor physical, motor or psychological development and where there is evidence that emotional stress is the cause. This may be positive, in the case of emotional persecution, or negative, by the denial of normal affection.

Places and modes of presentation

At home

Most child abuse occurs within the family. When the family has close ties with other relations, such as grandparents, the plight of a child may be brought to light by their concern.

The choice of the individual to be made the target of a disclosure of child abuse depends upon the age of the child and the nature of the abuse. Physical and sexual abuse is often revealed to the general practitioner or the paediatrician. Emotional abuse presents more rarely in this way, largely because of doubt as to the appropriate person to whom a relative should turn.

Those professionals who visit families in their own homes, such as health visitors and social workers, may suspect child abuse, but they are rarely the target of a disclosure. This is because they are often visiting following initial concerns about parenting skills within a family. Such parents have often come from backgrounds in which they were abused; they see the specialists as adversaries rather than supporters, since their colleagues are remembered as being associated with the stresses of childhood.

At clinic or nursery

Children under the age of four or five are subjected to frequent physical and developmental checks. When they are reared in a deprived environment, they may be given an early placement in a day nursery. Careful observation of these children can lead to the detection of child abuse, but it is never easy to decide when a child's development is compromised as a consequence of child abuse. When obvious non-accidental injury is present it is less difficult, but such cases are a minority.

In school

Abuse of the schoolchild creates considerable problems in recognition. Children most at risk come from families where those in authority are viewed with suspicion. Teachers devote much of their time and skill to winning the confidence of their pupils and this requires befriending them. The older the children, the more secretive they become about their bodies, so the school nurse and the school medical officer have an important responsibility for the recognition of the physical evidence of abuse. Although teachers are often the first to suspect abuse, it is never easy to observe physical injuries while children are changing their clothes. The behaviour of schoolchildren, however, shows typical age-related patterns with which the experienced teacher is familiar. Unusual or deviant behaviour can be the most important mode of presentation of child abuse and the teacher is the best-placed professional to suspect it.

Professional balance

Whenever a case of child abuse is reported in the newspapers, there is an outcry of horror, directed first at the perpetrator and, usually later, at the social services staff for failing in their task. These reactions reflect our protective instincts towards children and have more to do with revenge than any more positive motive.

Anyone concerned with the detection and management of child abuse must preserve a balance between sensitivity to the plight of the abused child and respect for that child's place within his or her family. An understanding of family dynamics depends not only upon training but also on experience, both professional and personal. It is often said that cases should be managed by more senior staff for this reason. I would prefer to stress that each worker should remember that child abuse, although a crime, is above all a psychopathological disease, to be recognised and treated. The safety, growth and development of the child are paramount, but the abuser is to be treated rather than punished. There is no profit for anyone in child abuse, only pity and misery; punishment has no place as a deterrent.

Adverse influences

Parental background

The observation that abused children grow to become abusing parents has become something of a cliché. Its very glibness tends to obscure the truth that lies behind it, because one needs to have experience of such families to understand how this happens.

Children reared in the shadow of physical or emotional violence develop a distorted view of parent-child relationships. Their character has been moulded by these bitter experiences and, in later life, they gravitate towards others with similar backgrounds of abuse. Of course, there are many influences on the nature of their social contacts. When such adults become parents and experience stress, they may return to the deep-rooted and dimly-remembered patterns of parenting learned in their own childhood. Their children are more likely to be fed, struck, cuddled or rejected on a whim and without warning. The primacy of a parent's desires in this kind of family is absolute.

Sexual abuse, principally inflicted upon girls, is a serious and potent modulator of family dynamics and often leads to impairment of ultimate mothering skills, as well as psychiatric illness. It is often unsuspected as a root cause, as it is so cloaked in secrecy. As a consequence of such abuse a girl may grow into adulthood with deep and conflicting ideas about her role as a child and as a mother; she may have low self-esteem and ambivalent attitudes to male and female sexuality. Such mothers, especially if they become single parents, may abuse their children emotionally.

Deprivation

Every parent knows that, when their children are at their most irritating, the presence of additional stresses, such as conflict at work, can make the urge to strike out almost irresistible. Those with families who live below the poverty line and for whom each day is a struggle to survive, have a low tolerance of intra-family strife. Household rules become more strictly hierarchical and the transgressions of children are less tolerable.

Deprived families are more likely to abuse their children, but why is this not a global phenomenon? In our society, such families can see the evidence of affluence around them. Their natural feelings of frustration make them less able to cope with the demands of their children. In developing countries, the contrast is usually, but not always, less obvious and the local social structure more stable and homogeneous. In these circumstances, child-rearing follows an old and well-tried pattern.

Clearly the prevention of child abuse is inextricably linked with the alleviation of poverty.

Single parents

Not only does the evolution of sexual differentiation have profound genetic importance, it also allows the developing of a shared caring system for offspring. Parental interdependence has many valuable effects, not least a mechanism for the reduction of stress. 'A problem shared is a problem halved' is true; we tend to lose our sense of proportion in our inner debates about a problem. When it is discussed with another, difficulties recede and solutions appear.

Single parents, if socially isolated, are unable to share their problems. When relations support them, the handicap is lessened, but, when they have no close social contacts, stress increases and child abuse is more likely.

Intellectual impairment

Some adults who have limited intellectual capabilities make excellent parents. This has led some to assume that this is always true, but it is not so straightforward. When parenting skills have been learned in childhood, such adults are able to give appropriate social support. There is, however, a greater likelihood that parents with intellectual disability may come from deprived backrounds. In these circumstances. the upbringing of children may be unacceptably poor in quality.

Stress

Stress, whether acute or chronic, is a critical determinant of the quality of child care. There are several specific family pressures which are more likely to be associated with the subsequent ill-treatment of children.

The natural bond between a mother and her child is relatively fragile. We know that if, after birth, they are separated for more than two weeks, the link, although not necessarily broken, becomes so ravelled that it is hard to knit up again. Adverse perinatal events are important in this context, because the baby who spends weeks in an incubator may not be accepted back as the child he or she might have been. Such infants are more like foster-children, taken on trust.

Illness within the family, especially when chronic, is more likely to lead to child abuse. It may be the abused child who is sick, which can make it hard to tell where sickness ends and abuse begins. The child from an adverse background who develops, for instance, diabetes and requires careful parental management, can be neglected. These children may present repeatedly in crisis and it is often difficult to say whether their diabetes is 'brittle', or their care deficient.

Many sorts of marital stress lead to abuse. These may be emotional, psychiatric, or a consequence of separation or divorce. Sometimes they are due to financial hardship or unemployment: the insecurity of the parents making them intolerant of natural childhood transgression. The experienced specialist learns to examine, first of all, family dynamics and then to assess the nature of the outside pressures upon them. It is then possible to give an opinion on the quality of parenting and the likelihood of abuse as a cause of physical or emotional abnormalities in the child.

Recognition of abuse patterns

There are patterns of family behaviour, especially with respect to other members of the family group, which give valuable clues at to their relationships. Other papers within this collection, notably those by Arnon Bentovim, Rolene Szur and Helen Kenward, describe these family states in different ways. I have tried to suggest here how they may be recognised in isolation from the parent or guardian, which seems to me to be closer to the teacher's dilemma.

Age groups

Under nine months
Infants do not learn to roll over until they are about three months old. They are dependent on others to move them from place to place. Hence it is unlikely that they will acquire any injuries other than at the hands of those caring for them, although accidents are possible. Consequently, bruising in young babies should be assumed to be non-accidental, when no likely history of injury is obtained.

Some of the injuries with which such infants can present are horrific and the question of whether the baby has a 'brittle bone' disease or an hereditary bleeding tendency is often raised. These conditions are extremely uncommon, but it is part of routine medical care to screen for them.

Babies have a remarkable capacity to recover from serious illness or injury, but they are also more fragile than older children. Their lives may be snuffed out as a result of a brief but violent episode, because they cannot run away or hide from their attacker. Because of this, I do not think that a tendency to err on the side of caution, when a baby may be at risk, can be criticised.

Crawlers and toddlers
Once children become mobile, they acquire bruises with the greatest facility. Typically these are seen on the forehead and on those parts of the body likely to be knocked against furniture or the ground – elbows, knees, feet and so on. When toddlers are battered, it is often only possible to say that the bruising is *compatible* with non-accidental injury (NAI), but not that NAI is the definite cause. However, some sorts of injury can be ascribed with more certainty, such as strap marks.

Children in this age group may suffer from sexual abuse. Penetration of the vagina is possible by adult men in girls of one year, although the injuries to the child will be severe. Most sexual abuse is restricted to genital viewing or sexual fondling and this will not leave physical evidence of genital injury.

It is worth remembering, however, that many physically abused children have no visible bruising, but, when X-rayed, signs of bony injuries may be revealed. The lack of obvious physical injury in a child where cruelty is suspected does not, therefore, remove the need for X-rays.

Pre-school children

Once a child reaches the age of two and a half years, s/he may begin to attend nursery school. Unless they have been placed with a child-minder or a day nursery from an earlier age, perhaps because mother is working or because the child is judged to be at risk, this is the first time that the child will be seen regularly by someone outside the family. The opportunity for regular surveillance now presents itself.

Maltreated children in this age group may present either with abnormal behaviour or with injuries. Often, abnormal behaviour is thought, erroneously, to be a consequence of some inherent abnormality in the child. The possibility of emotional abuse must be actively considered. When a child who normally attends a nursery regularly is absent for a while unexpectedly and, when back at school, behaves in an unusual fashion, ill-use may be the cause.

Schoolchildren

Once children start full-time school, one imagines that they are at last in a position to let someone know if they are being assaulted, either physically or emotionally. However, this happens only occasionally. A child who comes from a violent and deprived background has usually experienced cruelty for as long as they can remember. In spite of its misery, their family may be a unit of tight interdependence, although the links that unite its members may be forged of fear.

Teachers require a special sensitivity to suspect that a child is under attack. The ability to recognise warning signs will depend upon their own experience, but can be heightened by a knowledge of what to expect.

Schoolchildren present primarily with behavioural abnormalities. Physical injuries may be detected, but the large difference between the expected number of cases and those actually registered suggests that frequently they are successfully concealed. Sometimes a child may present with a behavioural change, but, equally often, one becomes aware that a particular child has either been changing slowly, or has always been of a typical behavioural type. Although there are typical behavioural patterns, it is crucial to recognise that *any* unusual behaviour pattern may be the consequence of cruelty.

Demeanour

Children who have been subjected to chronic ill-use often show characteristic behaviour. There are several forms which this behaviour may take, depending upon the age of the child and the type of abuse.

A child who is treated normally will cry readily when physically injured or emotionally upset, whereas an adult is more likely to keep a stiff upper lip. The emotional responses of chronically abused children are quite different. They generate fewer, if any, outer signs of distress and are more likely to behave so as not to invite injury.

Recognition of the signs of distress in such children is, therefore, more empathetic. One can describe typical behaviour patterns and injuries in abused children, but the ability to distinguish between the injury-prone child who comes from a 'rough and ready' background, but whose parents are reasonably caring, and the child subjected to chronic abuse, requires a sensitivity to the feelings of the child.

Children under school age

An infant under physical or emotional stress may become irritable and difficult to feed. They may cry continually and attempts to pacify them may be unsuccessful. It is often hard to be sure whether the child is in pain or is emotionally distressed. As they become older, if the cruelty continues, they begin to show the behaviour patterns which are more clearly defined in toddlers.

In the toddler group, children may show fear, not only of the individual responsible for their distress, but of similar types – fear of all men, for example. A more common pattern, however, is for such toddlers to show abnormally pliant behaviour. They may seek attention, often in a rather quiet, undemonstrative way, and be happy to be picked up and cuddled by anyone. This is abnormal because, at this age, children are usually highly selective in their reactions to adults, only allowing close contact with parents, close relatives and others with whom they are well acquainted (see Arnon Bentovim's comments on attachment behaviour in the next paper).

Toddlers are curious about almost everything, including genitalia. If a child shows inquisitiveness only, then that should be regarded as normal. But certain types of play, even in this age group, may betray an unreasonable knowledge of sexual relationships and therefore arouse suspicion of sexual abuse.

Slightly older children may begin to show one of two contrasting behaviour patterns. Some children become apathetic, sitting quietly for long periods in one place. They react minimally to others, seeming miserable, but not crying. Such children touch their parents rarely and with diffidence – one can almost visualise the blow with which this contact has sometimes been met. Other children show a developing aggression. As they grow and learn what they perceive to be normal human behaviour, they start to imitate it. They become more and more aggressive, first towards their peers, then towards younger and older siblings. As they grow in audacity and strength, so they transfer their reactions to adults.

Schoolchildren

If chronic maltreatment has not been recognised, the cause removed and the child treated by the time that he or she reaches school age, one of three well-defined types of behaviour may be seen.

Some children have by this time become quiet and repressed, almost to the point of invisibility. They are often small, undersized and underweight. They may be less well turned out than their peers and have a slightly dishevelled air about them. They respond to questions and obey instructions promptly, but rarely show any initiative of their own. Such a child may have physical signs of injuries suffered over a long period, but usually takes pains to conceal them, or to give plausible excuses.

Another group of abused children may also be small, but are very extrovert and aggressive to everyone. These children strike first, ask questions afterwards and clearly believe that the weak go to the wall. Here, too, there may be physical evidence of previous injuries, but these marks are not usually concealed and are often ascribed by observers to the consequences of the child's own actions.

Children who have been sexually abused may present in either of the two ways already described, or with a distinct behaviour pattern of their own. Unless schoolchildren have had some sort of sexual experience, they rarely use sexual imagery or play in anything other than a lavatorial context. Sexually-abused children, on the other hand, may try to translate their experience to others in their class, either by description or in play. Their attempts to involve other children are usually greeted with embarrassment. Alternatively, their experiences may separate them emotionally from their peers, so that they become unable to join in play and social intercourse (see Helen Kenward's paper on page 127).

The widespread exposure of children to sexually-explicit videotapes has induced this sort of behaviour in some children and encouraged them to experiment, but it has not yet been shown to affect children in quite the same way as sexual abuse by an adult. This is, I believe, more likely to lead to psychiatric disturbance and more abnormal behaviour. However, I have no doubt that a significant degree of abnormality is induced in children as a consequence of their exposure to pornographic films, which is, indeed, a form of sexual abuse.

Growth and development

The growth of children is a sensitive indicator of their state of health: 'Failure to thrive' is a diagnostic grouping which the paediatrician recognises and which has a series of potential causes, one of which is child cruelty. When emotional abuse occurs, sub-optimal growth may be the only clinical sign of upset.

It is often necessary to admit such children to hospital for a period of observation in a controlled environment. In the ward, where nurses and play-leaders give reliable attention and affection; where meals appear at regular intervals and are eaten with other children; and where the loving, but firm, discipline of the ward sister is authoritative, but predictable, children whose poor growth is a function of their environment, and not a consequence of a disease, will thrive. As a means of clinical investigation, admission to hospital can be very helpful in such cases.

Although the children who fall into this group are usually under two-and-a-half, some five- and six-year-old schoolchildren may present in this way and the cause of their poor growth is not always appreciated. Furthermore, some children may have a relatively happy childhood until the disruptions of parental death, divorce, remarriage or unemployment. They may be abused only when they have passed through infancy. If this happens just when they start or change schools, any alteration is in their behaviour may be ascribed to the move, rather than to child ill-treatment. Sexual abuse is more common in older girls and so has its effect in later childhood.

Patterns of injury

Matching the appearance of a specific injury to a particular cause – either an instrument or something in the child's environment – is the specialised skill of the forensic pathologist. On the other hand, the experienced paediatrician is familiar with the knocks, bumps and bruises which are common at particular ages, a familiarity shared with others who work with children, as well as with many parents. When an injury fails to match either with this 'normal' pattern, or with the explanation offered for it, suspicion of child battering should always be aroused. Sometimes the cause of the injury is obvious – one may see the overlapping fingermarks of repeated facial slapping, for example. On other occasions, the injuries may be unusual, such as those with regular, geometric borders; those in the perineal area; or those typical of child abuse, such as grasping injuries of the wrist or ankle.

When the cause seems unusual, but obscure, the forensic pathologist's opinion can be extremely helpful, and their investigative advice of great value. For example, a two-year-old black child was once referred to me with curious oval marks on her buttocks. Other signs of injury and her surrogate care pattern made NAI likely and I wondered whether the strange marks were either bites or sucking marks. The forensic pathologist agreed, but suggested that the marks be photographed in ultra-violet light, which helps to reveal bruising on black skin. Before the photographs were available, the little girl told us that her fostermother had beaten her with a stick. The pictures revealed that this was undoubtedly what had happened.

Characteristic and pathognomonic injuries
Some injuries have features which allow one to conclude that they are, without doubt, the consequence of an assault. The presence of a sharp outline, regular geometry, or a typical pattern to a bruise or abrasion, independent of underlying bony prominences, is likely to have been caused by an instrument. Beatings with straps, heavy canes, saws and braided whips are examples which I have seen from time to time. Similarly, beatings inflicted by hand or fist may be clear, as when there is bruising of both cheeks with evidence of overlapping fingermarks, or the marks of attempted strangulation, with fingermark bruising around the neck. Recent sexual abuse, both in boys and girls, sometimes falls into this group. Such signs are termed 'pathognomonic' and, under these circumstances, NAI is undoubted, although the perpetrator may be obscure.

More commonly, the injuries seen are characteristic of NAI, although not pathognomonic. This implies that, while the balance of probability may be strongly in favour of NAI, it is not possible to attribute the injuries to NAI without some supporting evidence. Typical examples of these are bruises caused by gripping of the arms or legs, fingertip bruises on either side of the spine, heavy bruising in unusual areas where no clear outlines are seen, scars left by cigarette burns and perineal injuries where, although the labia may be damaged, there is no sign of injury above the hymen.

Characteristic injuries depend heavily upon the explanation that is offered for the physical signs that have been found. When the explanation is compatible with the injuries, doubt often remains in the pediatrician's mind. More frequently, the explanation is either incompatible, or none is offered. When this happens, one may be on stronger ground in attributing the signs of assault to NAI.

'Normal' and compatible injuries
Children who are mobile may have bruises as a consequence of their everyday activities. Although one might imagine that one will find a continuous spectrum of minor injuries, increasing to the point where the degree of bruising is abnormally great, this is not the case. Three groups can be defined: normal bruising; bruising as a consequence of a

specific illness; and bruising acquired non-accidentally.

Normal bruising has a typical distribution which depends upon the age of the child. Bruising found on children under the age of six months is sufficiently unusual that an abnormal cause should be assumed. Babies are unable to roll until they are about three months old and cannot sit unsupported until about six months. Their consequent dependence upon adults implies that any injuries are at least the result of inadequate care and, at worst, NAI.

Once a child is crawling, bruising on the forehead becomes common. Bruising on or below the cheeks, on the neck, or in protected areas, is unusual and should be regarded with suspicion. Toddlers also acquire bruises elsewhere: on the legs, the outer arms and, sometimes, the outer thigh. Again, bruises under the arms, at the neck or in the perineum are peculiar and NAI should be considered.

Schoolchildren, especially boys, spend much of their time in vigorous play. Playground injuries have a typical appearance and most teachers learn to recognise them. Again, those parts of the body most exposed are most often hurt: shins and knees, outer arms, forehead and around the ears. Abrasions from falling over in the playground are frequent in this group. Some children injure themselves more often than others and behave in a way which might lead one to expect them to be hurt. One needs to remember that children may also be acquiring injuries outside school; repeated bruises acquired over some time and in unusual sites may be significant.

Some illnesses can create confusion with NAI, because they induce what appears to be bruising without an obvious history of an accident. Orbital cellulitis, an infection of the tissues around the eye, can make it appear as though the child has a 'black' eye. I have known this to lead to false accusations of NAI which the parents, not surprisingly, deeply resented. Disorders of blood clotting have typical forms and patterns of bruising. Subcutaneous bleeding which, to the paediatrician, is typical of an illness associated with bleeding, may, by the layman, be ascribed to NAI, as there is no plausible history of injury and the site of bruising may be an uncommon one. Allergic conditions can be highly variable in their physical signs. Some drug sensitivities and food allergies cause peculiar rashes to appear on the skin in odd places. Skin sensitivity to chemicals can look just like burns. Some bacteria can cause skin infections which look remarkably like scalds. It is, therefore, wise to seek the advice of a doctor who is familiar not only with the appearances of NAI, but also conversant with the manifestations of common diseases.

When injuries are thought to be neither of a normal sort, nor the consequence of a distinct illness, and where explanations are either lacking or incredible, then NAI should be assumed to be the cause. However, if the signs are neither pathognomonic nor characteristic but only compatible with NAI, it is unlikely that a firm decision on their nature will be arrived at on the first occasion, especially if proceedings in court are considered. When a series of repeated incidents of a similar nature occur in the same child and no likely explanation can be found, the diagnosis of NAI is more tenable. There have been several cases in which parents have been found in court to have injured their children, but the child has proven subsequently to have an underlying disease. There is no substitute for examination by an expert and the clinical information on such children should be as full as possible.

Child sexual abuse

Helen Kenward has given a practical and moving account of the problem of child sexual abuse (CSA) in her paper. My comments are intended to help the reader to place CSA within the wider context of cruelty to children.

The recognition of CSA is an especially difficult problem. Sexual intercourse between an 8-year-old girl and her 35-year-old father is properly regarded with abhorrence. A sexual relationship between a 13-year-old girl and her 18-year-old brother who has a mental disability is a more complex moral issue.

CSA is considered to have taken place when a sexual contact, which may be visual only, takes place between an adult and a child under 16 years of age. In the first example I gave, no-one would disagree with the criminality of the act and the majority would want the child to be protected from her father, even if this meant their separation and, possibly, the break-up of the family. The second example is more subtle; one might find, on further investigation, that the brother depended heavily upon his sister and that their separation could destroy not only his future, but also hers and that of the rest of the family.

For these reasons, precise guidelines describing when CSA should or should not be considered to have occurred, can be a handicap. It is, however, essential that a sensible code of practice and the accepted local procedure is well-known to all those whose professional work may lead to their being made the recipient of a disclosure of sexual abuse.

The long-term effects of sexual abuse in childhood can be more serious than most people imagine. As I described earlier, women who have been repeatedly abused as children grow up with very low self-esteem and an abnormal image of family dynamics. Because they may find great difficulty in developing their own roles as mothers, rather like physically-abused children, they often associate with men who sexually abuse their own children. It is not uncommon for such women to aid their male partners in sexual abuse or at least to turn a blind eye, perhaps because they perceive this behaviour as normal. These observations underline the importance of the detection of child sexual abuse – not only for its prevention, but also for the psychological treatment of the affected children.

Between 80 and 90 per cent of children who are sexually abused are girls. They may be brought to a doctor with injuries to the genitalia. In such cases, just as in uncomplicated physical assaults, an explanation for the injuries should be sought and its compatibility with the physical signs considered. Common accidental explanations are that the girl was doing 'the splits' and either over-stretched her vulva or banged upon an object on the floor. Perineal damage can occur in this way, but, if there is evidence of damage above the hymen, accidental causes are much less likely. Although a cursory inspection of the injuries is sensible, when such an accident is reported, at school for example, and sexual abuse is thought to be a possibility, the child should be referred to the local paediatric team. There should be a proper procedure for the disclosure of sexual abuse and the examination of the child, which will take into account the needs of the forensic pathologists.

The signs which may alert one to the possibility that a child has been the subject of sexual abuse are principally those of unusual behaviour and they have been described already. However, any trusted adult may be made the target of a disclosure of sexual abuse and the way that this should be handled is suggested in the next section.

It has been generally agreed that such investigations should *not* be carried out in the nearest police station. The police and health services are in the process of establishing specially-designed centres for the management of such cases, where the children may be interviewed sympathetically and examined. However, once a suitable place for disclosure has been established, close co-operation between properly trained police officers and health care professionals has been found to work very well by those Health Districts which have pioneered this work.

Emotional abuse

It is worth repeating that the child who suffers from emotional abuse alone poses the greatest difficulty for those professionals who are involved in the detection of child cruelty. Although these children may be unkempt and have minor abrasions, there will be no sign of injuries which cannot be described as 'normal'. We all recognise, despite this, the behaviour of the child who may not only have been denied affection, but also subjected to the unrelenting stress of the demands of a tyrannical parent.

Every child has a right to be loved. Cherished rabbits and hamsters, kept as domestic pets, grow larger when they are stroked and cuddled than when they are ignored. Similarly, children who are denied normal physical contact with those who care for them do not grow as well as those children brought up within the affectionate environment of healthy family life.

I have described the typical behaviour of maltreated children and the need for empathic recognition. However, the greatest difficulty lies in the management of such cases. We depend upon the collection of unequivocal evidence of child abuse to create the pressure needed either to persuade parents to participate in programmes designed to modify family dynamics, or to convince the courts that cruelty has occurred and the child is in need of care and protection. When a child can be shown to thrive physically when placed in a controlled environment, but repeatedly to wilt when returned to his parents, one may claim that child abuse is a reasonable cause. Older children are less likely to show this pattern, however, and the need for careful family studies and psychological opinions on the child's behaviour may be crucial.

The characteristic behaviour of the emotionally abused child has been described already and is better and more thoroughly dealt with by Rolene Szur in her paper (see page 104). The greatest difficulty lies in knowing what action to take when one's suspicions have been aroused. A conflict often arises between a desire to protect the child from further abuse, if it turns out to be behind the problem, and a fear of upsetting parents, with potentially deleterious effects upon the child's schooling and social contact. Furthermore, we all tend to have a subconscious feeling that the parents have a right to manage the child as they wish.

I believe that an open approach to the family is the most appropriate policy. An experienced and well-trained professional can always find a way of discussing a child's behaviour with parents. I would advise anyone with suspicions about emotional abuse in a child, who feels that they lack the experience to handle the problem themselves, to seek help from a more experienced colleague.

Disclosure

When parents are asked about the possibility that their child has been subjected to maltreatment, an inadequately-trained interviewer, who has not seen many cases, can seriously impair the prospects for a satisfactory outcome for the child. The disclosure of child abuse has similarities with the confessional in the Catholic Church: each depends on mutual trust and the understanding of the listener; each depends also upon a degree of recognition that confidentiality will be respected although, in the case of child cruelty, this is rarely possible, given the legal requirements governing child care. Despite this, the creation of an atmosphere which encourages those caring for children to speak freely about their management is very important.

Training in disclosure

Those professionals who may, as a consequence of their work, be made targets for the disclosure of child abuse, must receive suitable training. Only a few programmes are as yet available for such people, and places on them are difficult to obtain. More training programmes are needed. It is to be hoped that the special needs of teachers, to be provided with initial and in-service training in child abuse recognition, will soon be met.

The content of a course should be designed to be as practical as possible. Although one can design a series of lectures which cover all the aspects of child abuse and its disclosure, it is more useful to help trainees develop their communiation skills through practice. Interactive videotape interviews and role-playing are of great value. They allow one to try out methods of questioning and to experiment with various situations and parent types, as well as with different patterns of child abuse. We should no longer expect men and women to learn by experience – one shudders at the thought of families whose lives have been ruined by people learning by their mistakes!

The professional work of different groups often plays a part in determining the way in which disclosure should be handled. A teacher may be well known to the parents and already seen as a friend, whereas a hospital consultant paediatrician will probably be a new and rather frightening person, whom they have never met before. It is more appropriate for each professional group to design courses which they believe are best suited to their colleagues, while co-operationg with those in other disciplines, in both formal and informal ways.

Who should receive disclosures?

The best opportunities for disclosure cannot be accurately predicted. However, it is important that each professional group has a procedure, well-known to everyone, which can be called into action at the right time. In practice, the most helpful information about what actually happened during a particular incident is likely to be collected very quickly. When a child has a pattern of injuries and a parent fabricates an accidental cause for them, the explanation tends to become more plausible as information about the nature of the injuries becomes more detailed. Obviously, a properly-taken history of the events, written down with a recorded time and date, and signed by the participant, can be crucial. Diagrams of any injuries, labelled, dated and signed in the same way, should be prepared.

Sometimes it is possible for the story to be heard on several occasions, although this is less than ideal. In other circumstances, such as CSA, the evidence from the child should be taken once only, when this can be arranged. Ideally, all disclosures should be videotaped. This serves several purposes. First, it may spare a child having to repeat a difficult and painful experience. Second, a doctor can view such a videotape when attempting to get some idea about likely physical injuries to look for, instead of asking the child. Third, videotape interviews can be very useful in persuading the perpetrators of child cruelty to admit to their actions. Fourth, when abused children are under psychiatric treatment, it can be extremely helpful for them to watch their own disclosures again. This approach may be used when, for example, a child is adopted. Watching the videotape serves to share the information between the child and the adoptive parents.

It should be clear by now, that each professional group, within, say, a local authority area, needs a trained team experienced in receiving disclosures of child abuse. The team should be made up of both men and women and must be of sufficient size to ensure that a team member is always available at any time and to cover any district. There should be rooms specially equipped for disclosure interviews, with concealed video cameras and recording equipment. One-way mirrors can also be useful. There must be a procedure, subject to regular review and well-known to all staff, so that everyone knows to whom they can turn when the possibility of child abuse arises.

Disclosure technique

The environment
Some disclosures must be taken as soon as possible, for example, after a serious assault; others can be delayed, such as when longstanding CSA is discovered. In the acute situation, whoever is best trained and available at short notice to take disclosure should do so. In less urgent cases, it is better to delay disclosure for the most experienced professional to take, provided the delay will not be harmful. It is worth remembering that an unnecessary degree of haste can be damaging.

When either an adult or a child is interviewed about the circumstances surrounding a suspicious episode, it is helpful to arrange that the surroundings put them at their ease. A comfortably-furnished room, with carpets, curtains, and armchairs set around a small coffee table, is best. A formal, starkly decorated office with a desk tends to be inhibiting. There should be toys for children to play with and arrangements of flowers. Sexually explicit dolls for the disclosure of sexual abuse should be unobtrusively available and one-way mirrors and cameras adequately camouflaged.

When feasible, two adults should always be present for disclosures. Both professionals must seem to be a natural pair from either the child's or the parents' point of view: a children's nurse and a paediatrician or a community doctor and a social worker, for example. One member of the professional team should conduct the interview, while the other listens and acts appropriately to the stresses of the discussion. It is not necessarily a good thing to be impassive in discussing unpleasant events. Although calm should prevail, anguish, distress and solace may all be important. Whatever is revealed, the interviewer should avoid expressing disapproval, unless there is a definite short-term advantage to be gained with respect to information-gathering. Inexperienced interviewers should be especially careful in this repect. I have known the expressions of understandable anger at a disclosure, about a parent's actions, seriously to damage the success of subsequent management.

Disclosure by adults

The nuts and bolts of disclosures are highly variable, depending upon the nature of the incident. It is usual to begin by describing the reasons, physical and psychological, for the disquiet that the interviewer feels about the circumstances surrounding the case. This is followed by running through the possible causes of whatever the child's symptoms and signs might be. At intervals, the parent may make comments and should be encouraged to say what they like. Eventually, they should be asked, first, for any explanations they may have for the signs and, second for any comments they may wish to make. Finally, assuming that NAI is still felt to be possible or probable, the potential actions that the professional team may take should be described to the parents, so they are aware of what may happen. If a case conference is to be called, the nature of the police involvement should be made clear.

There are a number of typical responses to a disclosure interview: anger frequently, sorrow occasionally and a lack of concern, not uncommonly. All these reactions should be noted and recorded. It is important not to press too hard for a positive response. Personally, I take only one or two versions of events from the same carer, in order to avoid confusion. Parents either know what happened and will or will not describe it, or they don't know and can't tell you. In my experience, a further history, taken as a consequence of new clinical information, tends to cloud the issue.

Disclosures by children

The story the child has to tell is very important. In many cases, it is better to let a younger child play (say in the hospital's children's ward) and, after they have settled, to discuss short sequences of the events with them, at intervals. This sort of disclosure is carried out expertly by children's nurses. In cases of sexual abuse, as I have already said, a more formal interview, by a specially trained person, is necessary.

I will not try to describe the interviewing technique for children in detail. It is largely a matter of experience and personality: some people simple cannot talk to children. In the same way that children are frightened by doctors who loom over them while carrying out an examination, dialogue needs to be conducted on the child's level if it is to bear fruit. In no way does this imply 'talking down' to the child, as children expect adults to behave in an adult way. The key elements are trust and confidence; if a child instinctively trusts a particular adult and has sufficient confidence in the responses that adult will make to a disclosure, then there will be little difficulty. Team leaders must ensure that all those who are entrusted with the interviewing of children are not only adequately trained, but capable of sympathising with children's moods and behaviour.

Actions

The dominant problem is the protection of the child from further physical or emotional damage. All other decisions must be based on this consideration. Although, in principle, this will mean the separation of the child from the perpetrator, it is important to remember that such a schism will initiate its own element of emotional trauma, which must be weighed against the benefits of protection.

The mainstay of child abuse management remains the case conference, which is usually called by the social work team. When a disclosure interview has revealed the possiblity of child abuse, the social services should be contacted so that they can arrange a meeting of all the interested parties at a convenient time. Ideally, they should include the GP, the Health Visitor, Hospital and Area Social Workers, Teachers, Paediatricians, Community Medical Officers and anyone else who may have been working with the family. In cases of child abuse, the police have a statutory duty to be present and their actions are not governed by case conference decisions.

At present, potential actions are relatively limited. The child may be returned to the family, either because there is felt to be little risk, or because there is insufficient evidence. A Supervision Order may be obtained, under which the Local Authority has a statutory right of access to the child and can require regular attendance at, say, a school or a day nursery. Finally, a care order may be obtained, putting the child in the care of the local authority, who may then place them wherever it feels most appropriate.

When a case is heard in a magistrates court, the local authority, the child, and the parents all have separate legal representatives, although the parents may choose not to be represented, if they wish. The court appoints a Guardian ad Litam, who oversees the conduct of the child's case as a surrogate for the parents. This ensures the independence of opinions about the child's best interests from both the views of the local authority and the parents.

The future

The Minister of Health has issued a consultative document on the future of child care legislation and there is a private members bill before the House of Commons on the same subject. It is likely that these measures will introduce changes which will make the law more punitive and less flexible in cases of child abuse. While the proposal of this sort of legal stricture is hardly surprising, given the recent spate of terrible cases in the press, it is unlikely that these alterations will have any impact upon the incidence of child abuse.

In general, three factors underlie the aetiology of cruelty to children: first, inappropriate parenting, brought about by adverse childhood experiences and a failure to teach family and life skills at school; second, deprivation and social disadvantage; and, finally, stress of many different kinds. Child abuse can be defeated only by improving the quality of life for all members of our society and by increasing the amount of teaching we given our children in proper methods of child-raising.

As many ideas about parental care are assimilated during a childhood of misery, a key element in prevention is the early detection of child abuse and effective measures to ameliorate the environment of affected children. Child screening programmes, safe houses, child abuse prevention centres, good parenting courses and day psychiatric hospitals are used all over the world to greater or lesser effect.

In Britain, children have little or no political recognition as individuals, but are seen as the property of their parents. Until we see them as our equals as people, with appropriate personal rights and freedoms, we will fail to protect them adequately from the suffering inflicted upon them by those who care for them.

Ideally, we all bear responsibility for the care of each child. As John Donne might have put it 'Each baby's birth invigorates me, for I am a part of mankind.'

Further reading

Doek, J E (1985). Presidential address. *Child Abuse and Neglect* 9 3-6.

'The rights of the child.' editorial in president of what *Australian Paediatric Journal* (1982) 18 pp.6-12

Helfer R E and Kempe C H (eds) *Child Abuse and Neglect: the Family and the Community*, (Ballinger, Cambridge, Ma, 1976)

Jackson, A D M 'Wednesday's Children – a review of child abuse' in *Journal of the Royal Society of Medicine* (1982) 75 pp 83-88

Krugman R D 'Emotional Abuse in the Classroom. The paediatrician's role in diagnosis and treatment' in *American Journal of Diseases of Childhood* (1984) *138* pp 284-286

Lynch M A and Roberts J *Consequences of Child Abuse* (Academic Press, London: 1982)

McClare, G 'The management of child abuse and neglect in schools: the Toronto Model.' in *Child Abuse and Neglect* (1983), *7* pp 83-89

McNeese M C 'When to suspect child abuse.' in *American Family Physician* (1982) *25* pp 190-197

McRae K N, Hurd J, Ferguson C A, Longstaffe S and Gutkin R 'The Winnipeg Children's Hospital child protection centre: a provincial medical initiative.' in *Canadian Medical Association Journal* (1984) *140* pp 981-984

Minority Rights Group 'Children: Rights and Responsibilities.' (London, Minority Rights group Reports, number 69, 1985)

Moutzakitis C M 'Characterisation of abused adolescents and guidelines for intervention.' in *Child Welfare* (1984) *63* 149-157

Turbett J P and O'Toole R 'Teachers' recognition and reporting of child abuse.' in *Journal of School Health* (1983) *53* pp 605-609

Whitfield R C *Education for Family Life: Some New Policies for Child Care* (Hodder and Stoughton, London, 1980)

Chapter 4

Breakdown of parenting function in abusing families: how can professionals think about these issues and be helpful?

Arnon Bentovim

Introduction

In talking about family breakdown I am referring to destructive interactions and failure of care which leads to a child being neglected, abandoned or misused. This may take the form of physical abuse, emotional abuse, failure to thrive physically, sexual abuse or states of induced illness. To be considered family breakdown, the extent of the abuse has to be such that professional intervention becomes necessary, and may even require the provision of alternative parenting.

This definition of breakdown of parenting function therefore relies on:

1   The presence of destructive interaction within the family, and interactions which are at the breaking point.
2   A state in the child showing evidence of the abusive pattern.
3   A professional network which either recognises the state in the child or has the state in the child brought to their attention.
4   A decision to be made that the severity of the state in the child is such that development is being avoidably impaired, or cannot be assured without the provision of alternative parenting – whether or not other forms of intervention have been offered.

The decision to separate a child from their family is rightly seen as a major one, and the first task for a professional is to make a thorough diagnosis. S/he needs to do so to understand, in order to justify the decision about the need for separation, and to begin thinking about what is in the child's interest in the longer term, and how far the family is capable of changing in order to create a different situation. Although the first step in the recognition of any severe abusive pattern is to prevent further abuse (whether physical abuse, sexual abuse, illness induction, failure to feed or thrive, severe neglect . . .) at the same time planning for the future must begin. Unless long term planning emerges from the immediate crisis, it will always be something to be done in the future.

Family breakdown processes

Family interaction patterns

In thinking about the processes of family breakdown it may be helpful to apply the model of family interaction developed by the Family Studies Group, Hospital for Sick Children, Great Ormond Street.[1] This describes the family strain patterns which predispose to breakdown. Although the model of family breakdown and child abuse sees the child as 'victim' and not 'responsible', we know from looking closely at patterns of family interaction, that the child can be stimulated to take part in destructive interactions. He can himself trigger off or provoke some of the responses that subsequently lead to what can be severe physical abuse or other forms of abuse. This is not in any way to imply that the child has a direct responsibility for his own abuse. No child can be responsible for an adult's abusing him when that adult has a role of responsibility and the child is basically dependent. However, unless one looks in a value-free way at interaction patterns occurring in the family, one will have no way of rationally thinking about what the treatment pattern should be for that particular child and family, nor identifiying what needs to change.

A child in a traumatic state following abuse shows a behavioural state – eg frozenness, intense anxiety, anger and fear – which can be misinterpreted as provocativeness. This, in turn, may trigger off further rejecting responses, whether from the parent or from the caretaker who tries to care for the child in separation. We need to have information on family patterns in order to make rational decisions.

We have found it helpful to talk about categories of:

a   *Family character:* divided into four areas – communication, affective status, boundaries and alliances.
b   *Communications:* to do with satisfactory patterns of continuity in the expression and reception of messages. In family breakdown we see patterns which are chaotic, fragmented and disrupted.
c   *Affective status:* related to the atmosphere within the family. Basically relationships should be supportive and there should be a satisfactory expression and reception of emotional messages. The family should not give a dead, panicky, perverse, attacking or undermining feel and should not foster either overt dependency or inappropriate degrees of separateness.
d   *Boundaries:* to do with the regulation of closeness and distance

within the family. To function well a family needs distinct family roles, satisfactory intergenerational boundaries, a clear sexual identity and autonomy. A family shows severe dysfunction when there is such intense overinvolvement or isolation that roles are unduly rigid, or blurred so that there is no sense of identity or separateness.

Alliances

To function well families require satisfactory marital relationships, parental coalition, satisfactory sibling relationships and parent-child and child-parent relationships. What we observe in family breakdown is scapegoating, isolation of children or the pulling in of a child into family relationships through inappropriate coalitions and alignments.

The effect on the child of being involved in a family which shows breakdown characteristics is profound. Moreover, the child's role can be considerable. In making direct observations one has the opportunity of assessing these patterns and understanding what the child's role is or has been; by intervention one may discover whether in fact such roles can change or whether the child is always required to be a scapegoat. Can there be different forms of emotional support, or a different form of communication, alliances and boundaries?

Other areas of significant family functions are their competence: their ability to resolve conflicts rather than ignore or displace them, and the capacity to deal with tasks at the point the family has reached in the life cycle, dealing appropriately with infancy, toddlers, school-going children or adolescents.

Family process

The final area of importance is the issue of family process. Family life should be supportive and not constrictive. What we see in families where breakdown occurs are characteristic sequences of interaction which are repetitive, destructive and quite compulsive. Despite asking the family to stop, or to do something different, they rapidly return to their original destructive patterns. One needs to explore the family background in depth to understand why something which seems so dysfunctional and destructive from the outside, and may even be recognised as destructive from the inside of the family, continues.

Assessment of family patterns

The assessment process

Assessment of family character, competence and process emerges from observations in a number of different contexts. There are the naturalistic observations of hospital staff, foster parents, and of course, the family's description of its own life. The information so obtained is inevitably limited because to be a participant observer of necessity restricts the field of observation. During the process of assessment, when the account of the problem and historical factors are being sought, it is possible to make observations of the family as it responds to the various issues that are being discussed. It is a common experience that children will enact with their parents the issues that are being talked about. Alternatively the family will enact with the professionals the sort of responses and patterns which are part of their character and competence.

A useful strategy is to focus on some specific tasks to elicit family interaction. These can arise out of the flow of clinical practice, eg 'Could you discuss between yourselves or with your social worker the reasons for the referral and assessment and what you all hope to gain from it?' The therapist can then withdraw from the meeting and observe through a one-way screen. There are other naturalistic tasks, such as 'Can you explain to your son or daughter the reason he or she had to be placed in care?'

In the course of a lengthy session there are many opportunities to focus on issues of control. Parents can be asked to get the children to settle down when there is noisiness, to work together to encourage the children to play, or do something constructive, or to help the children to draw their family, eg the kinetic drawing tests, or a family tree. All these are ways of stimulating patterns of interaction which indicate the way the family works.

Perhaps of even greater importance is the assessment of whether the family's patterns are rigid and unchangeable, or whether they can respond to requests to do something differently.

We are aware that the character of destructive interaction is such that short-term changes only will be possible. However, the family's reaction does give a clue about how they might respond to more intensive work. The therapist also can discover how he or she is being used by the family and can begin to sense the experiential life of the family.

Case example 1: Richard

Detailed examples of how a family in breakdown was described are given in Bentovim and Miller[1] and Kinston and Bentovim. A description of the response of a family in breakdown to a task interview was described in the former paper.

Richard, aged nine, was admitted to an in-patient unit because his parents had said very clearly that either this boy left the family or the mother would. As part of the case appraisal, a formal assessment to stimulate family interaction was administered. Family breakdown patterns were then revealed.

The parents worked with each other with considerable awkwardness and difficulty. They tended to interrupt and cut across each other when they were trying to discuss and talk to each other. John, the six-year-old, was included in tasks and attempted to help his parents, but Richard was consistently excluded. When father attempted to get Richard involved he refused to join and behaved in a frankly negative manner. The parents then joined together in an increasingly critical approach to Richard. As he became more withdrawn and oppositional, the parents were provoked to more bitter attacks against him, and the cycle escalated. John, meanwhile, remained a good boy and did not aid Richard, who was eventually written off as bad and unhelpful. Performance of tasks was severely disrupted by this scenario which was repeated during the interview and appeared to be uninfluenced by the nature of the particular task. This pattern was revealed in clinical interviews and attempts to get the parents to interact differently with Richard met with very limited response indeed.

Family breakdown in context

What sense are we to make of interaction patterns which seem so self-defeating? So often family breakdown patterns seem perversely repetitious and independent of external events. They require the collusive involvement, to a greater and lesser extent, of all members of the family, and are self-maintaining and self-defeating. The family cannot inhibit the cycle and the pathological patterns have a dominating and urgent quality which overrides the consequences. It is only possible to make sense of such pathological interaction by looking at and understanding the historical context in which the family lives.

This context relies on the history of the parents as children, as well as the history of the particular family. Because of the way in which professionals can become a part of the life of the family, we are particularly interested to know how the family has linked to the professional workers in the past. Often, if the parents have had a period of life in care, which to them has represented a safe refuge from abuse, then the family may feel pressure, at an unconscious level, to use this safe context; it becomes part of the family's expectations. Alternatively, being in care may stand for disaster. These factors need to be understood if we are to arrive at a proper understanding of the family, to identify whether change is possible and, if so, what form of change can be achieved.

In the case of Richard where there was such an extreme level of rejection it became possible to understand this rejection on the basis of the family's early history and attitudes. It appeared that the mother was sexually abused herself in childhood and as a result of this went into a long-stay hospital because of 'fits', her father was imprisoned and her parents' marriage broke up. She had a lengthy, difficult relationship with her own mother when she returned at the age of 11, after four years in hospital (having been admitted at the same age as Richard who was in hospital at the time of assessment). She subsequently married as a way of leaving home. There was further breakdown in her first marriage, and one of her three children, handicapped following meningitis, died in unexpected and unusual circumstances – a fall on a concrete floor. Her other two children were placed with foster and adoptive parents.

The father, on the other hand, grew up in a family where there was good care but considerable impoverishment. His basic life view, therefore, was to try, try again and never give up; the mother's view, on the other hand, was that if things don't work out you change, you get rid of people or stay silent. Dominating this family's existence seemed to be an active belief that children break up families, which arose, in the main, from the mother's own history. Thus it was considered better for Richard to be 'got rid of' or to 'get rid of himself' than for the marriage to break down and the mother to have to leave. The dominating meaning that the father gave to family life, however, stated that everything can be overcome. So Richard was caught between his parents' totally differing views and pulled and pushed at the same time.

This led to a constant pattern of negative behaviour on Richard's part as he attempted in more and more emphatic ways to help his parents by being so impossible that he had to be ejected from the family. His mother said, 'either he goes or I go,' putting her husband in an impossible position. Beginning to gain an understanding of the meaning behind the perverse, destructive interaction helps us to know what sort of work is going to be possible to help both the child and the family. In particular, it helps us establish what sort of changes are going to be requisite, so that we can know whether indeed Richard (or a child in his situation) can grow up without rejection and a degree of conflict which is bound to be repeated and reinforced in other contexts. In Richard's family it became possible to set the following goals:

1 for the parents to work together without scapegoating Richard;
2 for the children to be treated equally;
3 for the parents to resolve conflict without a child being involved in a sacrificial way.

Not surprisingly, in the more severe forms of abuse a family needs to be reconstituted in a safe context where intensive work can be offered to the family in breakdown and care given to the child. A residential or intensive day context can be helpful to this end.[3]

To illustrate these issues two further case examples will be given, one of which used a foster-care context, the other a hospital context for the work of assessment.

Case example 2: Tracey, a sexually abused child
This three-year-old was referred to a psychiatric day centre by a health visitor who was concerned at the difficulties her parents were having with her. She would not sleep alone, would not use the toilet and refused to feed herself. It was noted that her father, aged 68, was becoming increasingly concerned with her physical care, her mother, aged 48, becoming increasingly distant and depressed. She slept with her father and her health visitor was concerned with his physical contact – his way of creaming her bottom and drying her between the legs. Although there was no direct evidence, the issue of sexual abuse was considered. She was 'frozen' in her behaviour and did not respond to a 'play' visitor's work. Only the father and child visited the day centre.

A case conference heard all the observations and was concerned that this girl's developmental delay could be linked to the possibility of abuse. The parents were confronted with a concern that the pattern of mother 'opting out' and a father increasingly doing everything for the child's care could lead to abuse if abuse was not already happening. The parents, although distressed, appreciated the professionals' concerns and agreed to a period in care. Soon after this a wardship was obtained to ensure that work to test the resourcefulness and flexibility of the family system could continue. A contract was made for the girl to be placed with an experienced foster mother. The whole family would attend a day centre with the little girl; access would be facilitated by the foster mother and social worker. Work was centred on supporting the mother's caretaking, with the specific goals of mother managing – feeding, toileting and child care – to be carried out successfully in the foster home.

Family work focused on the effect of having a child in this particular family with its 'parent-child' pattern of relating between the parents. This predisposed to the distortion of father-daughter relating. A specific agreement was made under the terms of wardship that unless real change occurred within a period of six months an alternative family would be needed, to ensure that this child's development could progress satisfactorily. She had responded well to the foster family, and 'unfrozen' and her potential for normal development had been established.

Case example 3: Peter, a child who was failing to thrive
Peter was a two-year-old with brothers aged eight and five. His development at this age was six months retarded, and he had been in and out of a paediatric ward with failure to thrive. His growth failure earlier was thought to have been connected with allergies to various foods. The mother lived in the ward, and it was only when feeding by the mother was observed closely, that it was realised that she fed him inconsistently. She was constantly anxious that if she fed him 'sweets and puddings' it would 'diminish his appetite' or cause him to be 'allergic'. It was noted that food prepared for him appeared in the bins and on one occasion she was observed throwing it in.

The parents were confronted and it was put to them that the hospital must establish whether Peter could thrive with other caretakers. His development was six months retarded at two years. It was felt that the mother 'clung' to the child – and vice versa – and avoided issues in her marriage. She therefore had no capacity to foster his development – although he was the third of three children. Once it was established that Peter could put on weight with others it became possible to write a contract which specified family attendance at a day centre. Work on feeding, play and skills helping Peter to achieve independence, with proof of weight gain and skill improvement was essential. It was planned that this should occur in hospital, prior to increasing periods at home with the same aims – weight gain, independence and skills increasing. It was agreed that if the family could not create a situation for this child to thrive and grow and not be handicapped by severe failure to thrive or failure to develop psychologically, then an alternative family placement would be needed.

Attachments and family breakdown

The attachment dynamic

We also need a conceptual framework to enable us to think about both the family as a group, and the individual – in particular the individual child and his or her stage of development. When it has become necessary for a child to be separated from the family, this is inevitably a painful and less than ideal action. Goldstein, Freud and Solnit have talked about 'the least detrimental decision' in terms of a child's future care.[4] If a child has been caught up in processes which may well have damaged him or her then whatever is done for the child – whether return to their own family after a period of separation, or placement in a new family – must inevitably be less than ideal, but hopefully will be the least detrimental.

One of the problems which leads professionals to try to avoid separation where at all possible, is that the damaging effects of separation can themselves add to the destructive processes of the family. Such destructive processes not only affect the family, but may also be contagious – affecting professionals and alternative family groups. The child can become abused for a second or third time. Martin and Beezley's work[5] on what happens to abused children who have been in care, and the work of Rowe[6] and the Dartington Group[7] which looked at the effect of separation on children, emphasises time and time again that unless rapid interventions occur, then the consequence of separation on a child will be a life of further separations. A vigorous attitude towards attempting to ensure that a child is rehabilitated to their family is an essential follow-on from having to separate a child from the family following breakdown.

A conceptual framework which helps us considerably in thinking about children's needs is Bowlby's 'attachment' framework.[8] This framework is useful in the context of family breakdown because patterns of attachment between adults and children arise out of the specific interactions that occur between them. The intervention patterns described by Bentovim and Miller[1] as being at breakdown point, inevitably have an effect on the attachment pattern between parent and child. The intervention pattern affects the way the child himself sees, experiences and lives those relationships whether he is with his family or whether he has to be separated from them.

Attachment – a definition

Bowlby has described attachment as a conceptual framework.[8] Attachment behaviour results in proximity to a preferred individual who is differentiated from others in the field. That individual is perceived as being 'stronger and wiser'. Attachment behaviour has the form of following, clinging, crying, calling, greeting and smiling. Attachment develops during the first six months of life and attachment to specific individuals is evident on observation from six months onwards. Principal attachment figures develop out of the child's pattern of relatedness; in the presence of an attachment figure play and exploration are possible.

Attachment behaviour is most marked during the second and third year of life and diminishes slowly after this. But although attachment behaviour diminishes, the attachments themselves remain important throughout all stages of life.

Shaffer and Emerson[9] have described the way that attachments become established in the mind, and the way that having a second internalised attachment figure gives the child the ability after the age of three to be able to spend longer and longer periods away from the parents, in school or staying with relatives and so on. The time needed before the child has to 'refuel' these attachments by actual contact with the parent is extended as the child grows older. Even for the adult, primary attachments are important; when stressful events occur they are often accompanied by an increase in attachment behaviour and a desire to contact and be in contact with important figures, even if they have been out of direct contact for some time. Parks and Stevenson-Hinde[10] have shown the way in which attachments can play an important role through life, eg in marriage, divorce, illness and death.

Patterns of attachment vary considerably and each pattern has its own impact on the abusive pattern on separation, and is important in relation to the work that has to be done to achieve change. It is now possible to differentiate between three basic forms of attachment:

1   secure attachment;
2   insecure attachment – ambivalent form;
3   insecure attachment – avoidant form.

In describing the patterns of attachment, Ainsworth[11] has observed the way in which different children respond to strangers. In this particular procedure a child of one year is separated briefly from his own parent, and is first observed alone, then in the presence of a stranger for a brief period. There then follows a reunion when the parent returns to the child. The patterns of attachment which result discriminate between children, connected with clinical experience they can predict longer-term relationships (see also page 77). Main and Weston[12] have reported on the stable patterns of attachment patterns, and we will try to describe their important role below.

Secure attachment

Securely attached infants actively explore when they are with their mothers, and show little in the way of attachment behaviour. This is an important observation because it implies that if quite a young child seems to be playing actively, one might think he is avoiding contact with his mother. In fact this may be an indication of a good attachment relationship between the two. In the mother's presence the child does not have to keep checking back and 'fueling himself' at her lap to confirm his security. Thus active play and exploration indicate good attachment.

Following a separation episode, securely attached children of one year of age become upset. They explore very little in the absence of their parent and respond strongly on reunion. They seek bodily contact and they interact keenly, showing no resistance to such contact. In general terms, infants with a sensitively responding parent cry less, are generally positive in mood, can be easily soothed and comforted by their parent and are content to be put down to play. They are not interested in comfort from strangers.

The child who seeks comfort from relative strangers, however, who is apparently touch-hungry, following and clinging to whoever offers a parenting response, gives cause for particular concern. This child is not showing a secure attachment to a particular person, but rather exhibits an intense attachment need, focused on anybody offering a parenting response. The sign of more secure attachment is appropriate coolness and distance to a stranger and slow warm up and response if the 'attachment' figure gives permission.

Insecure attachment – ambivalent form

At one year the insecurely attached infant showing ambivalence before separation is highly anxious, and tends not to be at all explorative or active, even in his mother's presence. He is even more distressed by separation than the securely attached child and in reunion he will want close bodily contact. Yet at the same time one observes the child resisting contact and interaction. On looking at the interaction patterns closely, Main and Weston noted that ambivalent attachment occurs when mothers are insensitive; their babies want contact but, because of the mother's insensitivity, are unconfident about being held for as long as they need. A sense of anger and a mutual sense of rejection arise out of the interaction. Such children cry more, in general terms.

After an absence, these children respond negatively to physical contact and yet when put down remain negative. If the parental sub-system is a weak or vulnerable one, this negative behaviour on the part of the child can trigger off anger and rage in the parents. It is induced by long-term insensitive, out-of-touch parenting and describes the response of a child locked into the widespread pattern of chaotic communication, poor emotional expression, scapegoating closeness and distance.

Case example 4: The H family, Ambivalent – insecure attachment
A case which illustrates this issue is the 'H' family. Two of their three children, aged two and a half and five, had been removed before the birth of the third, now aged 18 months. As a result of strain, tiredness and marital tensions the mother had been threatening to kill the other two and had treated them roughly. Following hearings at appeal, the Court had felt rehabilitation was appropriate and the older girl was returned. By the time of our consultation a familiar scenario had been created. Mark had spent almost two years with his foster family and had been there from the age of six months. The local authority felt he had been with foster parents too long. The parents felt they had done

everything which Social Services demanded – including getting married – what more could they do!

Because of a further appeal, access was recommended in the parents' home after a long period of no contact. Mark was reported as being anxious before and after contact and we felt it would help if we asked the foster parents to help Mark to stay with his natural parents so we could see them together. Not surprisingly, in the intensity of seeing the parties together, we saw Mark clinging angrily and tearfully to his foster mother and pushing his natural mother away.

When we asked the foster family to help him stay with his natural parents Mark continued to cling and resisted attempts to get him to play with his own natural mother. We saw him rejecting his mother who blamed the foster parents 'You have made him like this, you have torn him away. I am his mother, he should not call you mother.' We saw the natural father trying to resolve the situation by snatching him. We saw Mark's disconsolate crying and the difficulties in understanding Mark's attachment to his foster parents. Although 'attached' to him in their minds, he was now in his mind part of the foster family.

Insecure attachment – avoidance form

This is one of the most worrying attachment patterns. It is marked by the distance and the very rigid boundary which develop between a particular child and a particular parent, or between the parents and the child in the family as a whole. Infants of one year who are showing avoidance attachment demonstrate little in the way of contact with the parent when playing alongside them, and on separation show little or no distress. They avoid contact with a parent and may move away, making sure that proximity and interaction do not occur. On reunion contact is avoided, they refuse to approach or look, even when coaxed. When the mother's behaviour patterns are looked at carefully they show rejection, aversion to body contact and a wooden-faced interaction with the child. This is obviously a dangerous form of attachment; if such a pattern continues throughout development it can lead to increasingly anti-social behaviour. Poor contact is shown to people who try to replace the rejecting parent and appropriate parenting and warmth are in turn rejected. It is thus possible for the infant and child showing avoidant attachment to induce further avoidant attachment in the parent, and in substitute caretakers.

It is also appropriate to note that it is possible for a mother who is wooden-faced and compulsive with one child to show warmth and intensive contact with another child. Avoidant patterns can grow and patterns of abuse emerge. Ainsworth[11] and Main and Weston[12] have shown that such avoidant attachment may well be initiated by the parent and precede avoidant attachment from the infant, in return.

Case example 5: Lisa, avoidant attachment

Lisa was a five-year-old described as 'provocative', 'tempting her mother to throw her across the room' when she wore the wrong clothes. She was described as 'uncuddly' from birth and (according to her mother) always fought her mother off. When they talked, it was noted that she stood woodenly answering her mother. When interaction was prompted – mother was asked to find something out from Lisa – the woodenness of their contact was noted. When asked to give her a cuddle the mother said that if Lisa fell she would ask for a cuddle – but only if her father was not there. Mother was asked to show us a cuddle; she touched Lisa but said 'It is not there, nothing'. She behaved quite differently with the younger boy, whose hair she ruffled affectionately. The cuddle she gave was wooden, stiff, rigid arms. Lisa gingerly climbed up and froze with her arms stiffly around mother's neck, paralysed and painful. This contrasted vividly with the warm moulding-in cuddle between father and Lisa, and between younger brother Charlie and mother. This quality of contact with father had a role in maintaining the frozenness with mother and vice versa.

Likelihood of the family to respond to help

In attempting to make a prediction of outcome we have found the following categories helpful:[13]

1   a prognosis of *hopeful* outcome;
2   a prognosis of *doubtful* outcome;
3   a prognosis of *hopeless* outcome.

Hopeful outcome

We can predict a hopeful outcome when:

a The family take responsibility for the abuse, rejection, or the state of the child and for their failure of care. They accept the need for treatment and agree to necessary separation and contexts for treatment because of their awareness of a need to be able to change to create a different context.
b There is some acceptance of responsibility, and an awareness that responsibility is held in the marital system.
c The children's needs are acknowledged as being primary, and there is lack of scapegoating or blaming of a particular child. It is important that there should be no blaming by other family members, for example other siblings who say that everything is 'x's fault. We can observe that with help and assistance better communication can occur and there is a potential for change in other systems in terms of boundary functioning,

affective relating, alliances, competence and relationships to the extended family.

d Attachments are clearly alive and although there may be some anxious or avoidant aspects there is potential for secure attachment between children and parents. During early periods of access there has been proper use of access and potential for growth of attachments seems to be present.

e The family has demonstrated an ability to work through difficulties with professional systems and there is potential for trust and bridge-building rather than fear and blame.

Cases of hopeful outcome, we suspect, are probably in a minimum in psychiatric contexts, but greater in number in health and social service agencies.

Doubtful outcome

This is far more likely to be the case in the more severe problems that we see. We would predict a doubtful outcome where:

a There seems to be an uncertainty about the parents taking full responsibility for the state of the child, particular form of abuse etc. There seems to be a continuing conflict between the adult's needs and the child care needs so that there is a continuing possibility and fear that the particular child who is being scapegoated remains at risk.

b Children remain unsure, attachments are ambivalent and continue to be insecure during periods of separation.

c There has been long-standing inadequate care and protection from main attachment figures and there seems to be a limited potential for change in communication, affective status, boundaries, alliances and competence. Relationships with professionals continue to be somewhat doubtful and the ambivalence, clinging and rejecting which is present between the parent and children continues between the parent and the professional sub-system. Access is likely not to be very well used – perhaps some missing of meetings, or access cut short by ambivalent or avoidant patterns.

Hopeless prognosis

A hopeless prognosis might be made where:

a Parents deny responsibility for the child's state, either totally or to a significant degree. Instead the child is blamed or rejected outright, or the professionals who should have been helping are blamed.

b Attachment is avoidant and continues to be so, access being poorly taken up or only perfunctory contact; there is no response to attempts by professionals to bring about change.

c There seems to be no progress with long-standing individual and family states, for example, alcoholism, drug addiction, psychiatric illness in a responsible adult which may not be acknowledged or treatment accepted. Communication, affective status within the family, boundaries, alliance, competence and relationships with professional systems remain at breakdown point, despite intensive investigation and attempts to create change during the assessment.

The following three vignettes may help to illustrate the process described above.

Case example 6: 'C' family – hopeful prognosis

The 'C' family are a reconstituted family in the sense that the father brought a daughter from his first marriage, the mother a daughter from her first marriage and they had four of their own children. Two of these four younger children had tyrosinosis. At the time when the family were seen, the father's daughter was living separately. Anne, the 12-year-old-girl, and the younger children were living in the family, the father was living away.

Some two months before the assessment Anne had come to her mother and had told her that her dad was 'touching her up'. Her mother had asked her to give details and had then contacted a social worker (with whom she was already in contact because of the father's daughter). They then linked with the police who charged the father and arranged for him to live separately. He had his own social worker. The family social worker and his social worker met with the parents as a couple to do some work on trying to understand the basis of how it was that the father had abused Anne sexually.

The father himself took full responsibility for his acts and had pleaded guilty. When the family were seen it was to test whether further therapeutic work was necessary and also to make an assessment as to whether the family could be rehabilitated. Anne was able to give a clear account of the abuse which had been vaginal touching and penetration with her stepfather's finger over a period of two to three years. All members of the family indicated a wish to be able to understand what had happened, so that they could get back together. The parents had already done some work on issues in the marriage, such as their difficulties in facing conflict and resolving it. Father had begun to think about his own family background and factors which may have led him to a sense of despair and being unable to reach his wife and having to use her daughter as a way of doing so. The professionals felt committed to work with them and were basically positive about the work that had gone on up to that time. There was no question that they put Anne's needs first, balanced with the family's needs for the parents to stay together for the sake of the younger children.

It was possible to help them as a family unit to have a degree of openness with each other which contrasted with the secrecy and hiding that had occurred previously. They were motivated to accept the possibility of attending a couples' group to do some work on their own relationship, and for Anne to attend a girls' group so that she could share with other girls who had had similar experiences. There was an acceptance generally of the need to change current patterns.

Case example 7: the 'J' family – doubtful prognosis
In the 'J' family, the youngest of four children was killed by the mother's cohabitee while the father was in prison. The cohabitee and the mother were charged but the mother contended that 'she was not responsible'. When the father was released from prison he and mother got together once more and the mother became pregnant again. The children had all been placed in care in a foster home, and the parents had regular contact with them in the social services department.

When assessed the children were seven, five and two-and-a-half respectively, and had been in care for 12 months already, a very lengthy period particularly for the girl of two-and-a-half who was 'unattached' to her own family and not fully attached to her 'short term' foster family. The baby of three weeks was a major focus for these children who were in limbo.

When the parents had been together previously, although causing concern through poor care, they had shown no active abuse before the episode. The family were able to accept a contract and showed some capacity to work together; they realised they had to accept responsibility for the death. The father had to acknowledge that his own acts led to him being in prison, the mother that she chose inappropriate partners. Both were aware that they should not blame each other. They were willing to go into an intensive day context for an assessment period and realised that if they could not convince the professionals in contact with them of their ability to change, their children would need alternative care long-term.

Case example 8: the 'L' family – hopeless prognosis
The 'L' family consisted of three boys who at assessment were eight, six and four – the youngest at six months had been killed 18 months previously by the mother – the night the father had come home from a job he had obtained after twelve months out of work. He had not woken to the baby's crying. The mother was imprisoned and spent much of her initial custody and imprisonment in psychiatric hospital as she had lapsed into a psychotic state after the death of her son.

She denied all knowledge of his existence, or thought he was still alive or had been killed by someone coming into the house. Father regularly visited the children's home where his sons were placed, and after 18 months the mother was released. At assessment, total denial was maintained. The couple were aware that if they could not take responsibility for the death of one of their children, no court could entrust the care of the other children to them. Yet at the same time they realised that if they *did* take responsiblity, they could not trust themselves to look after their three sons safely, particularly knowing how much anger, testing out and regressive behaviour would follow their children's rehabilitation.

To test the situation further we suggested they try to convince a residential unit to accept them for rehabilitation work. But they could not put forward any suggestions for change. They blamed the local authority social workers for not having helped sufficiently before the death. Finally the father informed the Court he felt his wife needed him, and that the children could not be looked after by them. The parents agreed to construct a life book to help them understand what had happened and accepted the notion that access would have to have as its aim the support of children's placement in a new family. It was also likely that to help the children they might need to stop access considering the age of the younger children. They were aware they would have to decide about agreeing to adoption, and that in this situation access would be in the hands of the adopters and could not be laid down.

Conclusion

It is essential to see the abuse of children as an issue for the family as a whole, and for the professional context where the family live. To be helpful, professionals must take a dynamic view of the family and its potential to be a safe place for the child who has been abused. Consideration of family interaction patterns and attachments will help the professional to make proper assessments of the prognosis for work. It should then be possible to know whether a child can be rehabilitated to their own family or requires the resource of long-term fostering or adoption to ensure that they have a family to grow up in without further abuse.

Notes and references

1 Bentovim, A and Miller, L 'Family Assessment in Family Breakdown' in Adcock, M and White, R (eds) *Good Enough Parenting* (British Agencies for Adoption and Fostering, London; 1984)
2 Kinston, W and Bentovim, A 'Creating a focus for brief marital and family therapy' in Budman, S H *In forms of Brief Therapy* (Australian paper) (Guildford Press, New York, 1981)
3 Bentovim, A 'A Psychiatrist Family Day-Centre meeting the needs of abused

or at risk pre-school children and their parents' in *Child Abuse and Neglect* (1977) pp 479-485; Pickett, J and Maton, A 'Protective Casework and Child Abuse, Practice Problem' in Franklin, A W (ed) *The challenge of child abuse* (Academic Press, London, 1977); Cooklin, A 'The Family Day Unit' in Fischman, C and Bosman, B (eds) *Festschrift for Salvador Minalum* (Howard University Press, Boston, 1985)

4 Goldstein, Freud, A and Solnit, A J *Beyond the best interests of the child* (Free Press, New York, 1973)

5 Martin, H P and Beezley, P 'Behavioural observations of abused children' in *Developmental medicine and child neurology* (1977) 19, pp 373-387

6 Rowe, J; Cain, H; Humdleby, M and Keane, A *Long Term Foster Care* (Bastford/BAAF, London, 1984)

7 Milham, J; Bullock, R; Hosie, K and Haak, M *Children Lost in Care* (Gower, London, 1986)

8 Bowlby, J *Attachment and Loss* (Vol: Attachment) (Hogarth Press and Institute of Psychoanalysis, London, 1969)

9 Shaffer, H R and Emerson, P E 'The Development of Social Attachments in Infancy' *Monographs of the Society for Research in Child Development* Vol 29 (serial no 94) (University of Chicago Press, 1964)

10 Parkes, C M and Stevenson-Hinde, J *The Place of Attachment in Human Behaviour* (Tavistock, London, 1982)

11 Answorth, M D 'Attachment, Retrospect and Prospect' in Parkes, C M and Stevenson-Hinde, J *The Place of Attachment in Human Behaviour* (Tavistock, London, 1981)

12 Main, M and Weston, D A 'Avoidance of the Attachment Figure in Infancy, Descriptions and Interpretations' in Parkes, C M and Stevenson-Hinde, J *The Place of Attachment in Human Behaviour* (Tavistock, London, 1981)

13 Elton, A; Tranter, M and Bentovim, A *The Assessment of Family Breakdown – Treatability* (to be published)

Chapter 5

Parent-child interaction in abusing families: its possible causes and consequences

Kevin Browne and Sarah Saqi

Regularly the report of a nasty incident of cruelty to an infant or a child murder makes its way on to the front pages of our daily newspapers, then to a special inquiry and back again to the press. This is after much painful analysis and discussion to discover where procedures for managing cases of so-called 'non-accidental injury' have broken down. In this process lies much mystification and evasion.

Mystification is implicit in the semi-official term of 'non-accidental injury'. Quite obviously it is meant to sound like 'accidental injury'. Its true meaning may be obscured further by the abbreviation to NAI – clearly, like VD, too unmentionable to be openly acknowledged.

As a society we prefer not to recognise the fact that many children are either wilfully or, more usually, impetuously attacked physically and painfully by their own parents. Indeed, in a nation which uses physical punishment both institutionally and in the home[1] the condemnation of those whose discpline has 'gone too far' seems almost like self-condemnation.

Evasion is also involved in the assumption that when a child is injured this is actually due to some fault in the system of official communication and management. We should face the fact that it is also the fault of the family in which the injured child resides.

If we did this honestly we might actually prevent reoccurrence, if not occurrence. A study by Hyman[2] shows that nearly 40% of cases of child abuse coming up for case conference have already been known to the relevant authorities either on account of previous injury to the child under review or to one of his siblings. This is a common finding throughout the child abuse literature, yet one apparently little appreciated by magistrates.

While on the one hand mystification and evasion blur the public's and professionals' full understanding of child abuse, on the other, simplistic explanations make the solution of this society-pervading problem appear too easy. Thus the first Report from the House of Commons Select Committee on *Violence in the Family 1976-7*, laid special emphasis upon 'bonding' in the days immediately following the birth of a baby. However, we know from follow-up studies of infants who have suffered early post-natal separation that most observable effects disappear within the first 18 months.[3,4] Furthermore, many abused infants are not so separated.

By contrast, the 'social-situational approach' to child abuse proposed by many American researchers[5] states that certain stress factors may serve to elicit and maintain abusive patterns of parenting. It has been suggested that these 'predisposing' factors may form a basis for identification of families 'at risk' of abusing their children. However, a more pertinent question is why the majority of families under stress do *not* abuse their children.

From our own work, we have found that approximately 7% of Surrey families with a newborn infant have a high number of 'predisposing' factors for child abuse. On follow-up only $^1/_{17}$ of these 'high risk' families went on to abuse their children within the first 24 months after birth. This is less than expected when one considers the findings cited by Susan Creighton in Chapter 2, which show that most child maltreatment occurs to children under five, with the exception of sexual abuse (see Figure 2.3 on page 29).

Thus we believe that stress factors associated with families are not a sufficient causal explanation for child abuse.

Causes of child abuse

Figure 5.1 presents a tentative model of the causes of child abuse and neglect. It assumes that the 'situational stressors' are made up of the following four components:

A *Relations between parents:* intermarriage, marital disputes, step-parent/cohabitee or separated/single parents
B *Relation to child:* spacing between births, size of family, parental attachment to child and parental expectations of child
C *Structural stress:* poor housing, unemployment, social isolation, threats to parental authority, values and self-esteem
D *Child-produced stress:* unwanted child, problem child, a child that is incontinent, difficult to discipline, often ill, physically deformed or retarded

The chances of these situational stressors resulting in child abuse or neglect, mediate through and depend on the parent-child interactive relationship. A secure relationship between parent and child will 'buffer' any effects of stress and facilitate coping strategies on behalf of

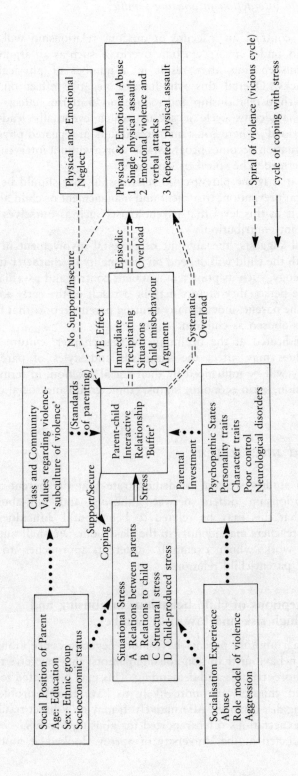

Figure 5.1 The causes of child abuse and neglect
(Adapted and modified from Gelles[6])

the family. By contrast an insecure or anxious relationship will not buffer the family under stress; 'episodic overload' such as an argument or the child misbehaving, may result in a number of physical or emotional attacks. Overall this will have a negative effect on the existing parent-child relationship and reduce any buffering effects still further. Hence a vicious cycle is set up which eventually leads to 'systematic overload', where constant stress results in repeated physical assaults. The situation becomes progressively worse without intervention and could be termed 'The spiral of violence'.

It follows that it is the parent-child relationship that should be the focus of work on prevention, treatment and management of child abuse and neglect. It is at this level that psychologists such as ourselves can make a significant contribution.

As the model suggests, the amount of parental involvement in the relationship with the child will depend on personality or character traits and their pathology, such as poor temperament control and psychiatric disorders. These personality factors may be a result of the early social experiences of the parent; indeed many abusing parents report that they were themselves abused as children.[7]

Finally, as indicated at the beginning of this chapter, culture and community values may affect the standards and styles of parental behaviour. They will be influenced by their social position, in terms of age, sex, education, socio-economic status, ethnic group and social class background.

Parent-child interaction

From our own studies we aim to demonstrate that the parent-child interactive relationship differs between abusing and non-abusing families, and that this may be related to behavioural difficulties in children which teachers may identify in the classroom. We shall outline two areas of work which exemplify different approaches to an investigation of parent-child relations.

Maternal perceptions of child behaviour in abusing and non-abusing (high risk and low risk) families

It is believed that abusing parents have more negative conceptions of their children's behaviour than non-abusing parents; they perceive their children to be more irritable and demanding. This may be related to the fact that abused children are more likely to have health problems, eating or sleeping disturbances. Alternatively, it may be a direct result of the unrealistic expectations often reported for abusing parents.[8]

A study conducted at the University of Surrey[9] looked at mother-infant interaction in abusing families compared with high risk and low risk control groups. The control families were designated high or low risk on the basis of their scores on a 12-point checklist of factors found to occur in child abusing families. Checklist items included: age of mother; time period between pregnancies; post-delivery separation; evidence of prematurity/low birth weight/handicap; family with separated or single parent; socio-economic problems; history of violence; record of psychiatric problems; and socialisation difficulties.

The sample consisted of over 30 families believed to have 'physically abused' their infants (aged between nine and 24 months), together with the same number of 'high risk' and 'low risk' control families with an infant of the same age and sex. The families were also matched for ages and occupation of parents, ethnic origin of child and type of housing.

Each family who agreed to participate received four home visits. During the weekly visits the mother and child were observed at play and the mother was asked to complete a questionnaire with reference to her child's behaviour.

The questionnaire was based on the 'Behaviour Checklist' devised by Richman, Stevenson and Graham[10] and covered four main areas of behaviour: sleeping-eating patterns, activity, controlability and interaction with others. In total 14 questions were presented, each with three items on which the mother was asked to rate her child's behaviour according to the description that she believed best applied over the past week.

The response to each question was scored 0, 1 or 2, 2 being the most negative perception of the child's behaviour. The findings of the questionnaire are presented in Figure 5.2. It shows that the abusers accumulated higher scores than both the high risk and the low risk families in terms of negative perceptions, with the low risk being the most positive and scoring the least.

Figure 5.2 Behaviour checklist scores by case type

	Low risk	High risk	Abusers
Score: 0 to 7	64.1%	40.0%	31.3%
No of cases	25	14	5
Score: 8 to 14	35.9%	57.1%	43.8%
No of cases	14	20	7
Score: 15 to 28	0.0%	2.9%	25.0%
No of cases	0	1	4
Chi-squared = 18.79, p < 0.001			

Figure 5.3 Number of life stress events in the last 12 months* (percentages)

	Low risk	High risk	Abusers
0-3 factors	68.4%	35.3%	16.7%
No of cases	26	12	2
4-22 factors	31.6%	64.7%	83.3%
No of cases	12	22	10

Chi-squared = 13.171   2 df   p < .001

*From the Parenting Stress Index (Abidin 1983)

This may be related to the fact that the low risk group had experienced significantly fewer life stress events (from the Parenting Stress Index[11]) over the past 12 months, as seen in Figure 5.3.

Table 5.3 confirms the validity of the 'social situational' approach as the high risk group mirror the abusers in the number of life stress events. However the parent under stress still requires a certain level of misconception about her child to become a potential child abuser, as exemplified in Figure 5.1 where the high risk group have more positive perceptions about their child than do the abusers.

It has previously been suggested that the child contributes to its own abuse.[12] Our work does not support this notion, for example we found no significant differences in children's health records. We consider that the abuse may be attributed to the fact that the parents have unrealistic expectations of their children. They interpret certain age-appropriate behaviours as deliberate or intentional non-compliance, concluding that this behaviour is an indication of the child's inherent 'bad' disposition. Thus abusive parents may see their child's behaviour as a threat to their own self-esteem, which then elicits a punitive attitude and an insensitive approach to parenting.

Children's perceptions

Earlier, a small project had been carried out by Hyman and Mitchell[13], which compared abusive and deprived children using the Bene-Anthony Test of Family Relations. This test consists of cut-out figures representing family members. Into boxes attached to the figures the child posts messages which reflect his feelings for his family members. Battered children avoided the mother's box, expressing significantly fewer feelings for her either of a positive or negative kind than the control children. Equally they denied that she had positive feelings or negative feelings for them. These differences were found among children who had been receiving help for two years in comparison with other deprived but *not* physically assaulted children. Although this small study was carried out on only 13 matched pairs of pre-school children we were sufficiently disturbed by the results to set up a more direct comparative investigation of mother-child interaction in abusing and non-abusing families.

A video study of mother-child interaction in abusing and non-abusing families

What goes wrong in the abusive mother arises, to a large extent, from her own personality difficulties which make it hard for her to respond appropriately and sensitively to her infant's behaviour. This in turn begins to affect the child's responsiveness to her and so a vicious spiral is set up.

It was to examine these ideas that we decided to undertake a direct observational study of abusive mothers and their infants between the ages of six and 24 months. We aimed to compare their responses to a standardised strange situation with those of 'matching' mothers and infants of the same ages and social class in whom no abuse was in any way suspected. In both groups we were looking at the sort of interaction the mother sets up with her child, the degree of attachment the child exhibits when the mother leaves the room and returns, how the mother copes with brief separation and reunion, and how the mother and child react to a stranger.

We filmed and analysed the results of 23 matched pairs, with the permission of all those involved. The subjects for this study were seen at a NSPCC clinic. They were shown into a room which they had not seen before, and told that someone would join them in a short while.

The video procedure lasted for 8.5 minutes. Four episodes were involved (see Figure 5.4).

Figure 5.4 Video-recorded standardised situation

INTRODUCTION	Episode A	Mother and infant alone in strange room	3	minutes
TRANSITION B	Episode B	Mother and infant joined by stranger	30	seconds
SEPARATION	Episode C	Mother leaves infant in the company of the stranger	3	minutes
REUNION	Episode D	Mother returns – reunion with infant and stranger	2	minutes

| | | | 8.5 | minutes |

One method of analysis used has been to look at the amount of interactive behaviour occurring. At this level we are mainly interested in whether or not there is interaction (regardless of its content), that is, whether the mother smiles or talks to the infant regardless of whether he or she responds with vocalisations, smiles or gestures. Types of interaction have been analysed in the following manner. If a *general interactive initiative* is shown (ie behaviour directed towards another), it can have one of three possible outcomes:

- it may result in the respondent reacting with another interactive initiative (*mutual interaction*);
- it may result in the respondent reacting with a non-interactive behaviour (*causal interaction*);
- it may receive no reaction at all (*failed interaction*).

For example, if the mother is eating and the child reaches for the food (interactive initiative), the mother may give the child some food (mutual interaction), stop eating and attend to the child (causal interaction) or continue to eat (failed interaction).

The interaction analysis demonstrated that abused female infants and their mothers have interactions that are less reciprocal and fewer in number than their matched controls, whether in the presence or absence of the stranger. By contrast, abused male infants and their mothers showed little variation from controls. Overall differences were only evident for interactions with the stranger where there were fewer general initiatives and mutual responses from abused infants in the presence or absence of their mother (see Figures 5.5 and 5.6). Thus we found a number of sex differences in our data which are not yet fully analysed. In this instance it seems likely that the greater responsiveness of the mothers to their girl children is associated with the greater amount of distress in the males, which will be discussed later. As Moss has shown[14] while initially mothers of males interact more with them than with girls, if the boys are persistently fretful the reverse effect occurs and their mothers become decreasingly responsive.

Another way in which we have analysed our data is in terms of the frequency analysis of the behaviours, using a three-second time grid. These behaviours have been grouped together into broader categories so that, for example, the category 'aggressive play' would include banging the tray of the high-chair, banging a toy, dropping or throwing toys, etc.

As with the interactive analysis a number of differences have emerged.

In fact, out of 17 categories used, 11 produced significant differences and out of the six remaining ones we believe, with hindsight, that three were not strictly appropriate, as the child was restricted to a high chair.

Again we have picked out the chief findings for graphic illustration (see Figure 5.7). As *column 1* shows, the main behavioural difference in

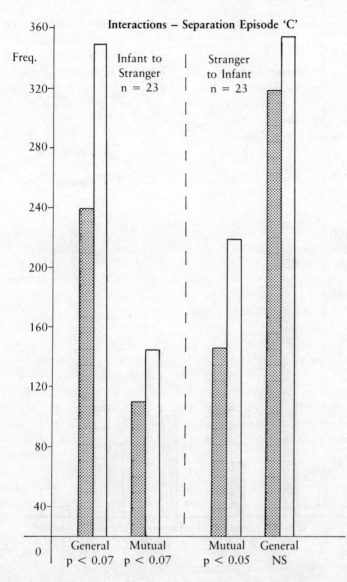

Figure 5.5

the introduction episode before separation, was in facial expression. The control children smiled, laughed and reflected happy expressions or 'positive affect', more than was true of their abused counterparts ($p < .03$ females, $p < .07$ overall).

In the separation episode one marked difference (*column 2*) was the

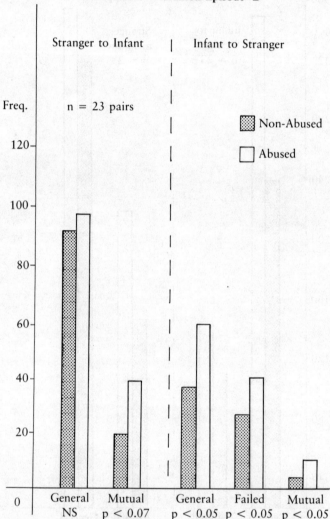

Interactions – Reunion Episode 'D'

Figure 5.6

much greater amount of aggressive play revealed by the abused children (p. < .07) while levels of passive play were similar for both abused and control groups. Another difference was the much greater visual interest in the toys shown by the control children illustrated in *column 3* (p < .05). However, the chief differentiating behaviour in this separation episode was the highly significant involvement shown by the control infants with the stranger (*column 4*). We have already talked

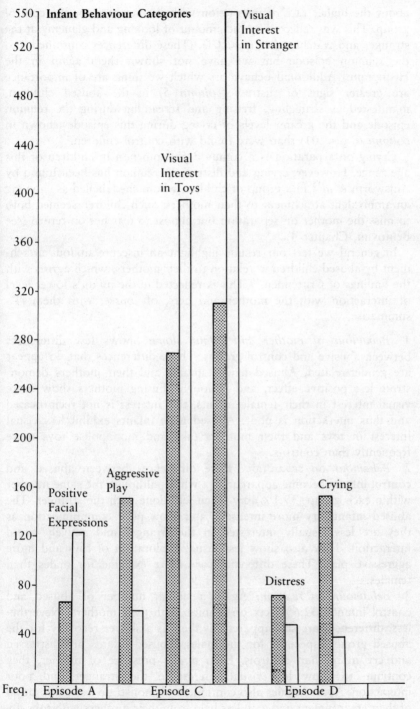

Figure 5.7

about the higher rate of interaction with the stranger for the control group. This was reflected by the amount of looking and glancing at the stranger and watching her (p < .01). (These differences continued into the reunion episode but we have not shown them again in the Histogram.) Additional behaviours which we think are of importance are greater signs of distress (*column 5*) in the abused children, manifested as struggling, fretting and screaming during the reunion episode and the greater levels of crying during this episode (shown in *column 6*, p < .01) than were found with control children.

Crying on separation is a common phenomenon in children of this age range. However, crying and distress on reunion has been found by Ainsworth *et al*[15] in a group of children whom she labelled as showing an ambivalent attachment to their mothers. Such children seemed both to miss the mother on separation but almost to fear her on return (see Bentovim, Chapter 4).

In general we feel our results highlight an insecure/anxious attachment by abused children in relation to their mothers, which agrees with the findings of Crittenden.[16] This is reflected in the infant's lower level of interaction with the mother and hers, of course, with them. To summarise,

1 *Behaviour of mother and infant alone:* Shows few differences between abusive and control groups. Those differences that do appear are gender-related. Abused female infants and their mothers demonstrate less positive effect, and although abusing mothers show more visual interest in their female infants, this interest is not reciprocated and thus interaction is poor. Abused male infants exhibit less visual interest in toys and their mothers take and monopolise toys more frequently than controls.

2 *Behaviour on separation:* Here differences between abused and control infants become apparent as a whole, although the same number within each group (39.1%) cry when left alone with the stranger. The abused infants cry more intensely, and show poor communication as they are less visually interested in the stranger and actively avoid interaction. They also show less visual exploration of toys and more aggressive play. These differences are more extreme for males than females.

3 *Behaviour on reunion:* Again a similar number of abused and control infants (32.6%) cry on reunion with their mothers. Nevertheless, differences are still apparent as there is a slower recovery for the abused group, especially for the males. Abused infants are distressed and cry more than controls. Even in the presence of mother, they continue to show less visual interest in the stranger and poor interaction. Abused males also continue to demonstrate less exploration of their environment and gain less help from their mothers with toys. By

contrast mother-infant interaction for female infants is inhibited by fewer vocalisations and less positive affect from their mothers.

It should be noted that whether infants cry or not, abused individuals show more signs of disturbance and have less confidence, both with the stranger on separation and with their mothers on reunion.

From the results presented, it can be asserted that the abused infant is less inclined to interact, either with the mother or with another strange adult. Evidence suggests that it is the mother who must set the pace of interaction in the early months of the infant's life.[17] Thus the failure to set up synchronous interaction by an abusive mother will have a cumulative effect. It is alarming to discover that the abused child's lower level of reciprocal interaction with the mother has already, before the age of two years, diminished their confidence in strangers and led to social avoidance.

The following sequence analysis shows that the abusive mother fails to 'frame' her infant's behaviour in the way Fogel described. She does not participate in the same amount of reciprocal interaction with her infant and what interaction there is, tends to interfere and contradict expressions of affection. Such a finding has also been reported by Burgess and Conger in the home environment.[18]

The sequence of behaviour during mother-infant interaction

Recent studies on parent-child relationships[19] (eg Martin *et al*, 1981; Cohn and Tronick, 1982; Dowdney *et al*, 1984; Phelps and Slater, 1985) can be distinguished by their emphasis on temporal relationships and contingencies of behaviour, in interactive situations. Dyadic interactions are based on the interweaving of the participants' behavioural flow as time passes; it has been stressed by Browne[20] that sequential analysis is a powerful method of analysing this behavioural flow in order to show which behaviours most frequently form a distinct 'chain' of events. It was thought that sequential analysis could be used to establish that abusing mothers and their infants exhibit different interactive sequences from those shown by non-abusing mothers and their infants, and this may highlight exactly where the communication between an abusing mother and her infant is breaking down.

To test this hypothesis Browne[21] used video data from 23 abusing and 23 'matched' non-abusing mother-infant pairs to sequentially analyse three-minute recordings of mother-infant interaction, observed while they were alone in a strange room. The method of sequential analysis applied was that outlined by Browne[20] to describe sequences of behaviour found within the individual mother and infant, in addition to the sequential flow of interactive behaviour between mother and infant. For the mothers' sequential behaviour, flow diagrams were produced to illustrate the main temporal relationships between different behaviour items at a 1% level of significance (Figure 5.8).

It is evident that the order of occurrence of certain behaviour items is similar, and indeed, no significant differences in the frequency of these acts could be found between the two groups. However, there seems to be a difference in alternatives for the maternal sequences. The non-abusing mothers seem to be more aware of the infants' interest in toys and less concerned with the infants themselves. This suggested that they have a less coercive style of interaction in comparison to abusing mothers who act intrusively, as indicated by previous work.[22]

For the infants' sequential behaviour, flow diagrams were also produced to illustrate the main temporal relationships between different behaviour items, again at a 1% level of significance (Figure 5.9).

It is evident from these results that the abused infants are ambivalent, as predicted by previous work.[22, 16] They mix distress behaviours such as crying or fretting with toy-related actions, while non-abused infants have two distinct 'chains' of behaviour which do not significantly link up: one chain consisting of toy-related behaviours and the other exclusively dealing with distress, making for less confusion during mother-infant interaction. The non-abused infants' behaviour sequences also contain more interactive initiatives.

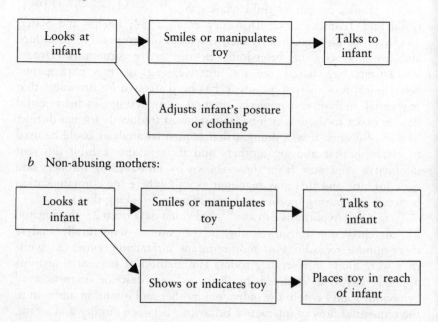

a   Abusing mothers:

| Looks at infant | → | Smiles or manipulates toy | → | Talks to infant |

↓

| Adjusts infant's posture or clothing |

b   Non-abusing mothers:

| Looks at infant | → | Smiles or manipulates toy | → | Talks to infant |

↓

| Shows or indicates toy | → | Places toy in reach of infant |

Figure 5.8

a Abused infants:

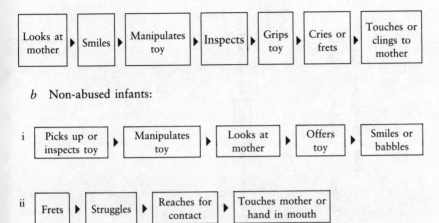

b Non-abused infants:

Figure 5.9

Finally, Browne carried out an analysis of data which highlighted *interactive sequences* between the infant and the mother in abusing and non-abusing data.[21] Figure 5.10 illustrates the lack of sensitivity shown by abusing mothers. The author asked the question 'What leads a mother to obtrusively "adjust" her infant's clothing or posture?' Non-abusing mothers significantly responded only to the signal of *frets* from their infants, which resulted in a change of behaviour if they successfully adjusted the right thing. In contrast, abusing mothers significantly responded to a wide range of behaviours with adjust, none of which indicated the infant's distress. Ironically, the abusing mothers sometimes induced distress in the form of *struggle* and *frets* from their infants as a result of their untimely interventions. Indeed, on the majority of occasions the abusing mothers interrupted exploratory behaviour in their infants. If this became a habit, it would have serious consequences for the infant's development.

Figure 5.11 demonstrates the ambivalence of abused infants while in their mother's arms. Whereas non-abused infants visually explore the environment in such a secure situation, abused infants cry and fret and passively hold on to a toy or their mother.

Overall, these findings are in agreement with the predictions made from Bowlby's 'Attachment Theory' outlined in chapter 4. They also support the conditioning model put forward by Sluckin.[23]

Given the preadaptations and cognitive means for interactive development the infant requires the opportunity for interactions. The importance of a turn-taking pattern of parent-infant interaction has

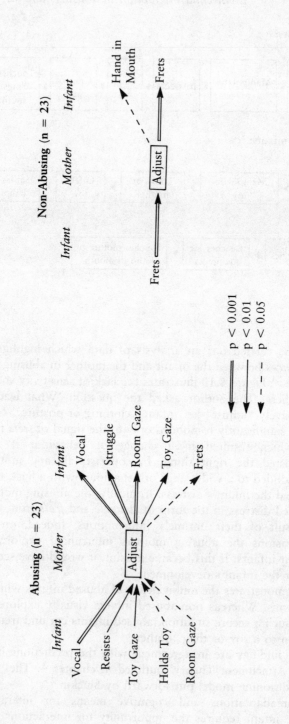

Figure 5.10 Infant to mother interaction

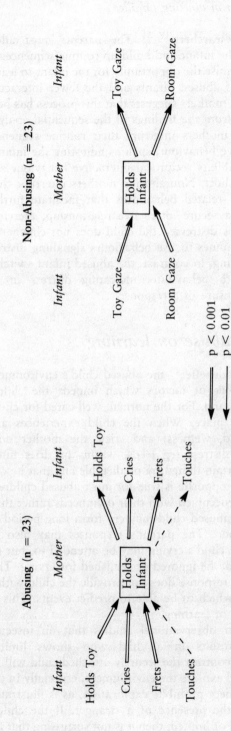

Figure 5.11

been stressed by many researchers.[17, 24] The parents must allow themselves to be paced by the infant and build up routine sequences of a predictable nature to maximise the opportunity for the infant to learn.

The developmental lag of abused infants and the fewer interactive responses shown by abusing mothers suggests that this process has been distorted.[22] This is evident from the findings of the sequential analysis which shows that abusing mothers interrupt their routine sequences with coercive, non-interactive behaviour, such as adjusting the infant's posture or clothing. This inhibits reciprocal interactive behaviour and cuts the 'interaction bout' short. Non-abusing mothers interrupt their routine sequences with toy related behaviours that facilitate further interaction. This produces a secure interactive relationship, therefore when a non-abused infant is distressed the child does not change his style of interaction but continues to use behaviours signalling distress until a response is forthcoming. In contrast, the abused infant switches from toy related action to behaviours indicating distress in an ambivalent fashion, being unsure of a response.

The effects of child abuse on learning

According to Martin and Rodeheffer[25] the abused child's environment is characterised by a number of factors which impede the child's capacity to learn and understand. For the normal, well-cared-for child, the world is a predictable place. When the child experiences any discomfort (eg hunger, cold, wetness) and cries, the mother does something to alleviate the distress (eg feeds, warms or dries him). Thus the child learns that certain things are predictable and that he can cause events to happen. The opposite is true for most abused children, whose parents tend to be preoccupied with their own needs rather than those of their children. The abused child may cry for a long period of time before anything is done. The parent's responses may also be inconsistent − sometimes the child's crying may be attended to, but on other occasions, the child may be ignored or punished for crying. This inconsistency in the parental response does not provide the child with a logical or rational basis on which to be able to predict events. This in itself limits the development of learning.

We know from our own observational studies that an insecure mother-child relationship results in a child who shows limited explorational behaviour. By contrast the securely attached child will be more likely to investigate and explore the environment, especially in the presence of the mother. Anxiety prohibits exploration, as is illustrated by the child's response to the presence of a stranger. If the child's natural curiosity is restrained or limited, then it is not surprising that his ability to learn is also limited. Piagetians have emphasised the importance of searching and manipulating objects in one's environment as precursors to intellectual development. For the abused child these precursors are limited or nonexistent. The neglected child may often be restricted to a playpen for hours or even days on end, while the physically abused child may devote most of his energy to staying out of trouble. The role of the parent as the child's primary teacher is thus a limited one in abusing families.

Martin stresses the important function of the parent in encouraging the child to think and reason about his environment. Language skills develop as the result of interactions between caretaker and child. For adequate language development a child needs to be able to communicate freely with those around him or her. This communication is a two-way process where the child should be able to express himself without restraint and also receive immediate corrective feedback as appropriate.

In abusive families, however, independence of thought is rarely encouraged. Children are expected to respond in rote fashion to questions asked of them. As a result not only is the child's linguistic ability affected, but also his belief in his own competence. Abused children are often reared in environments where there is little cognitive stimulation and support, but where a lot is expected of the child. Abusing parents have distorted notions of what they require from their children, often without consideration of the child's actual stage of development. Because of the exceptionally high standards of behaviour expected, most abused children fail and are therefore punished.

The world of the abused child is therefore a very strained and anxious one. He spends most of his energies looking for ways of avoiding parental wrath. Instead of being able to explore and experiment with the environment, the abused child has to constantly monitor his or her actions to ensure that they are in accordance with adult demands. Opportunities for creativity and learning are minimal or non-existent. It is not surprising therefore to find that abused children exhibit learning and behaviour difficulties.

The consequences of an abusive relationship

A considerable number of developmental problems follow child abuse. However, it should be emphasised that for a large proportion of cases, child 'battering' continues even after identification.

Most of the follow-up studies carried out to date reflect the repetitive nature of child abuse. A study of 78 non-accidentally injured children by Skinner and Castle,[26] reported a 60% re-battering rate. Morse *et al*,[27] reported a 35% rate and in a later study with Friedman[28], gave an even higher re-battering rate of 73%.

There can be little doubt that both previous injury to the abused child (prior to the time of diagnosis), and subsequent re-injury is very common indeed, although estimates vary considerably from survey to survey.

Cognitive consequences

Most research available seems to indicate that physically abused children have lowered intelligence levels and may also exhibit delays in language. We believe that these consequences are a result of pathological styles in parent-infant interaction, which are set up early in the relationship.

Indeed when assessed at the time of identification, many abused infants showed a delay in mental and motor development.

Appelbaum[29] compared 30 physically abused infants to 30 non-abused infants matched for age, sex, race and socioeconomic status, on the Bayley Developmental Screening scales. The average age of the infants was just over a year. The results indicated that there were highly significant differences between the two groups, with abused infants scoring on average four months below the controls. Abused infants showed particular evidence of delay on the motor scales, scoring 5-6 months below the control group.

Other studies using the Bayley Scales to assess abused and neglected infants compared to their matched controls have obtained similar results.[30] However a study by Gregg and Elmer[31] which followed up a group of abused infants and a group of infants with accidental injuries, found no difference in intellectual ability eight years later. At the start of the study, all infants were under 13 months. Standardised developmental screening indicated that 42% of abused children, compared to 18% of the accidentally injured children, were judged retarded. However, eight years later no differences were found between the two groups as measured by ratings of school files. This developmental lag of abused infants is thought to arise through inhibiting influences in the abusive environment and to ameliorate for most cases when there is effective therapeutic intervention.[32]

Studies conducted on older children indicate delays in educational attainment. For example, Kent[33] asked caseworkers to complete a questionnaire about groups of abused, neglected and low income school children. The data showed that 53% of the abused group, 82% of the neglect group and 28% of the controls were judged as doing below average or failing work at school. Furthermore available IQ scores for the neglect group revealed that 78% of the neglected children had IQs less than or equal to 89. This was also true for 44% of the abused group.

The point which needs further exploration is the extent to which initial impoverishment affects school adjustment, and the extent to which IQ gains are reflected in achievement. In this connection Martin[34] says, 'Learning, competency, exploration, initative, autonomy, are not valued in most abusive homes, indeed they may be the basis for physical assault by the parents' (p 103). Furthermore, Martin shows that even in those children with unimpaired IQs, 43% showed language retardation with an average difference of 14 points between language scores and intelligence scores. Since language is a key function in educational advance, especially in reading and learning, the likelihood of educational retardation in abused children is strong and worthy of investigation.

Perry[35] administered the Peabody Picture Vocabulary Test to abused children with an age range of two to 11 years, who were matched to low income controls. Pairwise comparisons (N=21) of the subjects' performance on the test indicated that the abused group scored significantly lower.

The linguistic abilities of abused children appear to be more affected even when the control group has recognised emotional problems. Morgan[36] compared 42 abused children with 57 non-abused children on the Illinois Test of Psycholinguistic abilities. All children were between six and ten years of age and were in special classes for the emotionally disturbed. The groups were matched for age, sex and intelligence. It was found that while the control group's mean profile was within normal limits, the abused group had scores suggesting deficits relating to linguistic competence.

Fitch *et al*[37] and Friedrich *et al*[38] using the McCarthy scale of children's abilities with pre-school children, found that the abused children attained lower overall scores on verbal, perceptual-performance, quantitative memory and motor assessments, compared with controls.

In conclusion, psychological assessment of abused children over three years shows that the majority are *not* mentally retarded (IQs below 75) although there is evidence for continuing language handicap. However, the children's school performance is not as good as expected from their IQ scores. This may be related to behavioural problems found in abused children such as enuresis, tantrums, low self-esteem,[39] aggressive and non-compliant behaviour towards peers and nursery teachers.[40]

Social and behavioural consequences

Research suggests that abused children are likely to exhibit emotional problems at home and at school. Again this may be related to early experiences with their parents. Gaensbauer and Sands[41] noted that even before the age of three, abused and neglected infants displayed more anger than controls. In addition, their anger was more easily evoked, more intense and less easily resolved than that of the control group. By contrast, Gaensbauer, Mrazek and Harmon[42] observed that the abused group appeared disorganised and lacking in energy in their play behaviour. However, there were differences between the infants depending on the type of abuse they had received. Those infants who had been deprived physically and emotionally, with little experience of caretaker-infant interaction, appeared emotionally blunted. They were socially unresponsive and inattentive to their environment. Also they were retarded in their cognitive and social abilities.

Infants who had experienced inconsistent caretaking, consisting of sensitive nurturing alternated with periods of abuse, exhibited ambivalent interaction patterns. Their social approaches lacked stability and under stress these infants would withdraw or display anger.

Extreme amounts of anger were only exhibited by those abused infants who had experienced frequent and harsh punishments from their caretakers. These infants were very active and had low frustration thresholds. Angry outbursts and destructive behaviour were displayed very frequently.

Many studies have noted that older abused children are aggressive in their interaction with peers and teachers. Green[43] examined 60 abused, 30 neglected, and 30 control children aged 5 to 12 years. Psychometric evaluation and psychological testing revealed that the abused and neglected groups had deficits in a wide variety of ego functions such as poor impulse control and low self-esteem. They also exhibited self-destructive behaviour. However, the abused children were aggressive, whereas the neglected children tended to be passive and apathetic. The abused group showed aggressive and destructive behaviour both at home and in school, where they would fight and bully others. The younger children tended to be hyperactive, while the older ones were involved in antisocial and delinquent behaviours.

Green also noted that the abused children were frequently sad and dejected, and had poor conceptions of themselves. The children regarded themselves with the same displeasure and contempt as was directed towards them by their parents. Because of these personality and behavioural problems, most of the abused children exhibited major difficulties in school adjustment. They showed limited attention span, frequent hyperactivity and cognitive impairment, all of which contributed to poor academic performance. In addition, their aggressive behaviour resulted in social problems with peers and teachers.

Reidy[44] studied behavioural and fantasy aggression in abused, neglected and control children. Abused children demonstrated significantly more fantasy and behavioural aggression in a free play setting than did the other groups. Furthermore, both abused and neglected children were rated as significantly more aggressive than were the controls on a behaviour checklist completed by teachers.

Kinard[45] compared 30 abused children between five and 12 years old with a matched sample of 30 non-abused children on tests measuring self-concept, aggression and socialisation with peers. It was found that abused children were significantly more punitive on a frustration task than the non-abused children. Measures of self-concept did not differ between the groups, although abused children showed a significant decrease in their motivation for socialisation.

Barahal[46] studied matched groups of abused and non-abused children between six and eight years of age. He found significant differences from controls on locus of control, where abused children were particularly likely to attribute outcomes to external factors rather than to assume personal responsibility. Abused children were also less able to identify and label others' emotions, although as with Frodi and Smetana's study[47] this did not prove to be significant when IQ differences between the groups were controlled. Nonetheless, abused children showed a tendency to be egocentric, whereas control children were more effective in understanding social roles than were abused children.

Unfortunately, six to eight year old children that have been abused continue to show poor self and school adjustment,[48] even when social work support has led to a measurable progress in reading.[49]

Recommendations and conclusions

It is clear that the available data indicates that abused children can suffer cognitive and behavioural impairments. We have discussed how the mother-child interaction may contribute to this. An abused child suffers not only from the abuse *per se*, but also from the effects attending abuse.

It is somewhat surprising that there is a scarcity of literature and thus of recommendations on treating victims of child abuse. Most practitioners in this area agree that the abusing families should be treated as a unit,[50] with the goal of keeping the family intact. However, it is not sufficient to evaluate treatment programmes on the basis of the occurrence or non-occurrence of subsequent abuse. Training parents to inhibit aggressive behaviour towards their children[51] may still leave unaltered the harmful context in which the initial abuse occurred. It should be recognised that in some cases treatment with the child remaining in the family may be ineffective and may in fact serve to perpetuate the 'abused become abuser' cycle.[52]

In view of the present socioeconomic conditions and relative scarcity of adequate treatment programmes, a primary focus should perhaps be the child's potential for development, not only the parent's prognosis for change. However, there is no simple answer.

Long-term foster-care may improve emotional and intellectual development while children with natural parents remain unchanged or deteriorate.[53] In contrast, short-term foster or residential care may enhance behaviour problems,[34, 54] as indeed can parental visits to such placements.[55]

What therefore can the teacher do? We believe that when a child shows evidence of learning or behavioural difficulties it is important that the teacher look further than the classroom situation. It is too global a statement to say that a child underachieved because he or she is from 'a deprived home'. Admittedly a poor home environment does not facilitate learning, but poverty *per se* does not necessarily retard intellectual development. Most important are the relationships within the child's family – especially the parent-child one. We would argue that it is 'poor parenting' in the physical and emotional sense that leads to underachievement. This is a feature which can occur regardless of socio-economic status. Teachers should not forget that abuse occurs across all social classes; it is just better hidden in the middle and upper middle brackets.

Acknowledgements
This research was carried out at the University of Surrey, and forms part of a study funded by the Medical Research Council. Grateful acknowledgement is made to Mrs Pauline Elliot (funded by the Leverhulme Trust) and to Miss Yvonne McDermott, MSc (funded by the MRC), who have worked enthusiastically on the presented material. Thanks are also due to the Health Visitors and Midwives of Surrey, who made a great deal of the work possible.

Notes and References

1 Newson, J and Newson, E 'Parental punishment strategies with eleven-year-old children' in Frude, N *Psychological approaches to child abuse* (Batsford Press, London, 1980) Chapter 5, pp 62-80

2 Hyman, C A 'Non-accidental injury' (A research report to the Surrey Area Review Committee on Non-Accidental Injury) in *Health Visitor* (1978) 51, (5), pp 168-174

3 Leiderman, P J and Seashore, M J 'Mother-infant neonatal separation: some delayed consequences' in O'Connor, M (ed) *CIBA Foundation Symposium No 33* (Elsevier Amsterdam, 1975)

4 Sluckin, W; Herbert, M and Sluckin, A *Maternal Bonding* (Basil Blackwell, Oxford, 1983)

5 Gelles, R and Pedrick-Cornell, C *Intimate Violence in Families* (Sage, Beverly Hills, 1985)

6 Gelles, R 'Child abuse as psychopathology: a sociological critique and reformulation' in *American Journal of Orthopsychiatry* (1973) 401 43, pp 611-621

7 Kempe, T S and Kempe, C H *Child Abuse* (Fontana/Open Books, London, 1978)
8 Helfer, R E; McKinney, J and Kempe, R 'Arresting or freezing the developmental process' in Helfer, R E and Kempe, C H (eds) *Child abuse and neglect: The family and the community* (Ballinger, Cambridge Ma, 1976); Rosenberg, M S and Repucci, N D 'Abusive Mothers: perceptions of their own and their children's behaviour' in *Journal of Consulting and Clinical Pathology* (1983) Vol 51, No 5, pp 674-682
9 Browne, K D; Saqi, S M and McDermott, Y 'Maternal Perceptions of Child Behaviour in Abusing and Non-abusing (High Risk and Low Risk) Families' in *Bulletin of the British Psychological Society* (May 1986) Vol 39, p A68
10 Richman, N; Stevenson, J and Graham, P *Pre-school to School, A Behavioural Study* (Academic Press, London, 1982)
11 Abidin, R *Manual of the Parenting Stress Index* (PSI) (Pediatric Psychology Press, Charlottesville, Virginia, 1983)
12 Kadushin, A and Martin, J *Child Abuse: an Interactional Event* (Columbia University Press, New York, 1981)
13 Hyman, C A and Michell, R 'A Psychological Study of Child Battering' *Health Visitor* (1975) Vol 48, pt 8, pp 294-296
14 Moss, H A 'Sex, Age and State as Determinants of Mother-infant Interaction' in *Merril Palmer Quarterly*, 1967, No 1, pp 19-36
15 Ainsworth, M D S; Blehar, M C; Wateres, E and Wall, S *Patterns of Attachment: A Psychological Study of the Strange Situation* (Lawrence Erlbaum Assoc, New Jersey, 1978)
16 Crittenden, P M 'Maltreated Infants; Vulnerability and Resilience' in *Journal of Child Psychology and Psychiatry*, (1985) Vol 26, No 1, pp 85-96
17 Fogel, A 'Temporal organisation in mother-infant face to face interaction' in Schaffer, H R (ed) *Studies in Mother-infant Interaction* (Academic Press, London, 1977)
18 Burgess, R L and Conger, R D 'Family Interaction in Abusive, Neglectful and Normal Families' in *Child Development* (1978) Vol 49, pp 1163-73
19 Martin, J A; Maccoby, E; Baron, K and Jacklin, C N 'Sequential Analysis of Mother-Child Interaction at 18 months. A comparison of Macronanalytic techniques' in *Developmental Psychology* (1981), Vol 17, No 2, pp 146-157; Cohn, J F and Tronick, E Z 'Communicate Rule and the Sequential Structure of Infant Behaviour During Normal and Depressed Interaction' in Tronick, E Z (ed) *Social Interchange in Infancy: Affect, Cognition and Communication* (University Park Press, Baltimore, 1982) Chapter 5, pp 59-79; Dowdney, L; Mrazek, D; Quinton, D and Rutter, M 'Observation of Parent-Child Interaction with two to three-year-olds' in *Journal of Child Psychology and Psychiatry* (1984) Vol 25, No 3, pp 379-407; Phelps, R E and Slater, M A 'Sequential interactions that discriminate high and low problem single mother-son dyads' in *Journal of Consulting and Clinical Psychology* (1985) Vol 53, No 5, pp 684-692
20 Browne, K D 'Methods and Approaches to the Study of Parenting' Chapter 12 in Sluckin, W and Herbert, M (eds) *Parental Behaviour* (Basil Blackwell, Oxford, 1986)
21 Browne, K D 'The Sequential Analysis of Social Behaviour Patterns Shown by Mother and Infant in Abusing and Non-Abusing Families' *Proceedings*

of the 10th International Congress of the Association of Child and Adolescent Psychiatry Dublin, 25-30 July, 1982

22 Hyman, C A; Parr, R and Browne, K D 'An Observational Study of Mother-infant Interaction in Abusing Families' in *Child Abuse and Neglect* (1979) Vol 3, pt 1 pp 241-246

23 Sluckin, W 'Human mother to infant bond' Chapter 7 in Sluckin, W and Herbert, M (eds) *Parental Behaviour* (Basil Blackwell, Oxford, 1986)

24 Stern, D N; Beebe, G; Jaffe, J and Bennett, S 'The infant's stimulus world during social interaction' in Schaffer, H R (ed) *Studies in Mother-Infant Interaction* (Academic Press, London, 1977) Schaffer, H R *The Child's Entry into a Social World* (Academic Press, London, 1984)

25 Martin, H P and Rodeheffer, M 'Learning and intelligence' in Martin, H P (ed) *The abused child: a multidisciplinary approach to developmental issues and treatment* (Ballinger, Cambridge Ma, 1976)

26 Skinner, A and Castle, R *78 Battered Children* (NSPCC, London, 1969)

27 Morse, C; Sahler, O J and Friedman, S B 'A three-year follow-up of abused and neglected children' in *American Journal of Disturbed Children* (1970) 120, pp 439-446

28 Friedman, S B and Morse, C W 'Child Abuse: a five year follow-up of early case findings in the emergency department' in *Paediatrics* (1974) Vol 54, pp 404-410

29 Appelbaum A S 'Developmental retardation in infants as a concomitant of physical child abuse' in *Journal of Abnormal Child Psychology* (1977) Vol 5, pp 417-423

30 Koski, M A and Ingram, E M 'Child abuse and neglect: Effects of Bayley Scale Scores' in *Journal of Abnormal Child Psychology* (1977) Vol 5, pp 79-91; Dietrich, K N; Starr, R H and Kaplan, M G 'Maternal stimulation and care of abused infants' in Field, T M; Goldberg, S; Stern, D and Sostek A M (eds) *High-risk infants and children* (Academic Press, New York, 1980); see also Hyman, C A; Parr, R and Browne, K D 'An Observational Study of Mother-infant Interaction in Abusing Families' in *Child Abuse and Neglect* (1979) Vol 3, Pt 1 pp 241-246

31 Gregg, C S and Elmer, E 'Infant injuries: Accident or abuse' in *Paediatrics* (1969) Vol 44, pp 434-439

32 Baher, E; Hyman, C; Jones, C; Jones, R; Kerr, A and Mitchell, R *At Risk: An Account of the Work of the Battered Child Research Department, NSPCC* (Routledge and Kegan Paul, London, 1976)

33 Kent, J T 'A follow up study of abused children' *Journal of Pediatric Psychology*, 1976, 1, pp 25-31

34 Martin, H *The Abused Child* (Wiley, New York, 1976)

35 Perry, M A 'Behavioural and cognitive status of abused children' Unpublished manuscript (Department of Psychology, University of Washington, Seattle, WA 98195, 1981)

36 Morgan, S R 'Psychoeducational profile of emotionally disturbed abused children' in *Journal of Clinical Psychology* (1979) Vol 8, pp 3-6

37 Fitch, M J; Cadol, R V; Goldson, E; Wendell, T; Swartz, D and Jackson, E 'Cognitive development of abused and failure-to-thrive children' in *Journal of Pediatric Psychology* (1976) 1(2), pp 32-37

38 Friedrich, W N; Einbender, A J and Luecke, W J 'Cognitive and behavioural characteristics of physically-abused children' in *Journal of Consulting and*

Clinical Psychology (1983) Vol 51, pp 313-314

39 Martin, H P and Beezley, P 'Behavioural observations of abused children' in *Developmental Medicine and Child Neurology* (1977), Vol 19, pp 373-387

40 George, C and Main, M 'Social Interactions of Young Abused Children: Approach, avoidance and aggression' in *Child Development* (1979) 50, pp 306-318

41 Gaensbauer, T J and Sands, K 'Distorted affect communication in abused and/or neglected infants' in *Journal of the American Academy of Child Psychiatry* (1979) Vol 18, pp 531-540

42 Gaensbauer, T J; Mrazek D and Harmon R J 'Emotional Expression in Abused and/or Neglected Infants' Chapter 8 in Frude, N (ed) *Psychological Approaches to Child Abuse* (Batsford Press, London, 1980) pp 120-135

43 Green, A H 'Psychopathology of abused children' *Journal of the American Academy of Child Psychiatry* (1978) Vol 17, pp 92-103

44 Reidy, T J 'The aggressive characteristic of abused and neglected children' *Journal of Clinical Psychology* (1977) Vol 33, pp 1140-1145

45 Kinard, E M 'Experiencing child abuse: Effects on emotional adjustment' *American Journal of Orthopsychiatry* (1982), Vol 52, pp 82-91

46 Barahal, R M; Waterman, J and Martin H P 'The social cognitive development of abused children' *Journal of Consulting and Clinical Psychology* (1981) Vol 49, pp 508-516

47 Frodi, A; Smetana, J 'Abused, Neglected and Nonmaltreated Preschoolers' Ability to Discriminate Emotions in Others; The Effects of IQ' *Child Abuse and Neglect* (1984) Vol 8, pp 459-465

48 Perry, M A; Doran, L and Wells, E 'Developmental Characteristics of the Physically Abused Child' *Journal of Clinical Child Psychology* (1983) Vol 12, No 3, pp 320-324

49 Gregory, H and Beveridge, M 'The Social and Educational Adjustment of Abused Children' *Child Abuse and Neglect* (1984) Vol 8, pt 4, pp 525-531

50 Bentovim, A 'Setting up a treatment programme' Chapter 11 in Frude, N (ed) *Psychological Approaches to Child Abuse* (Batsford Press, London, 1980) pp 163-180; Nicol, R; Mearns, C; Hall, D; Kay, B; Williams, B and Akister, J 'An evaluation of focused casework in improving interaction in abusive families' Chapter 14 in Stevenson, J E (ed) *Recent Research in Developmental Psychopathology* (Pergamon Press, Oxford, 1985) pp 151-169

51 See, for example, Hutchings, J 'A Behavioural Approach to Child Abuse' Chapter 12 in Frude, N (ed) *Psychological Approaches to Child Abuse* (Batsford Press, London, 1980) pp 181-191

52 Browne, K D and Parr, R 'Contributions of an ethological approach to the study of abuse' Chapter 6 in Frude, N (ed) *Psychological Approaches to Child Abuse* (Batsford Press, London, 1980) pp 83-99

53 Taitze, L 'Follow-up of children at risk' in *Child Abuse and Neglect* (1981) Vol 5, pp 231-239

54 Lynch, M A and Roberts, J *Consequences of Child Abuse* (Academic Press, London, 1982)

55 Scholz, J 'Competency of abused children in a residential treatment programme' in Meier, J (ed), *Child Abuse: A Practical Handbook for Understanding Treatment and Prevention* (Baltimore Press, 1982)

Chapter 6

Emotional abuse and neglect

Rolene Szur

One of the earliest documented cases of physical abuse associated with emotional deprivation was that of Kaspar Hauser, reported in 1832 by Anselm von Feuerbach, a distinguished Bavarian judge. More recently, in 1974 Werner Herzog's film[1] very movingly recreated this almost legendary story of the boy kept in a dark cramped cellar, who emerged when he had reached the age of about 16, hardly able to walk or talk, so that 'his whole conduct seemed to be that of a child scarcely two or three years old with the body of a young man'.[2]

'Soul murder' was the phrase coined by von Feuerbach to refer to the crime committed by the unknown man who had confined Kaspar and was therefore responsible for 'killing the joy in life and interfering with the sense of identity of another human being'.[3]

Some years later, after having been fostered with a kindly family Kaspar 'began more and more to reflect on his unhappy fate and to become painfully sensible of what had been withheld from him'. When asked what was now the matter with him, he 'replied with tears, that he had been thinking about what was the reason he had not a mother, a brother and a sister? For it was so very pretty a thing to have them'.[4]

What we refer to as emotional abuse is one factor that is common to all forms of abuse or neglect of children and infants. Indeed physical assault may leave fewer and less enduring scars than the relationships through which it occurred.

When attempting to distinguish emotional abuse as a specific entity, however, independent of any form of physical assault or deprivation, we are immediately confronted with an awareness that this, literally intangible, factor may be something which occurs along a spectrum that begins nearer home. Its roots lie in the common problems and unpredictabilities of personal relationships – of looking after small babies or large families. It may just be that one child has always seemed easy to love and another really difficult, and often there seems no obvious reason why this should be so. At this level it is also difficult to assess just how selectively individual children's personalities may themselves play some part in precipitating this, or for that matter, just how they will respond to their experiences in the long term.

It is necessary to give some thought to the more subtle and intangible aspects of this form of abuse. People responsible for physical or sexual abuse attempt to keep it hidden from others; in emotional abuse they often manage to keep it hidden from themselves. At some level, though, there is unease and guilt.

In order to do helpful work on behalf of children who are being emotionally victimised within their families, it is important to be able to reflect on, and try to identify with, the child's feelings – which may be confusion as well as distress.

Often this confusion in the child can seem disturbing or puzzling to adults who may, for example, find that an infant or young child is clinging desperately to an abusing parent. In terms of attachment theory this can be understood as 'anxious attachment'.[5] The infant is caught up in the terrible dilemma of needing to attach itself to a parent figure for protection from harm, when the very source of the threat is that same figure. These internal contradictions, the confusion between love and hate, or of neediness with terror and despair, constitute some of the problems of ambivalence such children have to struggle with. These factors must increase a growing child's difficulties in being able to trust, either externally or within his or her own personality, that the good and the positive can be protected from attack by the bad and the destructive, in others or in themselves. Anxiety in relation to strangers could thus be exacerbated.

There is a tendency to assume that *all* abused children will necessarily and always cling to their abusing parents. In at least two cases which come to mind this was not so. The common factor in these cases was the availability of another close and constant person to whom the child could turn. This appeared to help them develop a more secure capacity for making distinctions and to establish a relatively healthier and more reality-based split between good and bad, positive and negative. In one case the secondary attachment figure was an older sister and in the other a 'foster aunt'. It seems possible that these relationships helped to free the children to respond to further relationships.

Just as we need to identify with the child, it may be equally important to be a little introspective – to try to become aware of areas of feeling in ourselves which may parallel those of the guilty parents. For the majority of us the violence or viciousness of physical forms of assault must seem very remote. But there are probably few who have not at one time or another felt quite strong impulses to verbally wound someone, whether child or adult; as the saying goes, to 'slay with a look or a word.' Often, in order to help the child, one needs to understand and help the parents. Many feel both confused and guilty and will gratefully accept and respond to such help. For others, however, there may be total rejection of a child or a degree of very hurtful ambivalence, irresponsibility leading to a failure to provide the simple emotional needs of childhood.

If this rejection leads to babies or older children being placed in local authority care, either in response to parental requests or because of social services intervention, the emotional exclusion has led to physical exclusion also. In other cases a child may remain physically within the family, but in a position of feeling excluded or unvalued. Certainly this can be very insidious and undermining, and, if it persists, not dissimilar in effect to being physically excluded.

In some instances emotional neglect or abuse can have observable physical effects when parents fail to provide adequate nourishing care for the infant. This may result in 'psycho-social dwarfism', or failure to engage in interaction and stimulation of an infant, so that the baby becomes developmentally retarded.[6] Sometimes this occurs when a parent is severely disturbed or intellectually retarded, but this is not always necessarily or evidently the case.

Three boys

Berkeley

With this spectrum in mind I shall describe three boys, Berkeley, William and Derry. Berkeley was the 11-year-old younger son of striving professional parents and his mother's specialty involved long and sometimes unsocial hours. His older brother was academically successful but Berkeley was said to be unmanageable both at home and at school. (Later on we learned of truancy and absconding from school.) Following an almost self-inflicted traffic accident and some apparently hypochondriacal symptoms he was admitted as an in-patient to a child psychiatry unit. When referred for psychotherapy he did attend regularly but his manner was, with rare exceptions, taciturn and uninvolved, as if everything just bounced off his 'tough hide'. In the in-patient unit he was defiant and physically aggressive with the staff.

Berkeley's early history had included minor surgery in infancy, and it happened that during the current admission a further surgical repair was undertaken. His psychotherapist went to see him while he was convalescing and found him looking exhausted and in pain; in spite of his usually indifferent manner he seemed pleased by the visit. When presently she enquired about when mother was expected, this tough youngster answered with complete conviction, 'She isn't going to come, ever,' as tears welled from his eyes. It seemed as if re-opening the old physical wound had at the same time exposed a hidden psychic wound where the pain of his mother's absence was felt with the intensity and terror of a little child feeling totally abandoned. Perhaps it was something of this kind that had made it especially difficult for him to cope with his mother's busy career, while his brother was apparently unaffected. The therapist felt very moved by this sudden exposure of his vulnerability, though at the same time remembering how relentlessly he attacked any efforts to help him. He had made the staff feel as if nothing they had to offer was worth having. It seemed that the same kind of impasse had been set up between him and his family.

William

The second boy was a 5-year-old, William, who had spent most of his days since early infancy in a children's home. His mother was a very immature and inadequate young woman who would often promise to visit but then seldom actually arrive, and he had never known his father.

William too was a major problem of discipline and had been referred by the house-father for psychotherapy assessment. In sessions he sometimes smashed things after he had just carefully constructed them, or after drawing attention to some object as being a treasured possession. This was quite painful to observe, yet William remained apparently passive, as if needing to offload this pain on to someone else. Once, after doing this, he said, 'One day I'll run across the road and get killed. Then my mother will be pleased.'

Although the external and family circumstances of Berkeley and William were very different, as were their histories and personalities, yet certain parallels were there – in their destructiveness towards themselves and others, and in the undercurrent of despair. One might wonder whether Berkeley's early hospitalisation and painful surgery had taken on a meaning for him and his mother, equivalent to that created by William's early estrangement from his mother, in each case setting up a vicious cycle between mother and child.

The self-destructive aspects of these two children could be seen as characteristic of children who feel that a valued, good or loving aspect of themselves has been shattered with little hope of repair and who have some sense of inner worthlessness. Self-destructiveness is generally evidence of distress and I would agree with Sharon Morgan[7] who in listing indications that a child is being abused in some way, puts self-destructiveness high on her list, while at the same time adding the comment that many or most non-physical symptoms of abuse and neglect are likely to accompany stress even when it is related to other factors or crises.

Derry

A third boy, Derry, was, like William, living in a children's home, but doggedly pleading to return to his natural parents. Derry's case was an extreme instance of a family where one particular child appears to be singled out as the 'bad' one, repository of all inadequacy or malice, while in contrast the others appear to have acquired an enhanced sense of their own virtue. Sometimes it may be that such a child has an especially difficult or vulnerable temperament, though this is not necessarily so. Usually the wish or urge to victimise a child in this way is largely unconscious. In this case it was made distressingly explicit. Derry's mother had been refusing to have him back. She said that his behaviour was quite intolerable and proceeded to give examples. In interviewing the family the clinic team responded by asking what changes in behaviour would make her willing to have him back, when suddenly she snapped out, 'I can't stand him; I don't want him back, I don't *want* to like him!' Derry stared white-faced and rigid. (This child's face did have the painful 'frozen hypervigilance'[8] referred to in studies of physically abused children, different from the more familiar wariness and lack of trust in emotionally neglected children.)

How did these three boys fare?

Berkeley's parents were co-operative in that they attended family therapy and later, reluctantly, marital therapy sessions. Efforts were made to help Berkeley by a period in individual psychotherapy, but in the event a short phase of improvement and hopefulness was not maintained after discharge from the unit.

William however, who had spent practically all his life since infancy in a children's home, was able to make more progress than the other two. His was one of a number of instances where the quality of the support and understanding given him by his schoolteacher and also by his house-father seemed very important. He had been referred for psychotherapy fairly early, at age five (following a rather alarming incident). He responded well and was then fortunate in finding a very gifted substitute family.

Poor *Derry*, when seen at age 11, had already suffered physical abuse from his father and step-father and emotional abuse from his mother. He seemed then to be a very 'frozen child' intellectually and emotionally.

Frequently there is a feeling that a 'black sheep' child like Derry does not belong in the family but is an 'enemy alien'. Minor misdemeanours are interpreted as major crimes, any difficulties or quarrelling within the family are blamed on that child, their bad influence, the trouble they cause. It is more than difficult for such children to feel there is anything good in them, or that they are capable of doing anything well; or to have any image in mind of accepting, forgiving parental figures. Often, as with Derry, one discovers that the little scapegoat does in fact turn out to be the result of an extra-marital relationship, or the child of a former rejected or rejecting partner. Sometimes an adopted or fostered child may fall into this role. In many cases, however, there are no such external reasons, but more complicated origins in terms of personalities and family histories, as in the case of Berkeley.

Although Berkeley had seemed to have a comparatively more favourable situation and parental support, he proved to be incapable of defending any positive developments against attacks from something very destructive in himself. Of William one might think that a combination of circumstances had enabled some of the healthy qualities in his personality to survive and to benefit from the helpful elements available within his environment.

In the families where *all* the children are neglected, abused or exploited this behaviour may reflect some particular parental pathology. They may be reconstituting the deprived family life of their childhood, evacuating the remembered pain into their own children. At the same time they may feel persecuted by an image of the children's advancing growth and see it as a challenge to their dominance or a threat of revenge, and thus be unable to accept their progress or their affection. Alternatively, such parents may unconsciously need and expect loving care from the relationship, where physically it is *they* who must provide the care; emotionally, they are as incapable of offering it as are their young infants.

Thus, we can see how complex the individual interactions between personal characteristics, social circumstances and personal relationships can be in determining varying experiences and degrees of emotional neglect or abuse, and also what their eventual outcome will be.

Definitions

Given this complexity, how can we formulate a definition that will provide a starting point for further exploration, understanding and response? In essence, emotional neglect or abuse means that a vulnerable child is exposed to being emotionally starved and mentally stunted, so that essential childhood needs are either denied or perverted. In general this will be associated with some disturbances in personal, social and educational development.

The DHSS Memorandum of August 1980[9] concerning the central register systems relating to child abuse recommended that these arrangements be extended to cover mental and emotional abuse. This requires a definition that is more specific and immediately demonstrable. In terms of the Memorandum, inclusion in the register could apply to children under the age of 17 if:

- they have been medically diagnosed as suffering from severe non-organic failure to thrive;
- their behaviour and emotional development has been severely affected; where medical and social assessments find evidence of either persistent or severe neglect and/or rejection.

One authority in the field, Garbarino,[10] explicitly supports employment of the concept of abuse as 'deliberate behaviour that seriously undermines the development of competence' in the child, and represents 'actionable behaviour – first as a basis for initiating service, and second as a basis for legal coercion.' He lists four aspects of such behaviour:

In infancy

1 Punishing positive behaviour such as smiling, mobility, vocalising and exploring and handling objects
2 Discouraging bonding

In childhood and adolescence

3 Punishment of self-esteem
4 Punishment of interpersonal skills necessary for adequate functioning in non-familial contexts such as schools, peer groups, etc.

It seems to me that these formulations are helpful in directing attention to the important issue of the developmental aspect of child care and to the need for clarifying and promoting observance of at least some basic norms of what constitutes 'taking care of children'. However, insistence on formulations based on the use of terms like 'wilful' and 'deliberate' might be as likely to impede and confuse as to facilitate the pursuance of the best interests of the child. Legal proof of 'wilfulness' is less easily established in court than professional evidence of a child's avoidable psychological impairment. In cases where the main emphasis might be on therapeutic measures co-operation, rather than accusation and confrontation, might well have a more hopeful long-term outcome. Similarly the narrow focus on the parent's guilt that is implied within the limits of this definition fails to take into account necessarily contingent issues, for example, congenital disabilities, deficiencies or illness, physical or mental, in either parent or child; as well as social and economic circumstances. All of these may need state intervention, while not necessarily being linked with parental culpability.

In a paper presented to a BASPCAN Conference, following publication of the DHSS Memorandum, Hoxter[11] defines some of the difficulties of definition. She points out that when considering non-accidental physical injury, the nature of the injury, the cause, the victim and the perpetrator may all be identifiable. None of these may, however, be easily identified in cases of mental and emotional abuse, where there may sometimes even be some doubt as to who is the victim and who is the perpetrator. (A predicament of this kind was in fact often in the minds of workers involved with Berkeley and his family!) Often the severity of the injury and the way in which it will reveal itself may not be apparent for many years. Many variables affect the nature of the experience for a child including variations in 'the thickness of the emotional skin'.[12]

Following somewhat similar lines of thought, two North American writers, Patterson and Thompson[13] have tried to withdraw the attribution of criminality to the parents by removing the term emotional 'abuse'. This, they claim, places the main emphasis on identifying actions committed by the parents as criminal, instead of focusing attention on the state of the child and whether his or her particular needs are being met. Every parent must fail to some degree to meet even their own ideals of parenting. However, society needs to intervene in situations where there is an unacceptable degree of failure to provide an 'optimum psycho-social environment' for a particular child, as 'evidenced by the degree of dysfunction which the child experiences in coping with himself and the world around him'. The background to this suggestion includes considerations of a theoretical nature, but also issues of practice, which they discuss specifically in relation to the school setting.

Patterson and Thompson suggest, for example, that if a teacher draws attention to a child's difficulties from this point of view and along these lines it could make it more possible for most parents to see it as a potentially helpful observation. But implications of abuse or neglect would be seen as an accusation, which would therefore be likely to elicit more hostility and 'blocking', either openly or covertly, than understanding and, hopefully, co-operation in a shared aim. Patterson and Thompson refer to a suggestion[14] that emotional neglect be defined on three levels, in terms of

1 an ideal definition of parenting;
2 a functional mental health definition;
3 a legal definition.

This could prove to be a useful exercise in clarifying some of the areas of ambiguity in working with emotional abuse, since there is sometimes an imputation of interfering in other people's lives and lifestyles on the basis of a 'sectional' set of criteria, and with a relative lack of concrete evidence.

In venturing to explore what might serve as a working framework of this kind I have turned to psychiatric, educational and psycho-analytic sources.

The ideal definition

To present the *ideal* I select a few paragraphs from *Love, Guilt and Reparation* in which Klein describes 'a really loving relationship of a mother to her baby' which . . . 'may lead to an attitude where her first concern will be for the baby's good, and her own gratification be bound up with his welfare.' An important element in this maternal attitude would be a capability for 'putting herself in the child's place, and of looking at the situation from his point of view', but avoiding being 'too closely wrapped up and too much identified with him'. Klein adds that it is

'. . . psychologically quite inadequate to attempt to solve children's difficulties by not frustrating them at all. It is important to realize that the child's development depends on, and to a large extent is formed by his capacity to find the way to bear inevitable and necessary frustration and the conflicts of love and hate which are in part caused by them.' . . . (but) 'frustration which is in reality unnecessary or arbitrary and shows nothing but lack of love and understanding, is very detrimental.'[15]

No doubt others, parents and children, will have their own definition and ideal images of perfect parenting, but there can be few, if any, who would feel at all confident of always living up to them. To this extent there must always be some degree of failing or neglecting to fulfill completely and satisfactorily one's role as a parent. The issue then becomes one of degree, nature and evidence – the point at which the failure or neglect can be shown to be demonstrably damaging to a particular child's ability to cope with himself and his world. This issue can be defined in terms of mental health criteria.

The functional mental health definition

Emotional neglect occurs when there is a failure to meet a child's basic needs. These needs are defined by the Royal College of Psychiatrists[16] as:

1   Physical care and protection
2   Affection and approval
3   Stimulation and teaching
4   Discipline and control which are consistent and age-appropriate
5   Opportunity and encouragement to gradually acquire autonomy

Perhaps in terms of a mental health definition (as distinct from a legal one) one might wish to fill this out a little, and to add:

- appropriate physical contact;
- emotional support and containment at times of stress;
- recognition of the child as a separate individual.

Neglect implies an act of omission, of indifference; even if physical care is provided, affection, interest, a sense of being safely held in someone's mind, are missing. A lack of thoughtful discipline can convey a similar lack of caring. This sense of something missing can undermine a child's sense of self and of worth.

When the term *abuse* (or perhaps misuse) is employed, more actively negative attitudes and behaviour are implied. These could include:

Constantly *threatening* children with harsh punishments, eg that they will be sent away, severely beaten, even killed. Sometimes there may be grounds for believing that the threats might be carried out, but even where this does not appear to be the case, such threats touch on children's most primitive infantile terrors. Threats that the child's behaviour will lead to the death or suicide of a parent fall into a similar category of emotional abuse.

There can be a perverse element, so that a child's vulnerability and seeking for affection does not evoke tenderness and protectiveness, but the reverse, *bullying* and *cruel teasing*. Sometimes this means that there has been a fundamental denial of the existence of any feeling of love and dependency; often also a rejection of the distinctions between adults and children. Sometimes a parent relates to a child essentially as if he or she is a jealous brother or sister.

When children's efforts towards development receive more mocking and belittling for failings than any encouragement, it may be that the child is being used as if it were an external depository or representative of all the parents' feelings of impotence and failure, as inadequate, unlovable, or often a bad aspect of themselves and their internal experiences, which can then be attacked, sometimes quite ruthlessly. (In an extreme example of such attitudes, one woman attempted to poison her child when he reached his seventh birthday ie the age at which her own father had begun a sexual relationship with her. She said it was better for him to die than to suffer the loss of his innocence.)

In other instances a child may be being 'misused' in order to express parental fantasy. Sometimes this may involve an expectation of fulfilling a parent's grandiose ambition, so that in failing to fit in with this, the child becomes suffused with a sense of defeat and disappointment.[11]

In some cases a parent may wish the child to remain forever in an infantile relationship. (An extreme example of this was a child of three years old who was found confined to her cot, unable to walk and being fed only on baby food and sweets.) In yet others the situation may be reversed so that the child becomes a 'parent' to its own parents, (and apparently this occurs more commonly). This is often an expression of the parents' longing for the caring missed in their own deprived childhood. (A comparative study between physically abusing and non-abusing mothers carried out by de Lozier[17] found that the abusing mothers reacted especially strongly to even minor situations of separation, by feeling angry, rejected and rejecting, and unable to cope. These mothers reported a significantly higher incidence of separations, loss of caregivers and paternal absences in childhood than was found among the 'typical' mothers.) This example of parents' anxious attachment and detachment illustrates one of the many ways in which the experiences and images of family relationships can be transmitted through the generations.

In the kinds of family situations described above, children can find difficulty in discovering a real sense of worth, in knowing their own real needs and experiencing feelings of purpose and meaning, with spontaneity and conviction. This may interfere with their capacity for making other than superficial relationships and similarly for becoming involved in activities in a satisfying way.

Some of these problems are less severe and easier to recognise and treat than others; many of them will respond to therapeutic or counselling services offered to the children and families, hopefully while the children are still young.[18] But this depends, of course, on there being at least enough emotional and mental health, plus positive motivation, within the family to encourage them towards developing a better situation.

Legal definition

One could envisage a legal definition as being expressed in terms following on from the formulation of children's basic needs (as set out by the Royal College of Psychiatrists and quoted on page 112 above). Its objectives would therefore be:

1   to safeguard that all children in a family are entitled to having these general needs fulfilled;
2   to monitor whether an individual child's particular needs with regard to growth and development, physically, intellectually and emotionally are being avoidably impaired;
3   to ensure that full and proper use is being made of the educational, medical and social services available and necessary for the children.

In this context an example would be the case of a three-and-a-half-year-old boy who was referred to a child care consultation team in which Dr Arnon Bentovim was the psychiatrist. The boy had recently been taken into care. When brought by his social workers to the clinic he could not speak, only make sounds like those of an 18-month-old infant. His movements seemed restless, clinging or aggressive; it was very difficult to manage to keep him under some control. However he did become interested in trying to handle the coloured pencils when given some encouragement. He seemed to be trying to listen and follow, when spoken to, in an attentive way.

When subsequently his mother was interviewed she proved to be pathologically obsessed with a quarrel over property between her divorced husband and herself. Evidently a well-educated, intelligent woman, she was nevertheless totally unable to recognise her son's needs, denied his retarded development, and refused to accept that there was any cause for concern. She had become hostile to social services and also refused any counselling or psychiatric help. It was evident that by remaining with his mother the child would be exposed to emotional neglect and it was necessary for the court to rule that a more suitable environment be found for him. This was clearly a question of the child's need, and not an issue of the mother's guilt in legal terms. (Fortunately the boy improved and advanced very well in a substitute family.)

Personality difficulties associated with emotional aspects of child care

Behavioural observations of abused children

In 1977 Harold P Martin and Patricia Beezley[8] published a follow-up study of a group of 50 physically-abused children some four and a half years after the abuse was identified, selecting nine personality characteristics to be assessed. They found a high preponderance of a number of symptoms of emotional turmoil, including 'impaired ability for enjoyment' (66%); many behavioural symptoms, eg enuresis, sleep-disturbance (62%), low self-esteem (52%), hypervigilance, precocious behaviour, and school-learning problems, as well as children who were withdrawn or very aggressive.

The factors that correlated with the children's psychiatric symptoms were not the type or severity of the physical assault, but the quality of the family relationships.

This thoughtful study confirms the prevalence of emotional distur-bance among abused children; it draws attention to the need for psycho-therapeutic help and support both for the child and for the parents, either separately or together. Of course, many of the personality difficulties found to be common to the group are not, in them-selves, uncommon signs or expressions of disturbance or distress among children and can arise from varied circumstances. It could be misleading to construe them specifically as diagnostic indicators of child abuse.

Consequences of child abuse

In *Consequences of Child Abuse*[18] published in 1982, Margaret Lynch and Jacqueline Roberts provide a very fully researched picture of psychological and emotional features and characteristics encountered among 40 physically abused children and their families. Both supportive work and psychotherapy had been received by the children and the parents during a stay at the Park Hospital, and the book records a follow-up study of what was happening to them in the long term. One of their conclusions was that most of the families needed long-term support in order to maintain improvements gained, and they stress the importance of individual psychotherapy and follow-up for the damaged children.

The Tavistock study

Psychotherapy with severely deprived children was the subject of a multidisciplinary workshop at the Tavistock Clinic. A review of the 80 cases seen either at the Tavistock or other clinics, mostly in the Greater London Area, was published in 1983.[19] It had been considered at one time that such children would not be accessible or respond to intensive psychotherapy and the Department for Children and Parents had instead been offering consultation and support to the care-givers or substitute families. However pressure to help particular children, as well as more direct contact with them, soon brought a conviction not only of their need, but of their capacity to respond in their varied, individual ways. This experience therefore paralleled the findings of the two studies referred to above, in indicating the importance of direct work with the children.

A number of the findings in this study relate to understanding and working with children who have suffered from the experience of being emotionally neglected or abused. Only one of the referred children was living at home, 62 were in children's homes, and 17 in foster care. The sample included 53 children who had been severely deprived of parental care – over half having been separated from their natural families before they were four years old. Breakdown in fostering, often with multiple changes, had happened to a third of the group. Therefore, while 25 of the children had indeed suffered physical abuse, the greater number were primarily casualities of some form of emotional neglect, deprivation or rejection, rather than of physical damage.

Often deprivation was the result of the death or chronic illness of the parent. (As the term 'emotional abuse' carries the idea of negative intent, the question arises as to how and to what degree this would differ in the experience of the child as a helpless victim, when the suffering could realistically be seen as the consequence of external events ie unavoidable parental illness or death. It would not always be easy to disentangle these situations in terms of their overall effects, since in the inner world someone or something would be carrying the blame, perhaps another authority figure or a part of the self.)

Severity of disturbance was not the dominating feature of the group.

Often more positive or even chance factors were responsible for referrals, such as something especially appealing or hopeful in an unhappy child, or a special awareness in the staff of a children's home. An interesting finding was that despite the overall lack of continuity in their lives all of the 80 children had experienced some stability of care during some period. The importance of this as a factor in their capacity to make a therapeutic relationship, might be interesting to explore in more detail, and is in line with the findings of Kellmer Pringle[20], Wolkind[21] and Lynch and Roberts.[18] The place of this factor within the school system clearly deserves attention.

What was common to all these children, was their *more than ordinary difficulties in forming or maintaining relationships*. Although the nature of the particular difficulty varied it was very striking to discover how dramatically all the children managed to convey the intensely painful emotional experiences they had suffered, despite their individually different ways of communicating. It may be relevant here to focus briefly on the issue and nature of communication with children, especially emotionally deprived children, many of whom have very poorly developed verbal skills. We know that children do not necessarily convey their wishes, fantasies or actual experiences through words alone, but very often in more symbolic ways – as they play their familiar games, paint pictures and make up stories.

Other children, and adults too, will generally 'tune in' to these communications without necessarily putting them into words, either in their own minds or by responding explicitly. Often this kind of silent communication has the special quality of closeness and security that belongs to the communication between a very young infant and an attentive parent. When children are deeply distressed or disturbed and are referred for psychotherapy, they may need to have someone help them put into words some of their chaotic and conflicting experiences, in order to provide a means for thinking about them, instead of displaying their emotional turmoil solely through turbulent or 'mindless' activities. In trying to understand, together with the child, what the communications are about, a therapist uses simple words to convey what has been understood. In this way a kind of 'working relationship' can be built up, often of an intensely painful and stormy nature, but one through which the young patient's emotional states and damaging defences can be faced together and eventually modified.

For this to be viable, though, it is important to have a predictable and secure setting, ie a regular and consistent time and place in which sessions are held. This means that a therapist can give the child sole attention, what has been described as a 'space in the mind'.[22] During this time one would be trying to be receptive to the child's preoccupations and feelings and avoid being directive, within the limits of safety and tolerance. The opportunity to have this kind of individual attention and respect from an adult is a unique experience for many children, and does in itself have a healing quality, more especially for emotionally deprived children.

I have added these few sentences about the nature and atmosphere of the psychotherapy setting, partly to draw attention to the continuities with day-to-day experiences of communicating, and partly because I know and appreciate that in those schools where there is a visiting psychotherapist it may sometimes create problems for teaching staff to accommodate arrangements for special needs of this kind.

This workshop found that although

no single picture of *the* deprived child emerged, they showed a good deal in common in their reactions to therapy and in the progress which most of them could make, provided the therapist could stick it out in the initial phases.[19]

Although all of the children emerged as individuals, having developed their own ways of coping with stress and deprivation, there were a number of similar themes, and also particular clusters of defences. One could distinguish certain distinctive and recurring personality patterns, some of which are set out and briefly discussed below.

1   *A lack of trust* and of any expectation of continuity, as if the idea of an adult's continued concern or attention was foreign to many of the children. However, when somewhat better relations did begin with such children it was especially difficult for them to tolerate ordinary inevitable frustrations, absences or changes, since their underlying lack of trust would immediately convert such disappointments into a betrayal of their idealised longings.

2   An undercurrent of *anxiety about being suddenly dropped, 'unheld' or discarded*. This could be expressed during play, sometimes perilous games of falling, as if to project their anxiety into the watching adult, while also testing whether the adult would save them! Some seemed to treat themselves as if they felt worthless 'just rubbish',[19a] being excessively scruffy, or sometimes by actually soiling themselves.[19b]

One child who very often played these games would then deny her fear or need for help, as if showing that she felt she couldn't rely on or trust anyone to help her, 'she had to manage on her own, that was how she survived'.[19c]

3   Another problem which was not uncommon was an inappropriate and precocious *sexualisation* of relationships. Sometimes this might have been the consequence of sexual seduction or provocative exhibitionism in adults. In other instances it seemed a more naive expression of a desperate need for attention and affection or an attempt to manipulate adults into a false peer relationship.

4   One group was characterised by a very flat and *superficial* way of

relating, a '*two-dimensional*' quality, lacking a sense of genuine interaction. They tended to be 'promiscuous in a casual uninvolved manner' and to be experienced as unrewarding or frustrating by people who worked with them. Eileen, a 14-year-old girl, was described by the workers in her children's home as 'unbearable', because 'she made everyone feel such a failure. Nobody felt they could get through to her; nothing satisfied her; no occupation held her; no treat pleased her'[23] (Miller 1983). This recalls the characteristic of 'impaired capacity for enjoyment', frequently noted in the Martin and Beezley study quoted earlier, and which they describe as follows:

'(the children) lacked the ability to play freely, to laugh and to enjoy themselves in an uninhibited fashion. They did not complain even when frustrated or tired, which suggested that they had learned to accept an unrewarding world.'

Dr R Britton,[24] referring to the number of deprived children who were creating difficulties because of disruptive or aggressive behaviour, commented that sometimes this fighting spirit might indicate less emotional deadness and therefore more hope than seemed present in some of the apparently more superficial personalities.

There seemed to be a contrast in general, though not in all cases, between boys' more open and active attacks (or defences) against relationships and girls' more inward, passive resistance styles. How far this reflected social expectations or pressures is, of course, part of a wider issue. The Lynch and Roberts study found the girls to be at least as aggressively hostile as the boys in their group.[18]

5 Children who provided a very severe challenge in terms of management and communication were often those who openly and sometimes violently attacked others, verbally and physically. This *aggressive, violent behaviour* sometimes alternated with being mean or numb, and inaccessible, as if encased in heavy armour-plating. As one such youngster told his therapist, 'your face will be wet with blood before mine is wet with tears'.[23] In therapy a great deal of this aggressiveness can be better understood if one can recognise that it is taking place within the fantasy of being 'in the shoes of' some very cruel and frightening images, such as deserting or punishing parental figures. It may mean that while in fact engaged in attacking, in depth the child is aware of himself essentially as a victim.[19a]

6 *Difficulties in learning and thought disorders* were generally found to occur so often, that the Educational Psychologist in the team commented that it sometimes seemed 'to be taken for granted that all children in care would have learning difficulties and poor school reports'.[25] At one level this could be related to the comparative lack of thoughtful attention, understanding and social interaction which had been available. Many had suffered a degree of neglect, or been exposed

to confusions of environment, multiple family dispersals and arbitrary changes, without adequate adult help in trying to make some sense of it.

While drawing attention to the children's low self-esteem, the psychologist added that it soon became evident 'that teachers, care-staff and social workers often shared these low expectations of the children.' The possibility of remedial help was rarely considered, sometimes because of a mistaken concern not to label a child still more, sometimes because of uncertainty about the future. Holmes felt it was important to avoid falling into the trap of merely stating that the child was disturbed and underfunctioning because of a disturbed background; and tried to ensure that observations and results of testing were followed up by discussions with care-staff, teachers and social workers in order to gain some detailed understanding of 'how a child was feeling, as well as why he was failing', and to consider ways of helping him emotionally as well as educationally.

The most frequent referrals came at ages five or 11, ie soon after an educational change, which drew attention to the 'special sensitivity of deprived children to transitions that other children can manage more easily'. Children's motivation could rapidly evaporate if they began to feel that school was just 'another place where you can be forgotten and nobody cares'.

The experience of emotional neglect

So far we have been looking at emotional neglect mainly as an external event, defining it for purposes of recognition, intervention or legal action. Let us now try to understand something about the inner experiences and the in-depth relationships which together constitute these unhappy situations. What, for instance, does it feel like to be the child and what kind of parental images hold sway in his inner world?

A brief account of psychotherapy with one of these children may provide some glimpses. In a chapter entitled 'I'm bad, no good, can't think', his therapist describes Ian, aged nine.[22] Following unsettled early years with his mother, he had been taken into a children's home at age four, where he had remained for most of the time since. His mother, an immature and disorganised person, kept up some contact with him, he being the favourite among her scattered children, but he was not considered suitable for fostering or adoption.

Although at age 4 years he was considered to be developing reasonably well, over the following years the children's home found him to be deteriorating . . . His school . . . complained chiefly of his need for individual attention in order to sustain any concentration at all. Although he was able to write clearly, this would degenerate into scribble after a few words.

Although there was considerable disturbance in his general behaviour, the author focused on his 'difficulties in concentrating, thinking and producing written work, and his capacity to recognise, locate, and think about his emotions.' She felt that it was these difficulties which came to seem fundamental in indicating Ian's state of mind.

In the course of his life Ian would already have had to come to terms with the disappearance of two 'fathers' and some siblings, a number of moves, and finding himself in a children's home among total strangers, with his mother fitfully appearing and disappearing. One has the picture of a child whose parental figures have neglected and indeed shown little, if any, capacity to take thought for him and his feelings or even to be aware of what these might be. There has been no opportunity therefore to identify with parents as thinking and feeling, of having a 'capacity to process external events into internal experiences.'

A child in this situation has not only the burden of his distress to bear, but that of being left with extremely inadequate mental resources to cope with a degree of pain which would overwhelm the most favourably brought up child. His therapist comments that at times he seemed to convey that he felt lost 'in the grip of states of mind which had not evolved to the level at which he could talk about them.' On one occasion he was attempting to explain the relationships and whereabouts of the different members of his family, when he suddenly broke down, saying 'It's hard to know – if you know what I mean!'

Alfredo: disruption at school

I shall conclude by telling the story of Alfredo, a 13-year-old Italian boy attending school in a large city in Southern Italy. This is going far afield, but sometimes such distancing helps to highlight certain issues so that they stand out more clearly. Teachers are, of course, familiar through their own direct experience with both the rewards and disappointments of working with disturbed and difficult children. Offering a picture of such an encounter, as seen by an outsider, may provide the chance of another perspective for discussion.

Mrs Paolina, who taught at Alfredo's school, was attending a multidisciplinary work discussion seminar[27] and she brought her worries about Alfredo to this group. She was concerned not only about the boy but also about some of the ways in which she felt the school's response to him might be inappropriate and unhelpful. Certainly he sounded like a very troubling child, but the process of discussing the brief history of this teacher's encounter with him illustrated for me some of the many ways in which a teacher-pupil relationship can in itself constitute something of a healing process – and also, unfortunately, some of the ways in which it can become one of the hazards which may tend to confirm negative developments.

Mrs Paolina described her first meeting with Alfredo when she went to act as a substitute teacher in a class. She was astonished to find this boy sitting in complete isolation in the middle of the classroom with the other children grouped around him in a circle. She noted that, to quote from her account, 'he is the tallest and fattest. My first impression is that he doesn't look too bright and has a furtive expression. In the hour I spent in class I recall Alfredo as a floating mine, torture for everyone. Within a few minutes two children are crying because he beat them up, then a pencil case goes flying through the air; finally Alfredo himself disappears.'

Following this first encounter Mrs Paolina discovered that Alfredo was the centre of an unpleasant situation involving a complaint from the boy's mother regarding excessive corporal punishment administered by his class teacher. Although the situation was unclear, the school was supporting the teacher, and Alfredo was now being treated as if he were a 'criminal'.

The next time Mrs Paolina met Alfredo was when she was assigned to take on what is described as a 'post-curricular work group'. She was upset to find that he seemed to trigger off a dynamic that she couldn't control in the class. He would slap, throw things, and chase around the class, while the other children called him names, 'fatso, queer, idiot!' There were daily complaints from teachers or pupils about his bad influence in the classrooms.

On making some enquiries about his family background the teacher discovered that his parents were known to have a very unhappy relationship, to the extent that the mother was apparently considered by neighbours to be quite distraught and totally preoccupied by the situation. Alfredo's appearance was generally shabby, sometimes with buttons missing, trousers tied with a piece of string. He gave the impression of a child 'whom no-one had time to think about,' as if the only communications he received were complaints, teasing or blame. Mrs Paolina realised that after a while she too felt a strong temptation to blame Alfredo whenever something went wrong.

At mealtimes Alfredo's eating habits were voracious; he seemed insatiable, gulping down everything including any left-overs on others' plates, as if he were a 'bottomless pit'. He was ill-mannered to a bizarre degree, and the dinner-ladies behaved towards him in a hostile and humiliating way. There was a serious risk that he would be excluded from school. One day he came to sit next to Mrs Paolina at dinner-time, wanting to help himself from her plate as he finished his. On an impulse, instead of correcting him, she gave him some of her food herself. This seemed to have the effect of satisfying him quite readily, so that he soon said he felt full and even managed to leave something on the plate.

One might see this incident as evidence that Alfredo's desperate need to fill up his insides with food, and with the food that others had, was also a desperate longing to fill his inner self with some of the good and sustaining feelings that others seemed to receive . . . He needed also to find someone who would not experience the impact of his hunger and despair as intolerable, but would be able to 'contain' it and in this way help him to do so too. I have used the word 'contain' here to refer to a process which is similar to the way in which the relationship between a child and a mother may operate – one in which the child's anxieties or aggression can be taken in by the mother, held in her mind and thought about, so that the child will then be receiving from her in turn a sense that his or her anxieties and aggression are bearable. They can be understood as thoughts and feelings, instead of having to be acted out between them in the kinds of negative interactions which often form the background to child abuse.

Some observations about Alfredo in the weeks during which his relationship with Mrs Paolina developed were of interest. He would often seek small, sheltered spots inside a cupboard or a desk in which he would hide, while leaving some clue that would allow Mrs Paolina to prove, as it were, that she wanted to find him, and also that she recognised his need for a feeling of being held in some protective way. This seemed to express a need for someone to help him in finding a positive or valued aspect of himself, which had been 'lost'.

Gradually Alfredo began to improve, becoming quiet and even ceasing to bother everyone. Before long he was able to join in the work of the class and managed to write and illustrate a story. There was a prince and princess. They had to struggle to find a way over very high mountains, but there was a happy ending and a picture of a many-coloured rainbow. Sadly this story does not have such a happy ending, since shortly afterwards Mrs Paolina was moved to a different assignment. Despite her attempts to explain the reasons for the move, Alfredo could not even look at her after her 'desertion', but would only shout 'traitor!' whenever they saw each other.

This brief account of the experience of a teacher working with a disturbed, emotionally abused and neglected schoolboy touches on a number of relevant issues. One of these is that Alfredo, who had become the victim of neglect and abuse within his own family, seemed to be precipitating similar responses within the school setting. It seemed evident that he was rapidly taking up the role of 'scapegoat' for the misdemeanours of his peers as well as his own, or for the frustrations and anger of kitchen staff, as also of the teaching staff. This seemed to have become the only route by which Alfredo felt certain of receiving attention or communications. It was therefore very important to be able to intervene in some way that could begin to reverse this spiral, however difficult.

One of the ways in which schools may help is therefore by their sensitivity to such processes. Are there, however, occasions when similarly negative processes may even seem to be generated or at least confirmed within the school setting? We saw something of this in the early encounters with Alfredo. Michael Rutter[28] referred to 'substantial evidence that the characteristics of children's schooling influence their development'. On the negative side he drew attention to the potential stresses for children in situations where school and home appear to have incompatible attitudes or expectations, as may be the case, for example, with children of immigrant groups. In other instances a child who seems intellectually or temperamentally slow, timid or eccentric in some way, for example, can become a repository for the projection of other children's anxieties and insecurities.

The story of Alfredo impressed on me the potential, within the day-to-day child-teacher relationship, of generating some reversal of adverse developments, by giving time and thought to understanding what is going on. It also drew attention to the way in which administrative demands may unfortunately seem to necessitate a disruption in such a relationship. It is interesting to recall here that research studies have shown the significance for children with a disturbed and insecure background of having some continuity of relationship with a concerned adult, even though this may not necessarily be the child's parent.[18, 19, 20, 21]

After her experiences with Alfredo (and hearing about other children discussed in the seminars) Mrs Paolina wondered about whether she and her colleagues might find it helpful to have a discussion group of their own at the school to exchange ideas with other colleagues in other professions about some of the more difficult children.

Certainly children who have suffered emotional abuse and deprivation do, as we have seen, present many difficulties to those who work with them. It may be that the greatest of these difficulties lies in being brought so close to such powerful feelings of humiliation, rage, despair and intensity of mental pain. We need to be able to 'hold' these feelings when they are 'thrown' at us by the children, to experience them within ourselves and resist the natural impulse, whether conscious or unconscious, to push them right back. Pushing them back would create only a repetition of the 'vicious circle' of the earlier damaging relationships. Nor would it be helpful or even possible to replace their present frustrations by granting every wish or conceding to every demand.

Only through the process of being able ourselves to suffer and contain the distressful feelings and think seriously about the real needs, may we be able to help the children to bear their own pain in more constructive ways, and perhaps to offer them some experience of a 'relationship with someone who can be relied upon to attend to suffering with both receptivity and strength.'[28]

Notes and references

1 Herzog, W *Kaspar Hauser* (1974) a film based on *Caspar Hauser* by Jakob Wasserman, 1928 (reprinted 1983 by Floris Classics, Edinburgh); see also Simon, N 'Kaspar Hauser's Recovery and Autopsy: A Perspective on Neurological and Sociological Requirements for Language Development' in *Journal of Autism and Childhood Schizophrenia* (1978), 8, 2

2 Feuerbach, A von *Caspar Hauser* (tr H Linberg) (Simpkin and Marshall, London, 1834)

3 Shengold, L 'Kaspar Hauser and Soul Murder: A Story of Deprivation' in *International Review of Psycho-analysis* (1978), 5, pp 475-476

4 Feuerbach, *op cit*

5 Bowlby, J *Attachment and Loss* (Vol II) (Penguin Education, Harmondsworth, 1978) pp 256-257)

6 Maccarthy, Dermod 'Recognition of Signs of Emotional Deprivation: a Form of Emotional Child Abuse' *Child Abuse and Neglect* (1979) 3 pp 423-428

7 Morgan, S R *Children in Crisis, a Team Approach in Schools* (Taylor and Francis, London and Philadelphia, 1985) p 132

8 Martin, H P and Beezley, P 'Behavioural Observations of Abused Children' in *Developmental Medicine and Child Neurology* (1977) 19, pp 373-387, 376

9 Department of Health and Social Security *Child Abuse: Central Register Systems* (1980) LASSL (80) 4, HN (80) 20

10 Garbarino, J 'The Elusive "Crime" of Emotional Abuse' in *Child Abuse and Neglect* (1978) 2, pp 89-99

11 Hoxter, S 'Emotional Abuse: how can we define it?' *BASPCAN Conference 'Neglect of Neglect'* (1981)

12 Trowell, J 'Emotional Abuse' *Health Visitor* (1983) 56 (7) pp 252-254

13 Patterson, Paul G R and Thompson, Michael G G 'Emotional Child Abuse and Neglect: An Exercise in Definition' in Volpe, R; Breton, M and Mitton, J (eds) *The Maltreatment of the School-aged Child* (Lexington Books, Massachusetts and Toronto, 1980) pp 59-69

14 Laurie, S S 'On defining emotional abuse: results of an NIMH/NCCAN workshop' in Lauderdale, M L *et al* (eds) *Child abuse and neglect: issues on innovation and implementation: proceedings of the Second Annual National Congress on Child Abuse and Neglect* April 17-20 1977 (US Department of Health Education and Welfare, Washington DC, 1978)

15 Klein, M *Love, Guilt and Reparation, The Writings of Melanie Klein,*, Vol 1 (Hogarth Press, London, 1937) pp 317-320

16 Royal College of Psychiatrists 'Educational Abuse' *Bulletin of the Royal College of Psychiatrists* (Child Psychiatry Section, 1982) 6, 85-87

17 De Lozier, Pauline P 'Attachment Theory and Child Abuse' in Parkes, C; Murray, and Stevenson-Hinde, J (eds) *The Place of Attachment in Human Behaviour* (Tavistock, London and New York, 1982) pp 95-118

18 Lynch, M A and Roberts, J *Consequences of Child Abuse* (Academic Press, London, 1982) p 108

19 Boston, M 'The Tavistock Workshop an overall view' in Boston M and Szur, R (eds) *Psychotherapy with Severely Deprived Children* (Routledge and Kegan Paul, London, 1983) a) pp 1-11; b) p 59; c) p 15; d) p 76

20 Pringle, M K *The Needs of Children* (Hutchinson, London, 1974) p 135

21   Wolkind, S N 'A Child's Relationship after Admission to Residential Care' *Child Care and Education* 3, No 5, pp 357-362

22 Hoxter, S 'Play and Communication' in Boston, M and Daws, D (eds) *The Child Psychotherapist and Problems of Young People* (Wildthorpe, London, 1977), pp 202-231

23 Miller, L 'Eileen' *Journal of Child Psychotherapy* (1980) 6, pp 57-67

24 Britton, R S 'The Deprived Child' *The Practitioner*, Sept 1978, 221, p 37

25 Henry G 'Doubly Deprived' *Journal of Child Psychotherapy*, 1974, 3, p 4

26 Holmes, E 'Psychological Assessment' in Boston, M and Szur, R (eds) *Psychotherapy with Severely Deprived Children* (Routledge and Kegan Paul, London, 1983) pp 67-75

27 Material presented by Mrs Carla Busato at a seminar organised under the auspices of the Tavistock Clinic and Rome University Department of Education (unpublished)

28 Rutter, M and Madge, N *Cycles of Disadvantage* (Heinemann, London, 1976) pp 267 and 326

29 Hoxter, S 'Some feelings in working with severely deprived children' in Boston, M and Szur, R (eds) *Psychotherapy with Severely Deprived Children* (Routledge and Kegan Paul, London, 1983) p 132

Chapter 7
Child sexual abuse

Helen Kenward

with a supplement
The police in the context of child sexual abuse
Detective Chief Inspector Richard A. Buller

Child sexual abuse hurts, it hurts the child, the family, the community, the perpetrator, and *you* the worker. The pain the child feels needs to be shared, dissipated, and left with someone; if you are that person, you have to understand it and learn how to handle it. Child sexual abuse is not something you should work with on your own; you need colleagues to co-work with, supervision to retain objectivity and people with whom to share your feelings. The best defence you have is knowledge and understanding of the problem; to gain this, you need to be prepared to listen and to have a clear idea of the process you become involved in.

Henry Kempe defines child sexual abuse as

The involvement of dependant, developmentally immature children and adolescents in sexual activities they do not fully comprehend, to which they are unable to give informed consent or that violate the social taboos of family roles.

Sexual abuse includes inappropriate touching; exposure to indecency and pornography; being required to participate in sexually stimulating acts including masturbation, prostitution, or pornography; heterosexual/homosexual forcible or other intercourse – vaginal, oral or anal. The legal definitions of offences under the Sexual Offences Act 1956, 1967 and Indecency with Children Act 1960, and possible consequences are outlined in Appendix A on page 138.

Jenny gives a vivid account of sexual abuse. She had remained silent for ten years before disclosing, through letters,

I was so unhappy I dreaded going home from school, every night it was the same routine, he used to threaten me if I told anyone he would kill me and mum. I once remember telling him he shouldn't be doing it but he said he enjoyed it and I wouldn't get pregnant.

Jenny's father masturbated over her, forced her to have intercourse and oral copulation, degraded and abused her.

He used to treat my bust like a punchball, I used to think he was going to kill me he was so heavy, I always thought this breath is my last one. I feel so lousy, unhappy, dirty, disgusting, embarrassed, cheap, sick, suicidal, tormented, and depressed. Why do I feel so guilty?

Sexual assault is a form of behaviour that arouses strong feelings, particularly among professionals who have to handle the victims and their families. If asked to express their feelings, they inevitably range from intense anger to compassion for all concerned. The responses are natural and most people experience some of them, but have to learn to cope with them. It is important that the child feels safe, protected, cared for and about, and that considerable warmth is shown. Everyone has a different manner in responding to children but however it is shown, the child will sense the honesty in the caring.

Many questions are raised in the mind of an adult who first comes into contact with sexual assault. In answering those questions, it must be remembered that we are still handling and talking about children. There is a tendency to forget the skills that are important in talking and working with those children once the label of victim has been placed on them. They have the same needs as all children, but more so, since they have often been betrayed by the very people in whom they should be able to trust.

Who are the victims?

Boys *and* girls are victims, although the exact numbers are unclear since boys in particular are reluctant to disclose abuse. The extent of the problem is demonstrated by Finkelhor (1979,80) whose findings indicate that 19% of women and 9% of men have been sexually assaulted and as a result have suffered long-term harmful effects on self-image and the ability to make sexual relationships. Other studies indicate a higher number. This paper will use 'she' to refer to the victims of abuse but the same responses will on the whole apply equally to 'he'.

Who sexually abuses children?

Offenders are both men and women, but more often men. They come from every class, creed, race, and profession, and many of them are married. Most were themselves abused as children and lacked affection and natural physical contact. There are two groups of offenders, those that abuse within the family setting, and those that molest in the community. It is recognised that children generally know the offender who becomes expert at hiding his behaviour from family, neighbours, friends, and colleagues; often the secrecy can be maintained for a long period because children are easily silenced by threat or promise from adults. The molesting adult often provides those needs attributed to good parenting, and the child becomes lulled into participating in sexual acts. The adult capitalises on being 'special' and leaves the child with the heavy price of guilt.

Paul, aged 12, was befriended by a valued friend of the family. They went camping and walking together. After a period of good friendship, Paul was sexually assaulted. Attempts at refusing further invitations were laughingly blocked by his parents and it took him two years to tell his older sister, who then told her teacher. Subsequent events were rapid and frightening, the arrest of the friend and his family's disbelief left Paul very distressed. Individual counselling and play therapy helped Paul understand the adult's responsibility and his own position as a victim. The last session was spent answering any questions Paul might have. The questions themselves are a good indication of the long-term effect of such an assault.

When people look at me, will they know? Will I be homosexual? When I have a girlfriend, will I know what to do? Will I be able to be a parent?

Paul's questions reflect his stage of development but also indicate the confusion that was aroused by a loving, caring adult initiating him into a sexual relationship he was unprepared for, and did not wish to undertake.

How do I recognise a child who is sexually abused?

It is important to understand that sexual abuse sets a child apart. She is involved in a situation which may be very confusing; she may feel both guilty about what has occurred and responsible for it. She is often torn by divided loyalties since the abuse may well take place within an otherwise loving relationship.

The most important tool an adult has in interpreting a child's behaviour is knowledge of normal development and behaviour. Teachers are in an ideal position to observe and understand changes in a child, and in general children are quick to show their feelings. An abused child may appear withdrawn or engage in fantasy or infantile behaviour. Her relationships with her peers may be very poor. Lorraine talked about school and friends: 'How could I be friends and chat in the playground? They laugh and talk as if they know it all, but I do know it and I have to be careful not to give anything away'. Lorraine was sexually abused and degraded by her father for five years, everyone was worried about her but no-one did anything. When asked why she didn't tell, she said 'No-one ever asked me'.

The child may be unwilling to participate in physical activities, be lethargic, and tired. Anxiety and fear may well mean poor sleep and lack of energy. Many children will describe waiting in bed, afraid to go to sleep 'in case he comes again'; after the assault the pain, the silent tears and the tension mean that sleep is hard. With such knowledge who would be surprised that normal play fails to tempt a child?

A child may try to 'tell' by delinquent acts or running away. Unusual behaviour should always be questioned and space given to the child to share feelings as to why she is acting in this way. Some children will tell more overtly; giving the adult clear messages of sexual assault, if the adult will *hear*. It is important to listen with your feelings as well as your ears.

Susanna tried to tell her teacher a very important piece of news during 'show and tell time'. 'My mummy and daddy were in bed and my daddy said I had to watch'. The teacher, not wanting to hear, said – in Susanna's words – 'not now dear'.

Susanna tried unsuccessfully to tell and subsequently the teacher told her parents they should be careful she didn't walk in on them. Susanna's behaviour became more and more difficult and she caused considerable anxiety to neighbouring families. Eventually she was referred to a family centre for assessment where play with dolls and a doll's house gave her the opportunity to talk about her abuse. Susanna had been buggered and orally assaulted, she was a very frightened child who had to find a safe adult to protect her.

Many abused children develop a defensive body posture. Lorraine hunched her shoulders and held her head like an old lady of 70. A greyness of skin and lank hair were physical signs of a grossly abused child, physically as well as sexually. When trying to tell, many children assess the adult in a similar way, observed by others as well as myself. They freeze and make eye contact which seems endless, before beginning a devastatingly honest and lucid account of abuse.

There are a number of signs that offer forensic evidence, and it is essential that these should be recorded and collated by the police surgeon. Torn, stained or bloody underclothing and physical signs of pain or itching in the genital area should be looked out for. Bruises or bleeding in external genital, vaginal or anal regions, needs urgent medical attention. Pregnancy or venereal disease are danger signals, the latter having been observed in very young children. It should be remembered that any adult having concerns about a child must be careful not to ask leading questions that may well get in the way of further investigations. 'Who did that?' rather than 'Did your daddy do that?' Access to the family may well give clues to a child's behaviour; a parent of a child (especially at adolescence) may be afraid that the child may tell and use fear to ensure the secret is kept. 'He says he'll kill me or my mum if I tell' is a frequent cry. The child may be encouraged to engage in prostitution or sexual acts in the presence of a caretaker and some of the indicators for such a lack of boundaries are: parents who are experiencing marital difficulties, misuse alcohol or other drugs, are frequently absent from home, or have been sexually abused as a child.

Sexual assault should be suspected if the child shows an early and exaggerated awareness of sex, with either seductive interest or fearful avoidance in close contact with others.

Joanne, at four, caused considerable embarrassment to a visiting probation officer when she climbed on his knee and tried to unzip his trousers. Her mother casually remarked that Joanne would go to any man and seemed unperturbed by the child's attempts to masturbate against him. Joanne had been abused by lodgers and neighbours and mother had failed to protect her. During play sessions with mother and child, she disclosed her own abuse as a child, and showed a lack of understanding of why Joanne had been assaulted.

What do I do about it?

When a child tells you about sexual abuse or you begin to suspect it, it is important not to back off. The child needs to feel that the adult will hear and share the pain; at the same time there is a need to protect the child and stop the abuse. Each Area Review Committee will have a procedure for multi-agency response. All professionals should make it a point to obtain a copy, included in which will be a list of contact telephone numbers to go to for advice, support and help with decision-making in response to individual needs.

It is important that the safe adult the child has chosen to disclose to, knows what will happen next; or, if not, that he/she is prepared to admit that they will need to get help. The police maintain very strongly that they should be brought in right at the beginning, and they have the skills and resources necessary to investigate. Disclosure and investigation can be part of the therapeutic processes since the way children cope with the results of sexual assault depends to some extent upon the responses of the adults around them. Tina was a frightened 12-year-old who refused to go home. Her teacher was concerned since Tina's work had deteriorated and she had become very nervous. Social services were contacted and a social worker visited the school. Tina shared with the social worker that she was afraid of going home because her father wouldn't leave her alone at night. Tina was interviewed by a policewoman in the presence of the social worker and she later described the experience.

I didn't like the questions but felt safe to say all the things that had happened to me. They tried to find out if I was telling lies, I didn't like that but they had to be sure because it meant locking my dad up. They were all very nice to me and they believed me. I felt better straight away once I knew that someone believed me. The only thing is my mum didn't even though dad was arrested, so I had to go to a children's home.

The child will want to know what is going to happen if she tells, so the police interview needs to be described, making clear that the child can have someone with her and should not be afraid. The interview will have to be explicit, but the details can be given in the language the child is used to and she need not worry that anyone will make fun of it. One of the first tasks for the interviewing officer (whenever possible a woman for a girl, and a man for a boy) will be to establish the words used within the family. Young children will not be formally interviewed, the officer will take time to get to know the child and make them feel relaxed. The child will be encouraged to draw and the statement will be a series of answers to simple questions.

Forensic evidence is important and a medical will be needed, to provide corroborative evidence. The time scale is important, here, since such evidence is easily lost. It is necessary for the samples to be collected as soon as possible after the event. The child needs to be reassured that the experience may be uncomfortable, but won't take long. The police surgeon is in a unique position to reassure the child that what has happened has not permanently damaged them. Many children fear that the pain of being penetrated means extensive internal damage.

Christina drew a picture of herself with her eyes at the top of her head and great black tears rolling down the face. Her lower body was painted black. She described her drawing – 'If the eyes are up there, they can't seee what's happening and the body is black because that's what it feels like inside'. Subsequent disclosure, investigation, and medical, left Christina feeling a whole person. The doctor reassured her and she began to view growing up with pleasure rather than fear.

Many children feel let down by the adults around them when, having gone through the investigation, there is not enough evidence for any action to be taken. The subsequent management and help needed by a family requires skilled intervention. This can come from combined work by professionals from the areas of social work, child guidance, and education.

What will the child want to know?

The child will want to know what happens at a case conference and who will attend. It is important that the roles of individuals be explained and the nature of the conference discussed in terms appropriate to the age and ability of the child. In many areas the police automatically attend the conference and the issue of registration for sexual abuse is becoming more accepted. Children who share a painful secret will want to know who else is going to know. If the child is to learn to trust adults, then she has to know what is confidential and what is being shared. The older the child, the clearer the worker has to be as to why information is passed on and to whom. For a child who has been afraid and who has betrayed – in their eyes – a family secret, the thought of facing family members is awesome. No-one should make promises they cannot keep and it is often better to say you don't know or are not sure, than to give an enigmatic answer which you can't back up.

Sexual abuse has to stop, and the child must be protected. The statutory agencies can take a Place of Safety Order and place the child in a foster home or children's home, but they generally prefer that the offender be removed. The latter means that the non-offending parent has to accept what has happened and be prepared to ensure protection for the child. One of the problems is that the child did not feel able to confide in or trust that parent or, alternatively, may have tried to tell but been rejected. A great deal of work has to be done between the non-abusing parent and the child as well as between the abuser and child. The child will be reluctant to face the offender and will need to know that they don't have to until they are ready. If the child has to leave home, she will want to know where she is going and who will look after her.

As one considers the questions a child will ask it becomes clear that it is vitally important that the professional network communicates and formulates a local structure. Thus the child will get a uniform answer and each adult will have the answers ready. Once the immediate future is clear, the child will want to know about school; if she can return and what the other children will say. If the child participates in deciding what she wants said and who is going to know, it will ease her way back into the community. As far as possible the child has to be helped to take back control over herself and her body; being part of the decision-making will increase her self-confidence. Adults around who take the time and trouble to participate will need to give messages of liking and respect since abused children have been denied their rights and feel worthless. When the child begins to think of a future beyond disclosure, she wants to see her family; the issue of guilt is a major one, the emphasis has to be on placing responsibility where it belongs – with the adult. When there are other children in the family, they may well have been assaulted, too, and this often comes as a surprise to a girl who has been led to believe that she is the only one. The children often believe that theirs is the only abusive family and one of the ways of helping work through the issues is for them to join a victims' group.

The loudest cry from abused children is 'Why me'? There is no simple answer, if any, and they struggle with the feelings this arouses. Claire was the fourth child in a family of six, her parents separated when she was nine and her father sexually abused her from that time. Claire was deprived of her childhood and of the normal emotional responses she should have been able to expect from her brothers and sisters.

When she reflected on her adolescence it seemed the whole family had conspired to scapegoat her and she felt trapped. Threatened that her younger sister would be hurt if she didn't accept whatever she was handed, she became more and more isolated. Disclosure came accidentally through the innocent chatter of her five-year-old sister. Claire was left with a legacy of fear and bewilderment and was rejected by the others when she made a statement to the police. The family were angry that Dad was in prison and they were separated. Claire seemed to carry the guilt for all of them.

How do we meet the needs of workers, parents and children?

Adults working with victims may well feel uncomfortable about presenting sexual abuse information or wary of hearing a child's account of the abuse. They frequently feel they have inadequate knowledge and need to have access to material including case histories and research data. (Appendix B on page 140 is a bibliography of readily available material.)

Written material does not replace the need for colleagues to be available for advice and consultation. There are no real experts in this field, the problem has been with us for a long time but we are only just beginning to address it. Local colleagues do have resources and skills, they just have to develop them, to cease to be afraid and remember, above all, that children are involved.

Children who are vulnerable to molestation, who may already have been, or are being, exploited, need to learn about good touch, bad touch, and confusing touch. They need to know who is safe to tell and how to tell. They need to know how to say No and how to get away. It is important to provide self-esteem enhancement exercises for children to encourage them to practice saying No and to learn to be assertive. We have to teach all children safety skills involving accepting lifts, being alone at home, going off with someone, bribery and threats – active or implied. Children feel powerless in an exploited situation, they need to be taught they have the right to say No, that older people are *not* always right, and that secrets should be told if someone is being exploited.

The goals for working with victims and their families are

- to prevent further abuse;
- to help victims overcome the emotional results of sexual abuse – the self-destructive feelings;
- to help with family relationships;

• to rehabilitate the offender, helping him or her accept their responsibility.

The goals may be worked towards using combinations of individual counselling, family therapy, play therapy, marital counselling, and dyad sessions with child/mother, child/offender, and child/siblings. With abusive families growth is difficult unless each member of the family is helped to see their part in the structure.

The child's self-image needs to be fostered and reinforced. A variety of activities can be provided to allow for success and foster creativity. Tracy had never succeeded at anything until she was taken sailing. Once at the helm of the dinghy she became responsible for us both, the joy on her face and the strength she gained far exceeded our expectations. Children need love and care. Opportunity has to be given for the families to learn to show emotional care in an acceptable manner. Normal interaction between children and adults has to be taught and social situations exploited.

As one way of doing this the family centre held family 'Playdays' when workers, children and parents played together. John had abused two of his children and they were very wary of him. Finger painting, clay modelling and role play were activities they had never shared and John lost his diffidence when he saw other dads down on the floor. The professionals have to be prepared to act as role models for families who have had poor experiences resulting in sexual abuse.

It is important when working with parts of families to keep other members informed of stages of growth. Frequently, once the abuse has stopped, children begin to grow at a phenomenal rate; their parents have to be helped to cope with newly-assertive children who make demands on them. The parents' needs are often as great as the child's and the workers have to attempt to keep a balance. Appendix C on page 141 gives some practical ideas for activities with children and families.

Teachers are the single group of adults, outside the family, that has the most contact with children. They are in the unique position of being skilled in the developmental needs of children and of having a knowledge of normal growth and behaviour. Development of observational skills, sensitivity, and awareness of sexual abuse mean that children are more likely to disclose to them than to anyone else.

Children may feel no-one would believe them, they need to learn who to tell and how to tell, and to keep on telling until someone helps. Workers, parents, and children need to hear, and to remember that it is *never* the child's fault.

The police in the context of child sexual abuse

The purpose of the following section will be to review briefly the duties and procedures of the Police in the context of child sexual abuse. On the one hand, it is important to remember and allow for our pain when we become involved in these cases. On the other, good managers ought to be aware of the dangers of self-indulgence and lack of understanding of other agencies' procedures, particularly of police duties to respond to reported crime.

As professionals, we should remain aware of police responsibilities within the criminal justice system. They are liable for their inefficiency both through internal disciplinary procedures and in the wider contexts of the civil law. Similarly, we in the Social Services are liable for our acts of negligence. It is a fact of life that we should not lose sight of. It follows, therefore, that training in the realities of *varying* professional procedures on a multi-agency basis should promote a deeper understanding of the constraints placed on other agencies.

Rather than provide a detailed list of police duties, I thought it might be more revealing to consider some of the changes effected within the Police Service in recent years. Perhaps the responses will provide an insight which may help us come to terms with our uncertainties. Developments within Northamptonshire Police are symptomatic of national policy. I shall, therefore, confine my comments to the county force with which I work.

The force's training is continually being widened and now includes instruction/debate on the interviewing and treatment of victims and on rape trauma syndrome. The Detective Chief Inspector (Liaison) in his role as Child Abuse Liaison Officer is a participant in multi-agency initial and management training planning. Such courses include police participants with supervisory responsibilities. Furthermore, in-force training allows for contributions from partner agencies in this field. One significant recent change involves the introduction of mock interviews and role playing generally. This should enable the assessment and improvement of interview techniques.

The Northamptonshire Police place great importance on the need to assist and support victims of sex offences. It is the responsibility of the officer handling the case to ensure that the necessary support and assistance are provided. In rape cases this involves liaison with a Rape Crisis Centre in a neighbouring county, or local Women's Aid groups, as appropriate.

Perhaps, in the educational context of this response, an exploration of the police surgeon's considerations may enhance awareness here. All Northamptonshire police surgeons have attended the Women Specialists' or CID Course in respect of sexual assault training. During their attendance they will have had an opportunity to listen and talk with a representative of the Luton Rape Crisis Centre, who regularly lectures these courses. The speaker is herself a rape survivor and provides a tellingly poignant contribution to the courses.

Two female deputy police surgeons are retained by the Service. If a victim prefers medical examination by a female examiner, the duty surgeon will request one of these deputies to attend. If this is not possible, he can request the services of a female medical practitioner (for example, a hospital doctor or family planning clinic doctor) who will conduct the examination in order that the correct forensic samples are obtained and that the findings are properly recorded for evidential purposes. It should be stressed that all the male examiners are in active clinical practice as family doctors. There has never been a problem in the county in the choice of medical examiner for sexual assault victims. This may be due to the fact that although a police surgeon's rota exists, the Women Police Departments quite often exercise their discretion of choice in conjunction with the Investigating Officer and at times Social Services, regardless of the rota.

As for medical examinations, the force will shortly open a victim's support suite, with toilet and shower *en suite*, on one of the two divisions. A second such suite is planned for the other division, in the near future. The intention is to provide comfort, privacy and confidentiality in these distressing cases. The rooms selected for this purpose are set away from the main charge room and the rest of the station.

Apart from the Police Station, examiners commonly use their own surgeries, hospitals and even the victim's home. Indeed, a place of examination will be arranged to the mutual satisfaction of all concerned, ie victim, social services, doctor and CID. In respect of victim's support, the surgeon will not undertake any psychiatric care or treatment of sexually transmitted diseases. However, at the conclusion of the examination, an offer will be made either to contact the woman's general practitioner (it is surprising how many victims do not wish this to be done) or to arrange for follow-up support from the local hospital, especially the Sexually Transmitted Diseases Clinic.

In contrast to the practice of larger forces, the woman police constable involved in the initial complaint is often the officer who maintains contact and not only acts as a link between victim and police surgeon, after initial examination, but also develops a supportive relationship with the victim – of obvious benefit if a court appearance becomes necessary. Although an informal arrangement, more or less dictated by the fortunate circumstances of a small force, this does mean that surgeons are able to keep in touch with the progress of the case and the state of health of the victim as a result of the professional, yet caring relationship between police and victim.

All Northants surgeons and deputies are members of the Association of Police Surgeons of Great Britain, which lays great stress on training aimed at producing competent, impartial and caring professionals. Indeed, if a victim were to request their general practitioner to be in attendance during the examination, this would be arranged.

Finally, I would like to touch on one area which is indicative of the tensions involved between achieving appropriate sensitivity and the need for the Police to prove the case in court. After all, what possible purpose is there in subjecting the child victim to the trauma of a court appearance, if the case is to be lost through inefficient preparation?

I wonder how many of the other professionals involved realise that whilst a police offer attempts to deal sympathetically and tactfully with a sexual abuse victim, he or she is also required to deal with at least 30 evidential and practical considerations – and all the while, the clock is ticking away. Delay in response or questioning can result in the loss of forensic evidence or the loss of the person responsible. That person might offend again.

Appendix A

Buggery
It is an offence for a person to commit buggery with another person.
Section 12(1) Sexual Offences Act, 1956
There are two kinds of buggery:
 (a) Sodomy – sexual intercourse between males or between male and female per anus.
 (b) Bestiality.
   Punishment: life imprisonment – if with boy under 16 years, or female or animal.

   10 years imprisonment – if without consent on male 16 years and over.

   5 years imprisonment – if with consent on male 16 years and over, but under 21 years.

Indecency with children
Indecency means offence to modesty, impure, obscene or unchaste behaviour, for the purpose of the
Indecency with Children Act, 1960
It is an offence for any person to commit an act of gross indecency with or towards a child under the age of 14 years, or to incite a child under that age to such an act with him or another (*Section 1*):
   Punishment: Gross indecency on a child under the age of 14 years – 2 years imprisonment.

Unlawful sexual intercourse
It is an offence for a man to have unlawful sexual intercourse with a girl under the age of 13 years.
Section 5, Sexual Offences Act, 1956
> **Punishment** life imprisonment, attempts to commit offence 7 years.

It is an offence for a man to have unlawful sexual intercourse with a girl under the age of 16 years.
Section 6(1) Sexual Offences Act, 1956
> **Punishment** 2 years imprisonment (where the girl is over 13 years but under 16 years).

Indecent assault
It is an offence for a person to make an indecent assault on a woman.
Section 14(1) Sexual Offences Act, 1956
It is an offence for a person to make an indecent assault on a man.
Section 15(1) Sexual Offences Act, 1956
An indecent assault is an assault accompanied by circumstances of indecency on the part of the offender.
> **Punishment** 10 years imprisonment (amended by *Section 3(3) Sexual Offences Act, 1985*)

Incest
Incest by a man offence to have sexual intercourse with a woman he knows to be his –
  grand-daughter
  daughter
  sister (includes half-sister)
  mother
Section 10 Sexual Offences Act 1956
Triable on indictment
  Prosecution may not be commenced except by or with the consent of the Director of Public Prosecutions.
> **Punishment** Girl below 13 years – life imprisonment.
> Otherwise 7 years.
> Attempt to commit the offence – 7 years and 2 years.

Incest by a woman offence for a woman aged 16 and over to permit a man whom she knows to be her –
  grandfather
  father
  brother (includes half-brother)
  son
to have sexual intercourse with her by her consent.

Section 11 Sexual Offences Act 1956
Triable on indictment:
   Prosecution may not be commenced except by or with the consent of
   the Director of Public Prosecutions.
   Punishment   7 years imprisonment.
                    Attempt to commit offence – 2 years imprisonment.

Appendix B

Child sexual abuse – a bibliography

The books and articles in this list are recommended to professionals
seeking a broad understanding of the issues surrounding sexual abuse.

Books

Goodwin, Jean – *Sexual Abuse: Incest Victims and their Families*
   Wright, PSG
Finkelhor, David – *Sexually Victimised Children* Free Press
Mrazek & Kempe – *Sexually Abused Children and their Families*
   Pergamon Press
Nelson, Sarah – *Incest: Fact and Myth* Stramullion Paper
Forward, S and *Bruce*, C – *Betrayal of Innocence*, Pelican
Sgroi, Suzanne, M – *A Handbook of Clinical Intervention in Child
   Sexual Abuse*, Lexington Books
Adams, K and *Fay*, J – *No More Secrets*, Impact Publications
Rervoise, Jean – *Incest – A Family Pattern*, R and KP
Elliott, Michelle – *Preventing Child Sexual Assault* – Bedford Press
   CIBA – Child Sexual Abuse within the Family

Case Studies

Miller, K – *Please Love Me*, Word Books 1977
Hart, T – *Don't Tell Your Mother*, Quartet Books Ltd 1979
Wheat, P – *By Sanction of the Victim*, Timely Books 1978
Morris, M – *If I Should Die Before I Wake*, Souvenir Press Ltd 1983
Hayden, T L – *One Child*, Souvenir Press Ltd 1981

Appendix C Working with child victims of sexual abuse

Activities to promote growth

Emotional outlets

Water play	Child has control over the
Sand play	materials and can gain confidence
Clay	and a feeling of mastery
Papier mache	
Plasticine	

All are acceptable outlets for messing, aggression, and exploration.
Bean bags – an outlet for aggression and withdrawal.
Finger printing – a substitute for other unacceptable ways of smearing and messing. It encourages creative and personal expression, it can be calming to an aggressive child or relaxing to an inhibited child.
Creative art – finger and brush painting
                collage
                sculpture
The emphasis to be on the process rather than the product. The child needs to feel to express his own creativity through various media.

Large muscle activities

  movement and dance
  games
  music and song
These activities are to provide emotional and physical outlet through movement, verbalisation, and self-expression.

Self-expression through verbalisation

Stories	Puppets	
Picture discussion	Language games	Dramatic play

Listen to the child
Watch what the child does
Hear what he/she does *not* say
Reflect the child's behaviour
Care about the child, *protect* but do not *smother*.

Chapter 8

Case management and inter-professional liaison

David N Jones and John Pickett

The number and diversity of agencies and professions which necessarily become involved in a child abuse case has been found to be a source of complication and confusion in the response to individual cases. This often compounds the case management problems caused by the undoubted inadequacy of research into the causes and nature of child abuse. Both factors create significant problems in assessment and decision taking. In many respects child abuse cases are no different from other child care cases which necessarily involve a number of specialists from different professions, for example the co-ordination of services to seriously handicapped children or those with serious learning difficulties. Experience has shown, however, that a failure to give adequate attention to issues of communication and the relationship between the different groups of workers can cause major problems in child abuse cases, including the possibility of errors or misunderstandings proving literally fatal.

Teachers have faced criticism on grounds of their inadequate communication with other professionals in a number of the major child abuse enquiries. The Maria Colwell enquiry was critical of the education services, among others. The report makes fascinating, disturbing and instructive reading and should be a set text for all student teachers. Three issues emerged in relation to the education service; communication, record-keeping and awareness. The report criticised inadequate communication within and between schools and especially between schools and other agencies. The exclusion of the class teacher from discussion with other agencies was regretted: head teachers did not have the intimate knowledge of individual children which may have assisted other agencies and the comments of these agencies were often not passed back to the class teacher.

The report was concerned about the failure to pass on background information when Maria changed schools, although this would have had little relevance given the paucity of information in the official school records. Discussions with other agencies were not recorded routinely and the medical record lacked relevant social factors. At the enquiry it was recommended that schools should have a systematic written record of significant events and communications affecting children *at risk*. Communication with the education welfare officer was described as poor and unrecorded. The report concluded: 'there appeared to be no machinery by which concern about the welfare of school children automatically reached the Social Services Department' and wondered whether this reflected 'a lack of confidence in and understanding of the respective roles and responsibilities between schools and social workers'. The report also discussed the evident lack of awareness of and knowledge about child abuse. It recommended that there should be local, multi-disciplinary procedures detailing respective roles and responsibilities and giving advice on whom to consult if concerned about a child.

The Colwell enquiry report was published in 1974 and there have been considerable developments in services and understanding since then. There nevertheless remains a need for schools to remain alert to these aspects of the child abuse response, as demonstrated in the recent Beckford report.

Child abuse procedures and inter-agency communication have received considerable attention from local and national government and professional bodies. Guidance from central government and professional bodies and that provided in local child abuse documents all place emphasis on effective systems of co-ordination and communication. It is generally agreed that nobody should attempt to deal with a case of child abuse on their own. Yet working with colleagues from other professions and agencies, who may well be complete strangers, whilst being expected to take speedy decisions about emotive issues at a time of crisis, is a highly challenging and sometimes disturbing experience, especially for those who have no prior experience of such matters. There is a real danger that the interests of the child will suffer in the absence of effective policies and systems to guide and regulate such interprofessional contact. This paper comments on the problem areas and makes proposals for good practice, taking into account government and professional guidance.

The multi-disciplinary response to child abuse

Professional roles and functions

Throughout this century, and perhaps especially since 1945, there has been a trend to increasing job specialisation within the health and social services, with a consequent growth in the complexity of organisations, structures and individual case management. It is now common for complex, individual medical and social problems to be managed by a number of individuals with specialist but overlapping roles. The Court Report into child health services argued in 1974 that

'just as doctors and nurses must work together as a team in the health service, so the service must work in partnership with education and social services . . . The planning and development of an integrated health service must therefore be done in such a way as to facilitate at every level the closest possible relationship with these other services'.

The necessity for a multi-disciplinary approach in child abuse cases is self-evident. Almost all cases will involve a doctor, social worker and policeman, each with a defined area of individual decision which inter-relates with the others. There will probably be other professionals in contact with the family as well, who may not face the same immediate decisions about diagnosis and legal proceedings, but who will legitimately wish to influence the immediate decision-taking process and who may need to adjust their own plan of work in the light of the outcome. The degree of the complexity becomes clear when those potentially involved are listed, together with their powers and duties (see Appendix on page 162).

Professional differences

The objectives, purpose and ethos of the different professional groups (and their employing agencies) are subtly different and reinforced through training, although they all share a common, humanitarian concern. The early child abuse literature in the 1960s and 1970s often voiced concern about clashes of 'frames of reference' and professional perspectives, but research by Hallett and Stevenson and our own experience suggests that this problem is not as fundamental or serious as had been previously anticipated. Nevertheless the differing emphases cannot be ignored and can at times lead to tension and confusion.

Some of the perspectives seem comparatively clear-cut, for example the police operate within a justice framework which assumes individual responsibility for behaviour (and misbehaviour/crime) and at least a fair degree of conscious choice; on the other hand, psychiatrists or social workers might tend to adopt a more deterministic approach to understanding human behaviour, looking for background causes and influences, not to seek excuses or justifications but to explore causation as a basis for subsequent intervention. Another possible area of tension may be between those providing individual treatment for children, and teachers who have a concern for the progress of individuals but an equal concern for the progress of the class or group. This may result in impatience with the disruptive behaviour of a deprived or disturbed child and a wish to exclude her from the class, while the psychologist or social worker may focus exclusively on the needs of the individual and place less emphasis on the group needs.

These differences can be reinforced through use of jargon and technical language which may be unfamiliar to others involved or capable of differing interpretation. Particular problems arise with medical and legal terminology, but all professions share the problem. Jargon is often a useful and essential shorthand, but it can exclude the uninitiated. Jargon and technical terms are best avoided whenever possible, if unavoidable, the meaning should be fully explained, even if this seems to prolong discussion. Exclusion of colleagues by use of specialist language or other means can be a powerful, if not fully acknowledged, motive of individuals in multi-disciplinary groups (see below – personal feelings, group dynamics) but is obviously dangerous when planning the protection of an abused child.

Agency structures

The differing organisational structure of the various agencies may create problems of communication and decision. Some are extremely hierarchical, with important decisions always being referred up to a more senior level. This group certainly includes the police and in many respects also embraces Social Services Departments and schools (with the Headteacher holding considerable power). Differences in statutory, governing and authority structures are clearly influential. Local authority departments are accountable to committees of elected councillors who delegate powers and duties through senior officers and demand full accountability – for example, children in care are legally in the care of the Social Services Committee which delegates this responsibility to social workers. Hierarchies inevitably constrain freedom of action and decision to some extent; the expressed views of the individual concerned can be over-ridden by a more senior person. Some agencies have considerable delegated power, while medical consultants and family doctors are directly accountable to no outside body or hierarchy for their professional decisions.

Differences of structure are not often understood by those outside the agency and can lead to resentment, for example a family doctor can take an immediate decision about treatment but a social worker or policeman may have to seek approval for a decision. Some resent the delay this often causes and bemoan the bureaucracy involved.

Power relationships

The degree of influence any individual in a multi-disciplinary group can have over final decisions and outcome depends on the nature of the responsibility to be exercised, the actual or perceived expertise or knowledge possessed, and the force of the individual personality/ charisma.

Doctors have significant responsibilities for the health of the child and therefore his safety and placement, but no direct responsibility for legal action to protect him. The police have to decide whether or not to prosecute the offender and the Social Services Department or NSPCC have the duty to decide whether to initiate civil proceedings to protect the child. The SSD has the exclusive responsibility to decide where to place a child in care under a court order, except in wardship cases where the court can issue directions.

Teachers have very little power or immediate responsibility for decisions once they have referred a case of suspected abuse for investigation, although the response to the abused child in the classroom may be crucial to his future welfare and development. This powerlessness can be a source of considerable anger and frustration, especially when the decisions of others seem inappropriate. The result can be ill-feeling and bitterness which, if not understood and taken into account, can cause considerable problems for, and even harm to, the welfare of the child.

Power is also vested in individuals because they are perceived as knowledgeable or authoritative. It is not unknown for a doctor's opinion to carry more weight than a social worker's, for example, even when the doctor has no direct experience of the issue at stake. In one court case a doctor's opinion on future risk to the child was sought by the court and clearly given precedence over the views of the social worker, even though the doctor had never met the father who committed the assault on the child, whereas the social worker had been through an exhaustive programme of assessment involving a multi-disciplinary team. Resentment can also arise when an individual's own sense of authority is not acknowledged by others, for example in the teacher whose views about the developmental needs of a child who has been in the school for a long time are over-ridden by a social worker who has only known the child for a few days.

In many areas there seems to be a feeling of polarisation between the SSD and the other agencies in child abuse cases, particularly at the time of the initial decision taking. It is not unknown to hear other professionals express resentment that SSDs have taken no action in certain cases and inappropriate or excessive action in others. The prevalence of such feelings suggests that the cause must be at least partly structural. Referring agencies are usually generalist, whilst SSDs are problem-focused and have to assess each case to see if it attracts sufficient priority for intervention. The decision about priorities may not satisfy the referrer. The law also places SSDs in a powerful position in child abuse decision taking. They are under a duty to reach their own decision about risk and safety of children, although they should take into account the views of others. The lack of incontrovertible research findings on which to base decision taking means that social workers will always be vulnerable to criticism in the exercise of their judgement; a degree of tension between SSDs and other agencies is inevitable.

Teams and networks

A further difficulty arises because of the *ad hoc* nature of the professional group which has to ensure decisions are taken at the time of crisis. A group of people working closely together and in regular communication usually develops tried and trusted patterns of communication and a basis of almost intuitive understanding. In most child abuse cases, those involved do not constitute a formal team in this sense and may never have worked together before. They constitute instead a loose community network, whose only common link may be the abused child. The group dynamics may be further complicated by the existence of a core group of members who *do* work regularly together on such cases, such as the SSD Area Director, senior police officer and local authority lawyer, which might increase the sense of exclusion of the others. Despite this newness, the group must rapidly develop sufficient cohesion and mutual trust to be confident in sharing confidential information and in agreeing action. The sense of crisis associated with the incident adds a further dimension which may inhibit communication. It is perhaps to the credit of all involved that, despite these difficulties, our experience is that groups do usually manage to agree on far-reaching conclusions in a very efficient manner.

Group dynamics

Professional groups planning intervention following a child abuse referral are subject to the influences which affect all groups of people. There is now a considerable literature on small group theory, much of it derived from laboratory studies, producing contradictory findings which should be interpreted cautiously. Some of the findings are nevertheless relevant here. A number of studies have shown the pressure towards uniformity and the tendency of groups to reach a consensus. It is rare in our experience to find open disagreement in case conferences, although dissent is sometimes masked. Agreement usually feels better to those involved, but there is no guarantee that the basis of consensus will be appropriate. Some studies also suggest that the larger the group, the more acceptable are individual differences and the less likely a consensus. Other studies reveal that those with high status participate more in group discussion and have more influence on outcome, whilst lower status participants will have less commitment to implementing the agreed outcome. It is possible to conjecture that this dynamic might have influenced some of those who have been shown in public enquiries not to have followed a course of action agreed at a conference dominated by superiors. It is also clear from research and experience that absence of clear leadership in a group will result in its degeneration into cliques and factions, with a battle for leadership, lack of clarity in the outcome and general dissatisfaction. This can be seen clearly in some case conferences.

Multi-disciplinary groups are also strongly influenced by the nature of the subject under discussion. Not only is the subject of child abuse likely to cause a strong and unpredictable emotional reaction in some of the members (see below) but most of those involved will also have had detailed contact with the family, some for a considerable period. It is not the purpose of this paper to attempt an analysis of the dynamics of families which suffer child abuse, but it is clear from other studies that some such families exert powerful influences over their own members and also over those who intervene to attempt change. Families are highly resistant to change and have a repertoire of behaviours and strategies, usully unrecognised by them, which deters those attempting to intervene to provoke change.

Family members seek allies in this struggle and the professionals sometimes develop a strong identification with a particular member. This may be conscious, for example the probation officer supporting the client's perspective in the face of family, court and professional rejection, or unconscious, for example the identification of a professional having problems with their own children with the abusing parent. There are occasions when the professional group begins to mirror the family dynamics, with all its conflicts and tensions, a process which can be destructive for all involved and which can result in inappropriate decisions. Particular problems can arise when the abusing parent is very isolated in the family. The professional group sometimes absorbs and reinforces this overt family rejection but it can also rally to the defence of the outcast.

Professional groups are also prey to concerns about their own members. We have known a case conference to become completely preoccupied with supporting a distressed colleague and begin to lose objectivity and direction in planning the protection of the child. It is also possible for an individual to become the focus of collective anger and disapproval; it may be that the reaction against the police in some cases is a projection of collective anger about the need to make difficult decisions.

Problems arise when plans evolve out of these unconscious dynamics, which do not necessarily reflect the interests and needs of the child.

Personal feelings and individual differences

Managers and procedures can create the context for multi-disciplinary work, but the response of the individual professionals involved will determine its effectiveness. There are wide differences in knowledge about child abuse, some individuals have specialist knowledge and others no knowledge or interest. Frequent changes of staff can also create problems of effectiveness.

More significant than we may care to admit may be the irrational, emotional reactions of individuals to ill-treatment of children. Most professionals, however competent, seem to experience a sense of crisis following discovery of a suspected child abuse case. An Open University course on child abuse considered this area to be of sufficient importance to devote the entire first unit to it. Few professional training courses provide adequate, structured opportunities for students to come to terms with personal feelings and motivations. Often, indeed, staff and students actively avoid exploring this area because it is felt to be too personal. There are nevertheless important reasons for attempting an understanding of these processes in child abuse cases, particularly for those who chair case conferences or supervise staff. Individual responses to crises vary according to person and situation, but emergency responses are 'dangerous guides to cool judgement and wise action'. There is a particular risk of selective perception.

The Open University course commissioned a survey of a mixed group of 66 students, some pursuing professional qualifications in this field. They were asked to study some photographs of abused children and then to complete a questionnaire to test their emotional reactions. The most common reaction in all groups was pity for the child, followed by anger with the abuser. Over half were 'horrified' and felt the deed should not go unpunished. Incredulity, anxiety and sorrow were responses of a significant minority. Around 5% were unable to study the photographs closely. Some professional groups make a virtue out of denying or concealing emotion and there are operational reasons why this should be so. Personal reactions and emotions are universal and natural, however, and may catch the individual unawares. Their effect in child abuse cases must always be taken into account.

Individual reactions vary according to personality, experience, knowledge of the problem, skill and situation. In our experience as consultants to numerous multi-disciplinary groups, the following reactions can be seen:

- *Denial* that anything is wrong, often presented as 'all children in this area have bruises like that – if we call this case child abuse then all children on the estate will end up in care', or 'I have known this family for years – I don't know what happened but they are not that type of people'. Such comments may well be valid, but do not always fit the facts.

- *Anger* with the family for having 'let the professional down', for example 'I gave them all that time and helped them in so many ways and then they go and do this – well that's the last they're getting from me'. Or with a colleague for not preventing the incident.

- *Guilt* that more should have been done to anticipate the problem and prevent the incident or that the professional should have been more perceptive or skilful – 'It's all my fault'.

- *Fear* of personal and professional criticism and of possible damage to future career prospects (often associated with guilt). Or of getting caught up in systems and procedures over which nobody, let alone the individual, has any real control and which may swamp the family and individual.

- *Despair* that all seems so bleak with nothing apparently possible by way of help (occasionally justified but such feelings can defeat systematic appraisal of alternatives).

- *Horror* that such serious and possibly permanent damage could be inflicted on a child, freezing considerations of future action.

- *Jealousy* of professional colleagues now closely involved with the family and possibly being given the chance to develop a closer relationship than the individual who may have known the family for a long time, perhaps associated with

- *Resentment* that somebody else has the investigatory role and seems to be trampling over carefully nurtured relationships (an emotion frequently seen in teachers, and directed against social workers).

- *Omnipotence* a belief that 'I know best', 'I have the best relationship with the family', 'I know how to deal with this', 'Leave it all to me'. However true such feelings may be, in reality a group approach involving other individuals and agencies cannot be avoided and the child is put at risk by attempts at individual professional heroics, however well intentioned.

These tend to be initial reactions to the crisis, but they may persist for days – even weeks. People have different ways of coping with such reactions. Some plunge into a whirlwind of activity, which can become unfocused and unproductive. In contrast, others can become disabled and frozen. Most manage to sustain a reasonable balance, but all benefit from support and understanding from supervisor or colleagues.

The combined anxieties of families and professionals sometimes prompt statements of reassurance that all is not as bad as it seems, or that 'it will be all right in the end'. This sometimes leads professionals to deny the full significance of what has happened in their interviews with the parents, who often wish to believe that the abuse had not occurred. The need to show compassion and understanding is human and understandable, but false reassurance is dishonest and unhelpful, undermining the opportunity for effective work in the future. Future trust is often essential to therapeutic effectiveness and is undermined by an unwillingness to face the truth. Professionals must have an honest willingness to face reality alongside the family, in order to understand and to help.

Government and professional guidance

The government has issued a number of circulars of guidance to authorities and the professions about the management of child abuse cases. These have inevitably focused on questions of inter-agency and multi-disciplinary communication and co-ordination.

The publication of the report into the case of Maria Colwell in 1974 was pre-empted by a DHSS circular which remains the basis of guidance, although currently under review by an internal DHSS working party which issued a revised draft circular for consultation in May 1986. It has been followed to a greater or lesser extent by all authorities. Similar guidance has been issued in Scotland and Northern Ireland.

Non-accidental injury to children (DHSS, 1974) has had a significant impact on the pattern of service delivery to abused children. It recommended the establishment of Area Review Committees based on local authority or health authority boundaries and including senior representatives of all statutory and voluntary agencies involved with children and families. ARCs have been set up throughout the country and most have taken the terms of reference proposed in the circular:

advise on the formulation of local practice and procedures to be followed in detailed management of cases;
approve written instructions defining the duties of all personnel concerned with any aspect of these cases;
review the work of case conferences in the area;
provide education and training to heighten awareness of the problem;
collect information about the work being done in the area;
collaborate with adjacent Area Review Committees;
advise on the need for enquiries into cases which appear to have gone wrong and from which lessons could be learned;
provide a forum for consultation between all involved in the management of the problem;
draw up procedures for ensuring continuity of care when the family moves to another area;
consider ways of making it known to the general public that health visitors, teachers, social workers, the NSPCC and police may be informed about children thought to be ill-treated.

ARCs review general policy concerning child abuse. The circular also recommended a procedure for handling individual cases within such a policy. It recommended that 'a *case conference* for every case involving suspected non-accidental injury to a child should meet as soon as possible', and advised that there should be 'urgent consideration to setting up an adequate central record of information in each area' (*a register*). By 1976 all areas had established ARCs with case conference and register systems of differing types.

Non-accidental injury to children: Area Review Committees was issued by the DHSS in 1976 (DHSS 1976) and included an analysis of returns from ARCs about progress, together with further guidance. Among other matters, it advised that 'all areas which have not yet established a central register should now do so' and that separate agency registers should be amalgamated. The importance of case conferences was re-emphasised and the value of appointing a *key worker* to co-ordinate the agreed intervention was stressed. The circular acknowledged that all involved had to be bound by their own statutory duties and professional assessment, but advised that an approach based on the agreement of all concerned should be attempted, failing which all should be informed about any unilateral action by one agency so that others could adjust their plans if needed.

Non-accidental injury to children: the police and case conferences was issued by the Home Office and DHSS in 1976 (DHSS 1976). It advised that police should attend all case conferences discussing initial management of a suspected child abuse case. Guidance was also given to the police on disclosure of relevant criminal records.

Child abuse: register systems was issued in 1980 (DHSS 1980) and for the first time discussed other forms of abuse of children in this procedural context, apart from physical injury. This consolidated earlier guidance, the main innovation being the extension of the system to embrace severe and persistent neglect and emotional abuse, but not sexual abuse unless it came within the other criteria. Research by the British Association of Social Workers (BASW 1978) had shown that local ARCs were adopting a multiplicity of criteria for inclusion of cases. The DHSS called for uniformity, but this has not happened as yet. Local ARCs continue to adopt different definitions of child abuse and this can cause confusion, especially when families move between areas.

The British Association of Social Workers updated its guidance to social workers in 1985 (BASW 1985) and emphasised the importance of adequate pre- and post-qualifying training and continued supervision. The importance of a multi-disciplinary approach to case management was re-emphasised.

Child abuse – working together: a draft guide to arrangements for interagency co-operation for the protection of children was published by the DHSS in May 1986 following over two years of consultation. It reiterated the importance of a multi-disciplinary response to child abuse but expressed concern about the 'mechanistic' following of procedures without appropriate concern for the individual needs of the child. It suggested, for example, that case conferences had sometimes been held 'without a clear sense of purpose as if they were an end in themselves'. It went further than previous circulars in emphasising the central role of the social worker with statutory powers in the management and coordination of such cases. It advised that the key worker should always be a social worker with statutory powers (ie from a social services department or the NSPCC).

The draft circular suggested that Area Review Committees should be replaced by Joint Child Abuse Committees, directly responsible to the local Joint Consultative Committee (a statutory body including local councillors and officials from health and social services charged with planning joint initiatives in health and social services in the area). It argued that the involvement of politicians through the formal process of a statutory committee would add weight and significance to the decisions and activity of the former ARCs, which have no formal status. The draft circular proposed that child abuse registers should be retitled 'child protection registers', and advocated the appointment of child abuse consultants or advisers in every local authority.

The importance of regular staff supervision and support was underlined. It also recommended the inclusion of sexual abuse within the child abuse framework for the first time. The draft circular was issued in April 1986 for consultation and definitive guidance will be published in due course.

The context of multi-disciplinary work

The sections which follow comment on some ethical and procedural matters affecting multi-disciplinary work in child abuse.

Confidentiality

Discussion about confidentiality and civil rights of parents and children figured in the debate about child abuse in the 1970s and this was reflected in comparatively recent child care legislation and DHSS guidance to local authorities, for example in relation to parental access to children in care and the assumption of parental rights by local authorities under the Child Care Act, 1980. It would appear that in recent months the public has become more concerned about the protection of children and less tolerant of arguments in support of parents' rights. Given the emotive nature of the subject and the decisions to be made, for example to split up a family or to leave a child at home, possibly at risk of death, it is not surprising that strong feelings are generated. This debate has challenged traditional views about confidentiality, particularly in the medical field, but also in education. A consultant psychiatrist once said 'I don't care whether the child dies; my patient (the mother – who had told somebody else that she had attempted to smother her baby) has forbidden me to divulge any information and I am bound to adhere to that'. There is a fundamental question of professional loyalty – is it to the child or the parent?

The classic position on confidentiality is that whatever is said by or about a patient/client is confidential to the speaker and hearer unless it is explicitly agreed otherwise. However, increasing job specialisation and the trend towards team approaches in many professional fields can make this unhelpful and in some situations there is an explicit or informal understanding that information is given in confidence to the professional team but will go no further. This second position creates problems in child abuse cases because, as has been suggested above, there is not a formal and stable team but rather a loose network of professionals. There is the added complication that the network includes not only social workers, who have statutory powers and duties towards the child, but also the police, who have a duty to take an independent decision about possible prosecution.

Most codes of confidentiality acknowledge that there are times when other principles take precedence, either in the public interest or to protect life and limb, for example the British Medical Association recognises 'a doctor's over-riding responsibility to society' and the British Association of Social Workers code states that information will only be divulged by a social worker

with the consent of the client (informant) except: where there is serious evidence of danger to the client, worker or other persons or the community; in other circumstances, judged exceptional, on the basis of professional consideration and consultation.

It is nevertheless essential, not least in order to promote and sustain public confidence in the service, that relevant family members and others should know about the sharing of information, in most cases, and should somehow be involved in the process.

There have been a number of cases where teachers, among others, have found themselves in this sort of dilemma, when a parent or other informant mentions ill-treatment of a child by themselves, or more usually by another, but requests that this is not divulged or acted upon. This generates considerable stress for the individual and imposes a burden of responsibility which most people find disturbing and confusing. No person should leave a child exposed to continued risk, yet there are powerful taboos about breaking such confidences. In our experience, few parents in such circumstances are really seeking confidentiality. They are certainly seeking attention ('I have a secret – listen to me'). Usually they also want the problem to go away and, by raising the subject, hope that some action will follow, even if there is ambivalence. They may fear being identified as the informant and be seeking reassurance. There may also be a genuine fear of physical reprisal.

This dilemma has been called *the confidentiality trap* and obviously is best avoided. Most people accept that professionals have to consult others and making this clear from the outset does not usually inhibit discussion. In most child abuse cases, our experience is that, once the matter has been raised, the informant or parent is relieved to see somebody acting decisively, even taking control of what might have been a nightmare, but feelings will be mixed and there will be apprehension and ambivalence, possibly even anger.

An acting headteacher contacted a child abuse team for a consultation late one Friday afternoon. She explained that a mother had come in, very distressed, and had described moderate physical abuse of a child by the father. The mother was adamant that no further action be taken. The family was known to have considerable problems and the mother was very unhappy, but terrified of what the father would do if he discovered who had informed 'the authorities'. She asked that the school keep a careful eye on the children and compensate for any problems which arose in their work or behaviour. The teacher was very troubled by this and in particular by the mother's graphic account of what the father would do if he discovered that she had talked, even if only to the school. After a long discussion, the teacher decided to take no further action until she had had an opportunity to talk further with the mother the following Monday. She felt that the children would be safe over the weekend. There was no record of previous concern about child abuse in that family. Further enquiries on the Monday revealed that the father had previous convictions for violence, although not towards children, and that he had been violent to the mother. There were major financial problems and one child had been injured, albeit superficially. By deciding to respect the mother's confidence, the acting headteacher had taken a decision about the future safety of the children in the absence of full information, putting not only the children but herself at risk.

Breaching a confidence is always painful and a difficult judgement. It is necessary to take into account not only the immediate circumstances but also the likely consequences in other situations if it became generally known that the hearer could not be trusted. Yet inaction can be equally harmful. Ignoring a potent cry for help can be a profound disservice to the family.

Child abuse procedures

We have already noted that Area Review Committees have published procedural guidance for those likely to encounter child abuse cases. The need for such guidance is self-evident given the large number of individuals concerned (over 10 000 in a large city) and the dangers of misunderstandings and inadequate communication. Ground rules are essential to provide a framework for an effective and speedy response to concern about the welfare and safety of a child.

There is potential for good and harm in such procedures and there has been much discussion within social work about the risk that adherence to procedures is becoming more important than ensuring a sensitive, child-focused service (not least for self-protection). However a lack of procedures can also cause problems for the family, for example the sheer number of individuals potentially involved could swamp a family if all chose to visit around the same time and pursue their own enquiries: one family was visited by a teacher, family doctor, education welfare officer, health visitor, social worker and police representative within the space of four hours, following their earlier visit to see the headteacher. Professional intervention inevitably causes stress for the family, but this is sometimes unavoidable. However, unco-ordinated intervention can overwhelm a family and paradoxically increase the risk to the child. There must be accepted procedures to guard against excessive intervention and inappropriate personal responses by the professionals, whilst ensuring efficient and compassionate investigations.

The preamble to the *Manchester City Guidelines* summarises our approach:

Whoever becomes concerned about and therefore to some extent responsible for a child whose well-being is in question needs to know what to do in order:
1   To get his or her care and physical and emotional condition assessed and treated;
2   To prevent further and possibly more serious injury or suffering which is often an immediate threat;
3   To make sure that as far as possible his or her intervention does no more harm to family structures and relationships, including those with professional workers, than is necessary to ensure the child's safety and well-being;
4   To conform with the law and with professional standards of competence and conduct.
These guidelines are an aid towards achieving these objectives and are based on the assumption that the exercise of professional autonomy and independence can never be absolute and that the best interests of the child and family are best served within the context of multi-disciplinary teamwork, co-operation and commitment to the protection and well-being of the child.

For procedures to be useful and relevant to professionals, they need to be practical, agreeable to all agencies and acceptable to individual professionals, sufficiently detailed to give meaningful guidance, yet sufficiently concise to be clear and memorable. The guidance should identify whom to consult and to whom to refer concern, the location of responsibility for investigating suspicion (as few agencies as possible), the sequence of events during the investigations and what follows, the case conference outline (to assist all concerned when preparing for the meeting) and details of the operation of the central register.

The guidance can only address matters of process and inter-agency contact. It cannot give direction on individual case assessment and intervention. Professional assessment, decision and action remains the responsibility of individual professionals and their agencies.

All ARCs have established registers of abused children (sometimes misleadingly known as 'at risk' registers) as part of their procedural system. It is widely accepted that children should only be placed on a register following a review of the case by a case conference. Registers vary widely in their significance within the local child abuse system and in their effectiveness in identifying and protecting children.

The main purpose of any register is to facilitate and improve the protection of and services to children at risk of abuse, as is reflected in the DHSS proposal to retitle them child protection registers. Within this overall objective, five functions have been identified:

1   to provide detailed, readily available information about children who are known or suspected to have suffered abuse, within criteria agreed by all agencies and professions in the area covered;
2   to provide an aid to the diagnosis of a sequence of repeated injuries or events which might otherwise be seen as unrelated and not identified as a pattern of abuse;
3   to aid good communication between, and co-ordination of, agencies and to avoid unnecessary duplication of services to the child and family following an incident of suspected or confirmed abuse;
4   to provide a basis for regular monitoring and review of the child and family;
5   to provide statistical data about the extent and nature of the problem and to enable planning and development of services in the area.

Registers have attracted considerable debate and criticism since their inception in the early 1970s. In particular, there has been concern that case conferences have spent far more time considering whether a child should be placed on the register than on the nature and organisation of services to protect the child and enhance welfare (DHSS 1986). On the other hand, the register is no more, in one sense, than a record of children about whom there is sufficient professional concern for them to be identified through the formal process of multi-disciplinary consultation through a case conference.

The register is but a part of the whole system and should be concerned not only with the identification of children but also with subsequent review and monitoring. Professionals in all settings seem to find it very difficult to maintain communication with the many people in other agencies who share an interest and legitimate concern in the various child abuse cases known to them. The initial burst of multi-disciplinary activity soon passes and there is an understandable drift back into comparative professional isolation until a new crisis occurs. There is need for a procedure which ensures that this does not happen and that all concerned maintain a multi-disciplinary awareness. The register offers a means of doing this through systematic review by letter or meeting.

Some have voiced concern about the civil liberty aspects of child abuse registers, which have no separate legal status other than as professional records. This contrasts with the situation in the USA where registers have been established by law; there, named groups are legally required to register concern about possible child abuse, failure to report leaving the professional open to civil action for negligence. This is part of a wider debate about confidentiality and access to official records. Some have argued that data subjects should have a formal right of access to register data to review what is recorded and correct errors. Others argue that it is in the public interest that professional concern about children should be recorded and acted on when necessary, even when it cannot be verified through formal proof. Social workers certainly feel vulnerable to public criticism if they fail to act on reasonable suspicion. This debate is clearly wider than child abuse and even health, social services and education record-keeping.

Effective records are an integral part of an effective system for dealing with child abuse and vital as a formal record of work undertaken by publicly accountable agencies, but there must be high standards of confidentiality and parents should be aware of, and involved in, the recording process. *Effective and ethical recording*, the policy statement of the British Association of Social Workers, provides a basis for social work recording which might be of equal relevance to other professional groups.

Clear and acceptable procedures and a predictable response from colleagues are fundamental to the effectiveness of the child abuse system. This can release energy which might otherwise be devoted to procedural negotiations so that full attention can be given to direct work with the family and immediate decisions about family support and child protection. Such guidance must balance the rights of parents and children and the duties of professionals. In the final analysis, however, the effectiveness of intervention is dependent upon the skill and judgement of the professionals directly involved. When the parents and child are talking alone with the social worker, doctor or teacher, no amount of procedural guidance will ensure that the 'right' things are said or done.

Case conferences

The DHSS has recommended (DHSS 1974), with support from other Departments, that a case conference should be held in

... every case involving suspected non-accidental injury to a child. In this way, unilateral action will be minimized, and all those who can provide information about the child and his family, have statutory responsibility for the safety of the child, or are responsible for providing services, will be brought together.

This recommendation forms the basis of most current practice and is now generally interpreted to refer to other forms of abuse as well. This paper has already argued the need for a multi-disciplinary response to child abuse. The necessary communication will take many forms, but a formal meeting will be essential at an early stage and there may well be a need for subsequent meetings to review new information or review progress. The problems inherent in multi-discplinary working are often seen at their most intense in the case conference.

The case conference can be said to perform a number of functions:

- sharing information;
- promoting co-ordination of intervention;
- planning action and defining responsibilities;
- searching for and testing legal evidence;
- relieving individual stress;
- protecting the professionals/agencies;
- formalising the decision-taking process.

Conferences also perform a number of covert functions, such as seeking to manipulate another agency or pass the responsibility.

Conferences have been subject to criticism on various levels. Some advance *ethical criticisms* which question the rightness as well as the value of conferences. These include concerns about confidentiality and the potential erosion of individual professional responsibility and discretion, as well as concern about the civil rights of family members, in particular the right to privacy. Others have advanced *procedural criticisms* which do not question the need for conferences, but point to existing inefficiencies; for example that meetings are too long and poorly structured; that they involve too many people – or the key people are absent; that too many meetings are concerned with trivial cases; and that they degenerate into witch hunts. Such procedural criticisms must be taken seriously and steps taken to improve conference organisation if they persist. What is clear from all the formal enquiries into child abuse tragedies is that the case conferences are seen as highly significant forums and vulnerable to detailed review and criticism if things go wrong. It is therefore essential that ARCs give detailed attention to case conference organisation and in particular the chairing and the agenda or structure of discussion.

A significant number of ARCs have now organised training for case conference chairs. Some have agreed outline agendas for all conferences, which assist those attending to prepare more effectively. A lack of clear structure usually results in the conference degenerating into a sequence of disjointed individual statements which are impossible to draw together and evaluate, leaving an air of non-specific anxiety resulting in inappropriate or unjustifiable responses.

The case conference format used for some years in Nottinghamshire has proved helpful. It is based on the analytical framework proposed over 20 years ago by C Henry Kempe, but other models are equally acceptable and there may well be variations, depending on the theoretical framework adopted. This model proved adaptable over many years.

The conference starts with introductions and apologies. This may seem obvious but there are cases of meetings starting on the assumption that everybody knows each other when that is not true. It is also vital to record who was invited but absent and to note whether they have sent any verbal or written observations. The chair should then outline in a sentence or two the purpose of the conference and how the discussion will proceed. It may be helpful to acknowledge the possible choices to be made and alternative outcomes. The next stage is to identify family members by name, date of birth and relationship and to note where they are living. This phase of the conference introduces the key actors (family and professionals) and sets the scene.

The conference is now able to begin discussion of the incident or immediate factors which triggered the call for the conference. This is uppermost in the minds of those attending and best considered early in the meeting. Contributions are taken in chronological order so that a logical picture of the investigation is built up. Analysis of the sequence of events and family reactions at the different stages is an important part of the evaluation. There should be a clear distinction between reporting fact and analysis.

The conference can then turn to review the family history, relationships, dynamics and current circumstances. A more effective analysis seems possible if each family member is considered in turn rather than one person being asked to 'tell us all you know about this family'.

The final phase involves discussion of the evaluation/assessment. How this is handled will depend on the theoretical approach which is being used and the related therapeutic models available. By the end, conference members should have a clear idea of problem areas and positive family attributes as a basis for planning. The conference must conclude with clear recommendations and individual acceptance of responsibility for future action.

The 1974 DHSS circular recommended that conferences should reach 'a collective decision' but later recognised (DHSS 1976) that decisions 'cannot be binding on representatives with statutory powers and duties'. Each agency or professional has an independent duty to reach a conclusion on the matters within their area of responsibility. No individual or group can abrogate statutory powers or professional duties. Nevertheless there is a duty on all involved to attempt to agree a course of action, taking into account the needs of the child for protection and the family for assistance, as well as the views of professional colleagues. Inconsistency in the approach of the different professionals is confusing for the family and generates considerable stress which might provoke further risk to the child. Nevertheless this must never be seen to detract from the responsibilities of agencies and individuals; it is never a defence to argue, in retrospect, that a course of action seemed inappropriate but issue was not taken at the time because the conference decided otherwise.

Effective multi-disciplinary child abuse work

This paper has argued that, when considering the professional response to child abuse, it is necessary to give attention not only to the child, the family and their circumstances, but also to the professional network, its operation and its problems. For the system to work effectively and to protect children, while causing the minimum damage to family and professional relationships, the following should be present:

- agency and professional commitment to the child abuse management system;
- inter-agency cooperation and understanding;
- shared knowledge about the problem;
- shared knowledge about agency decision-making structures;
- sufficient agreement about the nature of the problem;
- ethical agreement/understanding;
- agreed and publicised procedural framework;
- well organised case conferences (trained chair people and a shared agenda);
- case conference attendance restricted to a maximum of ten if possible;
- sensitivity to use of technical language/jargon;
- appreciation of the influence of individual feelings on decision taking;

- appreciation of the influence of group dynamics on decision taking;
- clear and agreed demarcation of responsibilities;
- adequate recording of discussions and meetings.

All of this will remain ineffective unless there is a shared understanding that the purpose of the activity is to promote the welfare and safety of children. There must also be an adequate level of professional knowledge and skill to implement and monitor decisions which are made. Given this formidable list, it is perhaps reassuring that the objective is achievable and that multi-disciplinary groups are effectively helping children and their families throughout the country.

Appendix: Professional roles and functions

The list below is based on material produced for the Open University and gives details of those who may become involved in a child abuse case during the investigation stage or later. Their powers, duties and specially relevant skills in the context of child abuse are identified; other powers and duties are omitted. They also possess rights and duties as citizens, which are assumed.

Teachers

Powers None

Duties To exercise the duties of a parent (in loco parentis) not only to promote the general welfare and safety of the child, but also to refrain from abuse and ill-treatment.

Skills Teachers are qualified by training and experience to identify normal and abnormal behaviour and development in children.

Social workers – Social Services Departments

Social Worker (Area Team, hospital or other specialist setting), Team Leader/Senior Social Worker, Area Director/Manager/Officer.

Others who may become involved but who do not necessarily share the same powers and duties – Fostering Officer, Courts Officer, Residential Care Adviser, Officer-in-Charge and Residential Social Worker (community home), Day Nursery Matron.

Powers To institute civil proceedings in respect of children needing protection.

There is no power to remove or detain a child nor to enter a home to search for a child without a Court Order. The power to obtain a Court Order in such circumstances is not specific to social workers but available to all citizens, although in practice it is extremely rare for anybody other than a social worker to seek such an order, commonly known as a *Place of Safety Order*. The recent DHSS Child Care Law Review has proposed a different order which might be known as an *Emergency Protection Order*.

Duties To cause enquiries to be made about any alleged ill-treatment or abuse of a child. There is a general duty to promote and safeguard the welfare of children for whom the Department has a statutory responsibility.

Skills The following applies to all social workers regardless of the setting in which employed. Social workers are trained in a variety of methods and styles of work, including individual, family and/or group work and/or community social work. They are expected to have a knowledge of the welfare system and to know how to mobilise appropriate resources to assist an individual child or family. They have an understanding of normal and abnormal human behaviour and should be able to identify and assess signs of potential or confirmed risk to a child.

Social workers – NSPCC

Team Member, Team Leader, Regional Manager

Powers As above.

Duties 'To prevent the public and private wrongs of children and the corruption of their morals' and to take action 'for the enforcement of laws for their protection' (NSPCC Royal Charter).

Skills See above.

Social workers – Probation Service

Probation Officers, Senior Probation Officers.

Powers None specific to child abuse.

Duties To 'advise, assist and befriend' probationers. None specific, relating to child abuse. Expected to report breaches of probation orders to the Court, including the committing of further offences.

Skills See above.

Social workers – other settings

Social workers employed outside the Social Services Department, for example in the Education Welfare Service, Schools Psychological Service, some schools, voluntary agencies.

Powers None specific to child abuse.

Duties None specific to child abuse.

Skills See above.

Police

Uniformed officer, CID officer, Juvenile Liaison Bureau, etc.

Powers To institute criminal proceedings against an adult or juvenile who is alleged to have abused a child. Powers will change following the creation of the Independent Prosecution Service.

To institute civil child protection proceedings.

To remove a child to a place of safety for up to eight days on the authority of a senior officer, without recourse to a Court.

Duties To prevent and detect crime. To protect life and property.

Skills Experience and recognition of abnormal human behaviour and understanding of the law.

Nurses – Health Visitors

Powers None specific to child abuse.

In common with all other groups, there is no power to enter a home to see a child nor to examine a child without parental consent.

Duties To visit all young children to promote their welfare and development and to advise and assist parents to this end. Health visitors would also usually see a responsibility to older children in the household. Some health visitors are attached to schools as school nurses.

Skills Experts in the normal behaviour and development of children with an ability to identify and assess the abnormal.

Other nurses

Hospital nurses, community nurses, midwives, community psychiatric nurses.

Powers None.

Duties None specific to child abuse.

Skills Ability to assess and respond to/treat normal and abnormal health and behaviour, according to specialism.

Midwives in hospital and community have skills in the assessment of the response of parents and siblings to a newborn child and may be able to identify present or future risk to a baby or other child in the family.

Doctors – General Practitioners

Powers None.

Duties None specific to child abuse, but a general professional duty to promote the health and healing of patients. There is also an ethical duty on all doctors to respect the confidentiality of information provided by or about the patient, which can sometimes result in a dilemma when there is a conflict of interest between patients of the same doctor, for example between a parent and child.

Skills Ability to diagnose and treat illness and promote health and welfare. An understanding of normal and abnormal behaviour including the influence of social factors. Some doctors are also able to draw on experience of long-term contact with the family, although this may be less common than often argued, particularly in inner-city areas with mobile populations.

Doctors – Paediatricians

Powers None.

Duties None specific to child abuse but a professional responsibility to promote the health and positive development of children in their care.

Skills Specialists in the medical care and treatment of children and the contribution of social factors to health and development. Some have developed particular expertise in the diagnosis and interpretation of the causation of injuries.

Doctors – Psychiatrists

All settings, including child guidance.

Powers None specific to child abuse.

Powers under the Mental Health Act 1983 in respect of the detention and treatment of those suffering from a mental illness as defined under the Act.

Duties None specific to child abuse.

Skills Specialists in the diagnosis and treatment of psychiatric, emotional and relationship problems. Those in child guidance and other children's services have expert knowledge of the emotional, psychological and intellectual development of children and of parent-child relationships.

Doctors – other specialisms or settings

Specialists in accident and emergency, orthopaedics, neurology, radiology, etc., community medical officers, school doctors.

Powers None.

Duties None specific to child abuse. Professional duties according to specialism.

Skills According to specialism.

Psychologists (clinical or educational)

Powers None.

Duties   None specific to child abuse.
Skills   Specialists in the assessment and treatment of psychological, emotional and relationship problems. Those in child guidance and other children's services have expert knowledge of the emotional, psychological and intellectual development of children and of parent-child relationships.

Lawyers

Solicitors and barristers in private practice or employed by local authorities or law centres.
Powers   None specific to child abuse.
Duties   None specific to child abuse.
Skills   Knowledge of the law and of advocacy. Some lawyers, noticeably in local authorities, are developing considerable expertise in child care and family law and its application to child protection.

Housing Officers

Employed by local authorities or housing associations.
Powers   None specific to child abuse.
Duties   None specific to child abuse, but most local authorities now require housing officers to report cases where there is concern about child care and/or child abuse.
Skills   Some housing officers work extensively with families with housing and other problems and can identify children who are being abused or are at risk.

DHSS Officials

Powers   None specific to child abuse.
Duties   None specific to child abuse.
Skills   Some officials work extensively with families with serious financial and other problems and can identify children who are being abused or are at risk.

Voluntary agency workers

May be employed or voluntary (including playgroup workers and clergy, but see above for social workers).
Powers   None.
Duties   None.
Skills   Depends on setting, training and experience. Many playgroup workers have qualifications or training in child care and development and have similar responsibilities to teachers.

Further reading

The following have either been specifically mentioned in the text or were otherwise consulted during preparation of this paper.

Baher E *et al At risk: an account of the work of the Battered Child Research Department, NSPCC* (Routledge and Kegan Paul, London, 1976)

British Association of Social Workers *The central child abuse register* (BASW, Birmingham, 1975 and revisions)

British Association of Social Workers *Effective and ethical recording* (BASW, Birmingham, 1985)

British Association of Social Workers *The management of child abuse* (BASW, Birmingham, 1985)

Carter, J 'Co-ordination and child abuse' *Social Work Service*, 1976, 9, pp 22-28

Carver, V *Child abuse: a study text* (Open University Press, Milton Keynes, 1978)

Giovannoni, J M and Becerra, R M *Defining child abuse* (Collier-Macmillan, London, 1979)

Hallet, C and Stevenson, O *Child abuse: aspects of inter-professional co-operation* (Allen and Unwin, London, 1980)

Hey, A 'Organising teams – alternative patterns' in Marshall, M *et al* (eds) *Teamwork: for and against* (BASW, Birmingham, 1979) pp 25-36

Johnson, D W and Johnson, F P *Joining together: group theory and group skills* (Prentice-Hall, Englewood Cliffs, 1975)

Jones D N *et al* 'Central child abuse registers: the British experience' in *Child Abuse and Neglect, the International Journal*, 1979, 3, 2, pp 583-590

Jones, D N *et al* 'Child abuse: three perspectives on confidentiality: a social work perspective' *Concern*, 1981, 39, pp 20-25

Jones, D N; Pickett, J; Oates, M R and Barbor, P *Understanding child abuse* (Hodder and Stoughton, London, 1982; 2nd edition due 1987, published by Macmillan)

Kempe, R S and Kempe, C H *Child abuse* (Fontana, London, 1978)

City of Manchester Social Services Department *Child abuse procedures: City of Manchester guidelines* (1980)

Maton, A and Pickett, J 'Central registration of child abuse in Manchester' *Child Abuse and Neglect, the International Journal*, 1979, 3, 1, pp 167-174

Nelson, B J *Making an issue of child abuse: political agenda setting for social problems* (University of Chicago Press, 1984)

Nottinghamshire Area Review Committee *Child abuse: guidance notes on procedures* (Nottinghamshire County Council, 1984)

Pickett, J 'The management of non-accidental injury to children in the City of Manchester' in Borland, M (ed) *Violence in the family* (Manchester University Press, 1976) pp 61-87

Pickett, J and Maton, A 'Protective casework and child abuse: practice and problems' in Franklin, A (ed) *The challenge of child abuse* (Academic Press, London, 1977) pp 56-80

Roberts, B and Carver, V 'Personal attitudes to child abuse' in Carver, V (1978) *op cit*, pp 11-20

Rowbottom, R and Hey, A *A Collaboration between health and social services* (Brunel Institute of Organisation and Social Studies, London, 1978)

Sussman, A and Cohen, S J *Reporting child abuse and neglect: guidelines for legislation* (Ballinger, Cambridge Ma, 1975)

Tomlinson, T 'Inter-agency collaboration: issues and problems' in Borland, M (ed) *Violence in the family* (Manchester University Press, 1976) pp 136-145

Watson, D *A code of ethics for social work: the second step* (Routledge and Kegan Paul, London, 1985)

Wells, F 'Child abuse – three perspectives on sharing information: a medical perspective' *Concern*, 1981, 29, pp 20-25

Whiting, L 'The central registry for child abuse cases: rethinking some basic assumptions' *Child Welfare*, 1977, 56, 4: 761-7

Department of Health and Social Security (1974) *Memorandum on non-accidental injury to children* LASSL (74) 13, CMO(74) 8

Department of Health and Social Security (1976) *Non-accidental injury to children: reports from Area Review Committees* LASSL(76)2, CMO(76)2

Department of Health and Social Security (1976) *Non-accidental injury to children: the police and case conferences* LASSL(76)26,HC(76)50,HO 179/76

Department of Health and Social Security (1980) *Child abuse: central register systems*, LASSL(80)4

Department of Health and Social Security (1985) *Social work decisions in child care: recent research findings and their implications*, London, HMSO.

Department of Health and Social Security (1986) *Inspection of the supervision of social workers in the assessment and monitoring of cases of child abuse when children, subject to a care order, have been returned home*, Social Services Inspectorate, March 1986

Department of Health and Social Security (1986) *Child abuse: working together for the protection of children*, DHSS draft circular

Report of the Committee on Child Health Needs (1976), *Fit for the future*, (Court Report), London, HMSO, Cmnd. 6684

Report of the committee of enquiry into the care and supervision provided in relation to Maria Colwell, London, HMSO

Report of the panel of enquiry into the circumstances surrounding the death of Jasmine Beckford (1985), *A child in trust*, London Borough of Brent

Chapter 9
Strategies for prevention: education for good child care practice

Richard Whitfield

Overview

Many children are not receiving the consistent and dependable loving care which is essential for their optimum development. While the consequent demands upon the various remedial services become overwhelming, knowledge of the developmental needs of children and adults is insufficiently widespread in British society. Educational experience relevant to decision making about the parenthood option and the fostering of confidence and competence in the skills of childrearing and care at different stages of life are sparse. Parenthood and child care in the community tends to be seen as unproblematic and is generally taken for granted until severe disturbances in home environment, such as child abuse, become public. Educational institutions, including schools, have an important part to play, through aspects of their formal and informal curricula, in preparing and sustaining the next generation of parents, and in creating caring neighbours who have important roles to play in the overall care of children in the wider community.

This chapter extrapolates relevant research findings to suggest means by which varied educational contexts, given appropriate political backing, can make more specific responses which will help society, and particularly parents, to care more adequately for the children they choose to have. It emphasises proactive, primary preventive experiences for all who might have caring responsibilities for children and young people, thereby raising the cultural status of knowledge, dispositions and skills relevant to child care. Furthermore, the required educational initiatives have now become urgent.

The low cultural esteem of child rearing

Child abuse and its prevention are inescapably at the intersection of child/adult relationships and the physical, social and cultural environment. It is important to consider that context historically, and Eileen Vizard's chapter (pages 7-22) has provided a valuable perspective upon the present situation, which reflects aspects of the society's value systems.

A part of the contemporary cultural context of child abuse in Britain is the popular view that looking after children is more of a chore than a privilege. Children and young people tend to be more often portrayed as potential sources of nuisance and inconvenience to adults than as sources of stimulation, companionship and joy. Only recently this author overheard a young mother coping with a toddler at breakfast in an English hotel state her feeling to an overseas tourist that 'in this country having a child with you in many public places is like having a disease'. In a variety of ways, child rearing is perceived as a low status, unsophisticated occupation, one which rarely takes first place if other, alternative activities are available. There is still widespread ignorance about the nature and needs of children despite over a century of universal education and extensive research into child development. Across the social classes children are in different ways often treated as though they were commodities, property rather than persons in the making; too often they are the last, instead of the first to be considered when adults determine their 'grown-up' priorities.

Reflecting these general tendencies, the Minorities Rights Group[1] label children an 'unusual minority' for concern, drawing attention to the varied ways in which children's just claims for attention and resources are inadequately considered, nationally and internationally. It has to be be accepted that one international year for children (1979) could never be sufficient to change radically the many disturbing aspects of adult patronage which children experience.

A pilot open-air observational study (conducted in one town) of adults' behaviour towards each other and towards children in public recently found that adults displayed considerably less courtesy towards children than towards each other.[2] During three-minute periods of observation, 80% of adult-adult pairs had some positive speech or facial exchange. In contrast, no exchanges occurred with over half of the child-adult pairs, in some cases for up to ten minutes. In two fifths of the child-adult sample pairs, in those exchanges which did take place adults displayed insensitivity or hostility towards the children. Yule suggests that her picture of widespread rudeness to children in public is unlikely to be local and that there could be associations between this and the more obviously serious statistics of child abuse.

It seems to be the case that many parents, including those from apparently well-educated backgrounds, regularly find themselves unable to cope with reasonable manifestations of children's ignorance or curiosity. The structural stresses upon, and the individual preoccupations of, too many of us as adults seem to militate against our giving children the priority they require and deserve. Sometimes these stresses are concerned mainly with providing the economic base sufficient for the daily needs of shelter, food and clothing of the family group in a society whose affluent images reinforce the low esteem commonly held by those parents who are in real or marginal poverty. In contrast, the stresses experienced by professional family groups[3] are frequently the product of high achievement motivation in employment outside the home of either husband or wife or both. In these cases social and personal esteem is perceived to derive mainly from career success; feelings of guilt may arise from a regular short-changing of the children in terms of the time and energy required to meet their needs as developing persons. Unfortunately for children much substitute parental care (whether through children's homes, boarding education and short-term fostering, or through nannies and au pair assistance) does not provide, and perhaps in our society cannot generally provide, replacement *psychological parenthood* with strong and reliable bonds with both father and mother figures.

It is unsurprising therefore that some children perceive their parents as powerful but untrustworthy or uncommitted owners who tend to behave in an inconsistent and impatient manner, as though devoting relaxed adult time and attention to them and their developmental needs is *culturally* unimportant. Cultural priorities are, however, adaptable – albeit not overnight, nor without specific teaching and learning. Required too is a favourable political climate, for taking children, as non-voters, properly into account has political implications.

In relation to child care we know that transmitted norms of parental behaviour can be powerful determinants of almost conditioned responses of parents in the next generation. Role modelling of motherhood and fatherhood through the home environment seems strong, particularly in the context of a formal educational system which gives little priority to teaching and learning about human development within the perspective of varied social and cultural ecologies.

The presumption of this chapter is that some child abuse, including some of the most severe, is preventable, given prior learning about good child care practice. However, this learning and its associated teaching activities are not intended to be for a minority of actual or future parents who might be probable abusers, even if they could be reliably identified. Rather it is advocated that this learning should become available, through formal and informal educational opportunities, to *all* prospective parents, thereby raising the wider cultural priority which we should be giving to fulfilling the needs of all children. I believe that much lack of care and consideration for children is the result of ignorance of what children need for healthy development, combined with a lack of self-understanding and self-control under stress among those who have key responsibilities to provide that care. Hence abuse, in whatever form it is identified at the individual level, has structural roots derived from inappropriately targeted political and educational ideologies.

A framework for teaching and learning about child care

Since much severe child abuse occurs within the home and family, educational activities concerned with reducing its incidence are centrally a matter of 'parenthood-related education'. Increasingly, parenthood can be a matter of considered choice, and fortunately so if, ideally, every child is to be a wanted child from conception. Hence parenthood-related education must incorporate issues relevant to the decision, or otherwise, to procreate. The considered choice of non-parenthood, with all that its responsibilities involve thereafter, is thus a key aspect of concern.

It is conceptually and practically helpful to adopt an overlapping two-phase model for parenthood-related education (see Figure 9.1).[4] The first phase can be termed 'preparation for parenthood', the second 'growth and development within parenthood', or perhaps less helpfully 'parent education'. These may be likened to 'pre-service' and 'in-service' staff development and depicted pictorially by a Venn diagram, in which the overlapping area between phases signifies specific objectives and 'syllabus' topics which might occur in either or both phases.

Phase I: Phase II:

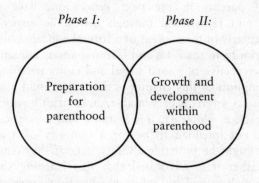

Figure 9.1 Basic changes in activities for learning within parenthood related education

More specifically *preparation for parenthood* may be defined as:

experiences incorporated within the education of young people individually, or of couples, which are concerned with helping them to become self-aware and to form stable relationships so that they may consider responsibly the option of parenthood in the light of its potential demands, rewards and disadvantages throughout the life cycle.

This definition stresses that, despite the many social pressures which encourage people in our society to become parents, parenthood must be seen as an *option* which can be responsibly and appropriately declined without loss of self-esteem. Thus the prevention of child abuse must contemplate less parenthood, and without stigma.

The definition also emphasises individual self-awareness, including possible responses to stress, as a necessary ingredient for forming stable relationships between partners and between them and any offspring. For such a dynamic to function it is usually necessary for parents to have reached a sufficient degree of independence (including independence from their own parents), trust and flexibility to accept each other, and to give of themselves. Attaining these conditions is, ideally, the consequence of appropriate passage through phases of psychological growth during childhood. Our relative neglect in actively promoting and evaluating the safe passage of many children through these phases of social, emotional and intellectual development is further compounded by insecure relationships in many families of origin, in which there are often insufficiently reliable adult models. As a result, partners and co-procreators may be chosen, consciously or unconsciously, as a means of attaining growth which should have been completed prior to procreation, or to supply important needs missed during childhood development.[5] Individual partners may thus exchange one form of dependence or insecurity in one generation for another in the next.

Growth and development within parenthood, phase two of the model outlined above may be defined as:

any educational or related assistance for parents which supports the physical, cognitive and emotional development of their children and of themselves in undertaking the parental role throughout the life cycle

This definition emphasises that parental responsibilities are rarely static but generally change through the various phases of the life cycle. Also emphasised is the fact that child welfare depends upon the psychosocial welfare of the parents.

The primary preventive framework now outlined suggests a number of operational aims which need to govern the activities of family life education more closely. There is concern to:

- increase knowledge of processes of human development from conception to old age;

- promote an awareness of different ways in which people can and do live together and care for each other, including the framework of marriage;
- develop and give practice in skills of interpersonal communication and care;
- promote knowledge and understanding of the inter-relations between the life of households and the wider society, including government;
- increase self-knowledge with a view to developing serious attitudes towards life decisions which involve taking responsibility for the care of others, in particular, decisions regarding mating and procreation;
- increase knowledge of diverse agencies which are available to support the lives of families and households.[6]

The second listed aim involves the study of modes of caring in different cultures so that the development of expectations may become less stereotyped, and an understanding of legitimate family diversity may thus be promoted within a framework of informed caring values. Overall these aims support the development of good child care practice which can be succinctly expressed as 'non-possessive warmth and a willingness and ability to take, and go on taking, trouble' with the diverse demands, roles and functions of the family home.[7]

The content of preventive experiences

For the two phases and aims outlined it is inappropriate to be exclusively prescriptive about what might be 'syllabus topics', while the very term 'syllabus' may have for some unfortunate connotations of rigid, didactic teaching methods. Since contexts for work in parenthood-related education are varied, here no discrimination is made regarding those topics which might be seen as 'core' or options within particular initiatives. The partially structured topic list below is however at least illustrative of the areas of concern; implicit is the assumption that both mothers and fathers have child care responsibilities, and that the nature of their relationships with each other is a generally significant element in the development of the child's identity.

Some important topics in parenthood-related education

i The nature of parental bonds, including marriage: perspectives provided from social history, theology and anthropology. Partnering as shared tasks, as companionship and friendship, and as a framework for procreation and child rearing: phases in the family life cycle.

ii   Families of origin: continuing impacts, and models of lover, mother, father, son, daughter; social class and cultural variations.

iii   Choice of partners – including hopes, needs and expectations; choice, vows and promises; the meaning and experience of being and staying 'in love'.

iv   Communication in courtship. Marriage and cohabitation; self-disclosure. Adaptation and acceptance; rituals (including sexual) as communication; openness and truth rationing.

v   Conflict, anger, violence, guilt, and love, companionship and sharing in family life.

vi   Decisions about parenthood; effects of children on parents and parental relations; children's perceptions of parental relations.

vii   Key elements in child development: phases and needs of childhood – biological, social and psychological perspectives and their behavioural implications during pregnancy, infancy, the 'middle years' and adolescence. Techniques for observing and assisting in areas of child development; socialisation, play, perceptual awareness. Deviations from norms of development.

viii   Time and energy for parenting activities; the growth of individuals and of relationships; ideals and coping with reality; compromising and avoidance of 'overload'; anniversaries and holidays.

ix   Economic aspects of marriage and family life; housing, employment, income, taxation and expenditure and their potential tensions. Employment, careers and family life; psychological absence.

x   Stressful life events (eg separation, bereavement, illness, redundancy, retirement, affairs, drug abuse, delinquency, house-moving) and their impacts upon parents and children; enriching strategies, including family counselling.

xi   Relationships outside the domestic group: eg neighbours and other friends, relatives, children's peers; their impacts upon family life.

xii   Professional services and child care: general medical practice, pre-school and school experience, social services and legal practice; support from voluntary bodies.

It is clear that the context of parenthood-related education involves a range of academic disciplines and practical crafts, illustrated in Figure 9.2. In this figure reference is made to moral reasoning and action; these are inevitably important in any discussion about the principles and practice of how people treat or care for one another, including children.

The challenge, in terms of teaching-learning techniques, of drawing these disciplines together for coherent experiences for parents or parents-to-be is significant, and it is to this challenge that we now briefly turn.

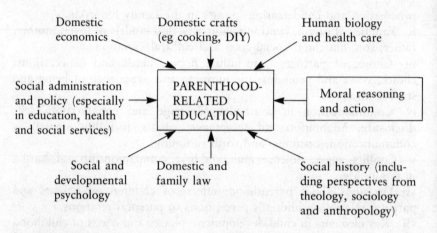

Figure 9.2 Academic disciplines and practical crafts related to the exercise of parental responsibilities

Methods and resources

The agenda for parenthood-related education is in part delicate and potentially controversial, not least in schools where statutory arrangements can often provide a captive audience without necessarily observing the formalities of proper consultation with parents and community. In our Aston University based study of preparation for parenthood in secondary schools there was some evidence of the exclusion of controversial topics about personal life from the curriculum because of the dilemmas which they present for teachers.[8]

More perhaps than most fields of learning, teaching methods for parenthood-related education must be sensitive to context, time and place. Since key objectives are concerned with the development of social competence, interactive rather than didactic teaching styles must predominate if the range of relevant learning is to be achieved. While research informed talks and information giving have a place, the emphasis needs to be upon group discussion methods, role play and simulation, couple communication, interactive assignments and, crucially, practical work with children, under supervision where necessary. These are unfortunately not universally the stock-in-trade of teachers beyond the primary school level, where there tend to be more tensions between the custodial, pastoral and pedagogic aspects of their roles. Hence developments in secondary schools and colleges need to be accompanied by appropriate in-service training so that teachers and lecturers can enlarge their repertoire and feel more confident about using a wider range of teaching strategies.[9]

Certainly it is misguided to approach education for parenthood as if people are purely rational and bound by their duties as adults, needing only to be better informed in order to succeed in their parental roles. With skill, non-didactic teaching methods may, however, be used to impart information in a manner in which participants' attention can be sustained. Information is always given in a social context, even if it is done through the mass media so that, at least in relation to social competence, it is never a neutral commodity.

The fact that many adults still seem to prefer to seek advice on family matters from friends and relatives rather than professionals and the media[10] has implications for the ways in which parenthood education is organised and conducted. In particular, levels of trust which are established between tutor or group leader and other participants need to parallel those in close friendships. Friends and relatives exchange 'home truths' and advice which may have powerful behavioural impacts regardless of their effectiveness. A part of parenthood-related education can therefore usefully include an examination of some prevalent 'myths' about parenthood and child care, such as those in the following list; it is worth remembering, of course, that myths generally embody at least some of the truth.

Some myths concerning parenthood and child care

Regarding babies and children	*Regarding parents*
Breast is best	Loneliness will be solved by having children
Babies do not understand words in sentences	The arrival of children improves difficult marriages
Babies often cry just to be naughty	Parenthood will fundamentally reform or change a person
Children should not be encouraged to play too much until they enter a play-group	Parents who love their children automatically know what their child is feeling or needing
Children, like pets, need care for life	
Young children readily accept all forms of authority	Parental attachment to children improves spontaneously given time
Young children rarely pick up their parents' anxieties	Given sound advice, patterns of parental behaviour can be easily changed

To be fair in a family all the children should be treated equally

Children should speak only when they are spoken to

Children develop in direct relation to the time and activities which the parents share with them

Concealment of true feelings from adults is intuitive from the age of 7 or 8

Girls react emotionally whereas boys react logically

Boys do not need cuddly toys

Television is very important these days for keeping children occupied

To children, childhood holds no particular advantage

Children have little to teach their parents

Spare the rod and spoil the child

Discipline should be based at least as much upon the needs of the disciplinarian as the needs of the child

It is always better to shield your child from negative feelings

One active parent is just as good as two

Working mothers harm their children

Fathers are more important for boys than for girls

Reference to sexual matters in the presence of young children should be avoided

Parents of adolescents should try to keep their own views to themselves

People who really love each other do not get angry with each other

Experience of the grown up world has little to do with childhood

Tutorial style in dealing with issues of this kind, whether with adults or young people at school, should be non-authoritarian and non-judgemental, with adequate space being provided for participants to gain insights at their own pace and in their own manner in relation to their unique experiences of home and family life, some of which may be painful. Hence some of the skills of counselling have central relevance to teaching methods in this field.

The broad field of 'family life education' has, in recent years, had a large number of scattered, piecemeal and uncoordinated investments in stimulus material. Included here are materials provided by the Open

University for community use,[11] by other publishers for use with the increasing numbers of pupils (so far almost solely girls) who select child development and family courses as 4th/5th years options in secondary schools, by those concerned with health education, by various voluntary organisations concerned with child and family welfare, and by broadcasting authorities.[12] However, these materials tend to give insufficient emphasis to questions of adult relationships surrounding children, and in particular to the bonds between parents which are so often relevant in child abuse cases.

Child development in the two-parent (or even one-parent) family does not proceed solely through child-parent interaction; children's observation of, and modelling from, the relationships (affectional or otherwise) between parents and other significant adults is extensive. The quality of verbal, emotional and sexual interaction between parents, and the general communication network inside the family, and between the family and the outside world, are significant to children's well-being. In addition, the importance of both men and women in role modelling, wider stimulation and the development of appropriate sexual identities of both boys and girls as they grow up is a central principle of child development.[13]

For both phases of parenthood-related education delineated above, considerable resource investment is needed so as to enable suitably experienced professionals and lay people from a variety of backgrounds to collaborate in different educational environments and provide supportive materials and staff development programmes. Harman and Brim's[14] book on education for childrearing is a key text, usefully supplemented more recently by Eastman's[15] review of family life education programmes.

A key element in developing parenthood-related education is the availability of suitably-equipped personnel to take on leadership roles. Desirable qualities in leaders are as much a matter of maturity, experience of biological and/or psychological parenthood, and relevant personal attributes, such as warmth, flexibility and genuineness, as of academic knowledge or specialist training. Just as a wide variety of subject disciplines are relevant to the content of this area of education, so a variety of professionals have potentially important contributions to make to their local communities, for example: solicitors, social workers, teachers, qualified counsellors, doctors, nurses, midwives, health visitors, clergy, and registrars.

However, it is most important that this subject is not rested so entirely in the hands of professionals that individual community members feel that they have no contribution to make. Concerned lay people should not be excluded from developments, nor their needs ignored, by those involved in setting up relevant training courses, not least because their experiences of parenthood and family life are as valid and central as particular professional skills. Indeed, if the status of the relevant knowlege and skills is to be raised, policy development has to be much more concerned with opening access than with restriction and exclusion.

Locations for parenthood-related education

Administratively there is a wide range of potential settings in which parenthood-related education can take place. This section gives a brief resumé of the principal settings that are available. As will be seen, most are far from being adequately exploited.

a Schools

Within secondary schools the minimal attention which is paid to aspects of preparation for parenthood tends to be associated with courses in health and sex education and in education for personal relationships. Nomenclature, content and approaches vary from school to school as a result of the largely decentralised curriculum systems which pertain in the UK. Some schools include relevant material under 'social education', 'active tutorial work' or 'life skills', while in a tiny proportion 'family life education' and 'preparation for parenthood' are co-ordinating themes.

The relatively recent national survey of preparation for parenthood in secondary schools, sponsored by the Department of Education and Science[9] found that a wide range of generally unco-ordinated family relevant topics appeared within many established curriculum subjects. Teachers' reports from over 200 schools indicated that over four subjects per school included some work relevant to preparation for parenthood, but in over two thirds of these this was seen to have only a subsidiary aim, as indicated in the following summary.

Primary aim to prepare for parenthood (217 secondary schools)
Compulsory: Within social and health education, religious subjects, group and tutorial work.

About 1 in 6 of subjects; either internally assessed or not assessed.

Optional: Within family and child subjects.

About 1 in 6 of subjects: mainly taken by girls in years 4 and 5 but under 10% of year cohort; externally assessed, usually at CSE level. (CSE entries nationally in this category in 1982 totalled 33 939, twice as high as in 1978 and twenty times greater than in 1974; for 1984 there was a further rise to 45 838 of whom only 278 were boys.)

Subsidiary aim to prepare for parenthood
Compulsory: Within social and health education, biological science and religious subjects.
About 1 in 3 of subjects; mainly years 1 to 3; either internally assessed or not assessed
Optional: Within social and health education, biological science and domestic and catering subjects.
About 1 in 3 of subjects: internal and external assessment.

Chance factors played the dominant part in the access of pupils to this kind of curriculum experience. Studies primarily concerned with parenthood and family life were almost solely the province of girls of average and below average academic ability, being taught by female teachers.

None of the local education authorities surveyed had an explicit policy towards preparation for parenthood and in almost all schools no member of staff was designated to co-ordinate and promote relevant curricular provision. Unsurprisingly, therefore, the boundaries of education and preparation for parenthood seemed far from agreed and lacked clarity among those teachers involved, many of whom had had little or no explicit training for that kind of work. Parenthood-related education thus currently remains marginal in the work of secondary schools. Some very useful related work does however take place in the primary sector, although this has yet to be surveyed specifically. This is not usually expressed explicitly in the curriculum, and it seems likely that much of it would be perceived as indirect and subsidiary rather than compulsory and direct.

Any major change in the purpose and substance of the school curriculum is, however, a complex matter. Despite some recent attempts by central authorities to specify the objectives and content of the core curriculum more precisely, and in a manner which is forward looking (DES, 1980, 1981)[16] the immediate prospects for any significant change of emphasis to bring parenthood-related education more to the centre stage seem slight. Much of the impetus of concern within the Department of Health and Social Security over a decade ago[7] has been lost, while the related wisdom of the Court Report on child health services[17] has not triggered coherent educational policies. Subjects perceived as more directly relevant to national economic well-being, such as computer education, and not so directly related to the practice of private life, are accorded far higher priority for new initiatives and supportive teacher education. So far at least the disturbing Aston Report and its recommendations[18] have had little impact upon policy and practice. Meanwhile there is no evidence to suggest that secondary school pupils perceive that the study of parenthood and family matters is either unmotivating or irrelevant to their needs (1983).[9]

b   Youth services

One fifth of men and one third of women now marry at the age of 21 or younger, while about 100 000 teenage pregnancies are recorded each year – and of these one in three is prematurely terminated. With high youth unemployment and related psychological problems[19] early marriage and/or pregnancy can be a means of achieving status and of gaining some perceived independence from home. However, there are many unwanted early pregnancies despite piecemeal attempts at sex education in the schools; a proportion of these trigger subsequent marriage, with childbirth often taking place under the further adverse conditions of poverty and parental alienation.

Despite such stark statistics, which reflect much wider needs, Pugh and De'Ath[11], as a result of a recent survey, conclude that

outside the school classroom, and particularly after leaving school, there are few opportunities for young people to discuss issues, choices or fantasies related to adult life, marriage, parenthood and families (p 113).

Their findings point to fragmentation and lack of unity of purpose in the youth services catering for the 14 to 21 age range; lack of provision for young married couples and teenage parents and for family life education more widely; over-emphasis on leisure activities and individual (generally remedial) counselling rather than mutual support and group learning. Similarly, in further education colleges, polytechnics, universities or the more recent youth training schemes, only isolated opportunities exist for intentional parenthood-related education; yet there is both institutional time and student demand for more.

c   Ante and post-natal services

As two become three, or more, through the birth of first and subsequent children, parental relations change their dynamic. Antenatal classes and post-natal follow-up properly focus upon foetal and early child care, and the process of birth itself. However, there are also opportunities in these settings to re-examine parental relations and the changing needs and mutual responsibilities of partners. The transition to parenthood tends to create additional stress in adult relationships as new demands are made on parental time and the family economy, but these can be counteracted by sensitive support and teaching[20] and so lead to widening interests and fresh shared pleasures. Learning new management skills and knowing in advance that difficulties, such as maternal depression and sexual lethargy, are not abnormal, can prevent undue distress in parental relationships during an important phase of potential growth, not least for the new baby. Creating appropriate climates to engage men as wholeheartedly as women at this stage of family development is a continuing challenge.

d Parent groups

In many communities the needs of children as they grow up form a natural focus for an array of parent groups associated with, for example, preschool activities (playgroups, parent-toddler groups etc), babysitting arrangements, family advice centres, parent-teacher associations, toy libraries, scouts and guides, youth and sports clubs. The natural child-centred focus of such groups is generally informal; it might in many cases benefit from more coherent planning of topics in parent education. The benefits of a relaxed responsiveness need not be lost in attempts to programme topics which are not immediately suggested by the partly chance experiences of individual group members. Provision of parent interest and support groups is, however, extremely patchy and many of those most in need often struggle on alone with the demands of parenthood. It is the experience of many parents (though still less so with fathers than mothers) that coping with the challenges and problems of parenthood is assisted by sharing and open communication in non-threatening environments.

Each of the locations for parenthood-related education outlined above may draw on useful stimulus material provided by the mass media: television, radio and magazines in particular. Video recordings, no doubt, have much potential in this sphere, for illustrating child development, identifying common problems and demonstrating coping techniques.

Problems of evaluation

One problem encountered in making a case for all primary prevention is that programme investment is long-term, and thus appropriate evaluative criteria necessarily have to be monitored over a long period. The organisation and funding of social research makes such studies rare, and, in the case of child abuse in particular, indices of its incidence are as yet unreliable. Evaluation tasks in the whole field of family life education are not confined to problems of measuring the knowledge and skills gained during adolescence at school or at marriage preparation or antenatal classes, where they, at least in principle, are possible; they are also concerned with how effectively these gains are later put to use at varying times when real family problems are confronted. As far as preparation for parenthood is concerned, the fundamental aims are in any case often mainly concerned with attitudes and values, and with increasing knowledge of sources of help at the onset of parenthood, rather than with the acquisition of particular skills for use in situations not yet encountered. As in all learning, the concepts of relevance and readiness are important.

Bearing in mind the diversity of activities which can take place in order to improve child care and parental practice, no simplistic standardised evaluation packages will be able to meet monitoring needs. However, among the needs and indicators which might be assessed are:

a the sources of advice and information of most use to parents about child care and family concerns;
b the knowledge of facts relevant to contemporary child care and family life;
c the estimation of attitudes towards child rearing and of dispositions to take on the long-term responsibilities of parenthood and the day-to-day care of other family members;
d the use made of child care and family services;
e the development of communication skills, including that of active listening;
f the variations in the pattern of the time spent by parents upon activities associated with child development;
g the variations in the patterns of physical and mental health of parents and children, and in the self-reported indices of parental potential and performance.

Even this limited list presents evaluators with daunting challenges, but, providing the approach to data collection and analysis is eclectic rather than rigidly psychometric or anthropological, taking evaluation seriously is likely to provide important feedback enabling programme development to rely on more than anecdotal evidence. In general, small scale studies may be more cost-effective at this stage in the development of evaluation technology, and this would be compatible with the requirement for accountability with regard to the finite resources expended upon action. Long-term longitudinal studies of the impact of parenthood-related education present researchers with problems of identifying causes in a multivariate context in which individual differences are likely to be marked.

Prevention's fundamental article of faith is that it is possible to learn more about life by means other than simply living and reacting to it; that scholarship and professional practice have given us insights into predicting events in people's lives, about gauging probabilities and risks, and into general patterns of human development. In other words, that we can learn at least something in advance of personal experience from the systematically recorded experiences of others, and, moreover, make considered choices from among recognised options rather than conditioned responses to early affective patterning.

Programmes aimed at the prevention of undesirable consequences of human action, whether they be targeted at inadequate parenthood, smoking, road safety or dietary control, are concerned to realign and bring into greater harmony the intellectual, emotional and practical parameters of human situations in all their variety. Fundamentally it is for this reason that techniques for prevention are necessarily diverse and that controlled monitoring and evaluation are both difficult and rare.

In the foreseeable future and perhaps permanently, it has to be accepted that teaching and learning activities with a preventive intent will be a combination of faith and pedagogical skill, only occasionally illuminated by 'scientific' evaluation since the resources which need to be devoted to the latter should be kept within realistic bounds in relation to the preventive activities themselves. Prevention is thus subject to the same constraints as the whole of the enterprise of education, reflecting, to use different language, the fact that the acquisition of wisdom is multifaceted and has limits to its predictability. Presently, primary activities designed to prevent child abuse and enrich child care have not been 'tried and found wanting'; they are manifestly wanted but have lacked sufficient social, educational and political conviction to have been seriously tried.

Issues within public policy: parents the key and prevention the priority?

An important and damaging side-effect of scientific and technological innovation has been the disruption of many of the natural structures of mutual support and neighbourliness that existed in former generations. Social life in industrialised urban societies is fragmented and mobile. Problems stemming from the increasing dislocation of the social ecology, and of family life in particular, are more psychosocial than intellectual.[20] Parenthood can provide a sense of self worth, of competence, of importance and respect; or it can be experienced as the reverse, a drag or millstone conveying a sense of no status, of denigration and of powerlessness; or indeed it can be felt as both of these in relatively rapid succession. Moreover parenthood is, implicitly, 'a job for life'.[22]

Implicit in this chapter is the presumption that it is *parents* who have the prime responsibility for child care. Despite the many contemporary changes in family structure and function, and the development of the Welfare State, the first line of support for children remains their parents; for most children there are no other equivalent long-term substitutes. In order to develop normally, all children need the enduring and sometimes what Bronfenbrenner[23] terms the 'irrational' involvement of one or more adults in their care and in joint activities with them. For the most part it is parents who, on a day-to-day basis, are most likely to believe in their own child's precociousness even when the child's behaviour irritates them, or appearances suggest something to the contrary. Parental concern needs in that sense to be unconditional, and in principle limitless, in contrast to the functions of most professionals which are specific and detached. However, the enduring involvement of parents with their children requires public policies which give resources, support, encouragement, stability, time and status to parenthood.

All educational initiatives seeking to prevent child abuse, in both its severe and more widespread, marginal forms, take place within the wider professional and political climate. The personal, social and economic costs of dysfunctions in child care in our kind of society are immense. Failing to take prevention seriously within public and voluntary services undermines not only the rights of children but also of other age groups who need to be given structured experiences and to acquire knowledge, insights and skills which are relevant to key aspects of personal functioning in an increasingly complex society.

Preventing avoidable pain and difficulty in childrearing could help to break cycles of emotional and other forms of deprivation. Crucially, however, it involves changing the status of the knowledge and skills most relevant to the development of persons in their contemporary environment. Furthermore, and as implied already, parenthood-related education requires a range of supportive social policies surrounding child care and family development. The frameworks of family law, of taxation policy, of employment opportunities, of housing, health and social security policies provide, or fail to provide, minimally permitting circumstances for the exercise of successful parenthood. Family matters tend to be taken for granted as areas for social policy, at least until they exhibit severe strain or disruption. Then, and often too late, overstretched remedial services with high unit costs come to the fore, at least for some. Yet life 'crises', which are often the precursors of child abuse, are not altogether unpredictable since they are associated with norms of maturation and development.

The prospects for sensitive, well-resourced and integrated social policies surrounding child care and family concerns in the UK are not encouraging. Despite the pro-family rhetoric of politicians of all persuasions, there is little or no real recognition that political decisions on public policy affect personal and private behaviour and circumstances. Balanced political concern for the quality of life *must* take the trouble to devote more resources to preparation for and support of parenthood. Without resources, whether provided centrally or locally, there can, simply, be little change of status regarding the knowledge, understanding and skills of most significance to our personal lives. Likewise, there can be little new training of personnel (whether professionals or volunteers) in the relevant disciplines and skills; few generally available courses (whether in schools, colleges or the wider community); no fundamental transformation in the priorities of the mass media; and no change in the underlying moral climate whose features cannot fail to be mirrored in home life.

We know that most young people, men and women across all social classes and income groups, regrettably remain ill-prepared for the challenges of rewarding parenthood. Procreation and parenthood have life-long consequences. In their various aspects they offer educational material which is inherently fascinating and which, if handled sensitively, can be attractive to a wide range of participants at different stages of the life cycle.

Currently we have a disturbed and depressing picture of the state of child care in Britain.[24] The features of this and the professional concern it generates are not new. The advice of the interdepartmental White Paper on violence to children[25] on education for parenthood has largely failed to be implemented despite the sponsorship at that time of no fewer than seven government ministers. Simultaneous concern for prevention expressed through the Open University initiative on child abuse[26] also seems to have dissipated. Moral indignation at the continuing revelations of child abuse is no longer sufficient.

The serious implementation of preventive strategies is, however, impeded by a view of child abuse which is more individual and pathological than structural, educational and cultural. All parents and other caregivers have a propensity to abuse the children in their care. Hence to presume that child abuse is inherently some sort of individual illness or abnormality requiring correction among a minority marginalises both the symptoms and any corrective action; it places the social work profession, in particular, in the unenviable position of having to predict and identify a 'disease' whose features are widely variable. Such marginalisation, readily eschewed by politicians, is detrimental to the cause of all children, concern for whom should be central in any nation's affairs.

This chapter has thus concentrated upon the primary prevention of child abuse, viewed chiefly as a social rather than an individual malaise. It represents a challenge to our curricular and cultural priorities in the light of the knowledge which we now possess about the major determinants of healthy human functioning, the limits of which are established during childhood. Legal, medical, psychiatric and social policy concern inevitably focuses on issues other than primary prevention; real cases of abuse have to be identified and remedial action taken. Prevention is thus centrally a matter for education, and therefore for appropriately informed teachers, in the classroom and elsewhere.

Perhaps the outrage felt by communities when severe child abuse is made public can prompt the teaching profession into directing its influences and skills to improve the quality of experiences which children are likely to receive within their home environments. We need many more teachers, including men, to take curricular initiatives in parenthood-related education. For that they will need proper professional resources and support, extensive in-service education and the goodwill of other professions, communities and their elected members. The outcome of serious attention to such developments could be not only less abuse and a greater valuing of children, but also less alienation between home and school or college, and enhanced impacts from the whole of the educational process.

If we fail to expand prevention, we will by-pass the challenge of breaking intergenerational chains of material, intellectual and emotional deprivation. The painful 'writing' is literally 'on the wall'; and the dilemmas and seeds of disturbance in some form or other are present in all of our homes. No less than a marked change in our cultural priorities will enable what we now know about human development to be of benefit to all children and those who care for them.

The need for action is urgent. Many of our children continue to suffer severe and avoidable deprivations; many more fail to achieve their optimum potential. Much of their pain, so often hidden, is our responsibility as 'grown ups'. But perhaps we shall only be able to face that responsibility squarely as parents, politicians and professionals when we have come to terms with our own periodic pain and emptiness – which reflects the search for security, identity and purpose begun in our own varied and problematic childhoods.

Notes and references

1 Minority Rights Group *Children: Rights and Responsibilities* (MRG Report No 69, London, 1985)

2 Yule, V 'Why are parents tough on children?' *New Society* 27 September 1985, pp 444-6

3 Evans, P and Bartolome, F *Must Success Cost So Much?* (Grant McIntyre, London, 1980)

4 Whitfield, R C *Education for Family Life: Some New Policies for Child Care* (Hodder and Stoughton, London, 1980)

5 See, for example, Skynner, R and Cleese, J *Families and How to Survive Them* (Methuen, London, 1983)

6 Whitfield, R C *Family Structures, Lifestyles and the Care of Children* (Department of Educational Enquiry, University of Aston, Birmingham, 1983)

7 See, for example, Cooper, J D in Department of Health and Social Security *The Family in Society: Preparation of Parenthood* (HMSO, London, 1974)

8 Grafton, T; Smith, L; Vegoda, M and Whitfield, R C 'Getting Personal: the Teacher's Dilemma' *International Journal of Sociology and Social Policy* (1982) 2 (3), pp 85-94. See also Grafton, T; Smith, L; Vegoda, M and Whitfield, R C *Preparation for Parenthood in the Secondary School Curriculum* Report to Department of Education and Science (Department of

Educational Enquiry, University of Aston, Birmingham, 1983); for a summary and post-publication discussion see *Education and Health*, 2 (3) pp 47-62 (Schools Health Education Unit, University of Exeter)

9 David, K *Personal and Social Education in Secondary Schools* (Longman, London, 1982); Grafton *et al* (1983) *op cit*

10 French, J and Whitfield, R C *Educating and Supporting Parents through the Media* Papers for the Health Education Council, the BBC and the National Children's Homes (Department of Educational Enquiry, University of Aston, Birmingham, 1984)

11 Open University, Community Education Division: course materials relevant to family life and child rearing (Open University Press, Milton Keynes, 1980-86)

12 See Whitfield, R C (1980) *op cit*; Pugh, G and De'Ath, E *The Needs of Parents: Practice and Policy in Parent Education* (Macmillan, Basingstoke, 1984)

13 See Bronfenbrenner and Weiss in Zigler, E F; Kagan, S L and Klugman, E (eds) *Children, Families and Government* (Cambridge University Press, New York, 1983). See also Whitfield, R C (1983, 1985) *op cit*

14 Harman, D and Brim, O G *Learning to be Parents: Principles, Programs and Methods* (Sage, Beverly Hills, 1980)

15 Eastman, M *Education for Family Life: a survey of available programmes and their evaluation* (Institute of Family Studies, Melbourne, Australia, 1983)

16 Department of Education and Science *A View of the Curriculum* (HMSO, London, 1980) and *The School Curriculum* (HMSO, London, 1981)

17 Committee on Child Health Services *Fit for the Future* (The Court Report) (HMSO, London, 1976)

18 The University of Aston in Birmingham 'Preparation for Parenthood in the Secondary School Curriculum. A study carried out for the Department of Education and Science' Department of Educational Enquiry, August 1983. Project Director: R Whitfield; Research Team: T Grafton; L Smith; M Vegoda; R Whitfield

19 Donovan, A; Oddy, M; Pardoe, R and Ades, A 'Employment status and psychological well being among school leavers' in *Journal of Child Psychology and Psychiatry* (1986) 27 (1), pp 65-76

20 See, for example, Clulow, C *To Have and to Hold* (Aberdeen University Press, Aberdeen, 1982)

21 Whitfield, R C (1985) *op cit*

22 National Children's Bureau *A Job for Life* (London, 1982)

23 Bronfenbrenner, U *Educational Analysis* (1980) 2 (1), pp 3-14; see also Bronfenbrenner and Weiss in Zigler *et al* (1983) *op cit*

24 Department of Health and Social Security *Social work: decisions in child care* (HMSO, London, 1985)

25 HM Government Interdepartmental White Paper *Violence to Children* Cmnd. 7123 (HMSO, London, March 1978)

26 See, for example, Chazan, M in Carver, V (ed) *Child Abuse: A Study Text* (section 24) (Open University Press, Milton Keynes, 1978); Pringle, M K in Frude, N (ed) *Psychological Approaches to Child Abuse* (chapter 15) (Batsford, London, 1980)

Chapter 10

School responses to child abuse cases: the reactive role

Peter Maher

Why should child abuse be a matter of concern for teachers?

Why should teachers play a significant role in detecting and reporting cases of child abuse?

What is it that makes the role of teachers significant in this area when there are other professional groups who are trained to deal with problems of child abuse?

Surely if teachers are there to educate their students, their involvement in such social phenomena will be of only peripheral importance?

I'm a teacher not a social worker!

Each of these questions or statements, offered by teachers, is an understandable reaction to the proposition that *teachers have a very significant role to play in child abuse cases*. These reactions are shared by other groups too and the questions need to be addressed before we can proceed to an analysis of that role. We need to understand why the role of teachers is unique and why that unique role is potentially so important. Only by understanding the importance of their input can we persuade teachers and other professional groups that this role needs to be offered a higher profile in dealing with cases of child abuse.

Such an analysis raises questions about the way that teachers work, whether in school with their students, with the families of the children that they teach, or with the communities that they serve. Questions are also raised about the relationship between the teaching profession and other professional groups who are involved in child care. This has implications for the way that teachers perceive and work with those groups, as well as for other professionals, social workers, psychologists, the health service, police and so on. What becomes clear from that analysis is that child abuse is an important focus for inter-professional work; and that there needs to be greater understanding and cooperation generally between all professional groups on a whole range of issues, not just over cases of child abuse.

A range of factors make the potential role of teachers in child abuse cases vitally important:

1   Children suffering abuse of one form or another are likely to exhibit some unusual behaviour. Teachers are trained in the normal development of children and are ideally placed, given this training and their prolonged contact with the child, to recognise abnormal or changed behaviour. Thus teachers may be the first to identify signs which may indicate that a child is suffering abuse.

2   An abused child may well look for someone with whom they can share their *secret*. Whether or not the abuse is actually perpetrated in the home, evidence seems to suggest that they will seek a neutral, trusted figure when they decide to talk about their problems. Teachers are often the very people that abused children turn to for help.

3   Reported cases of child abuse are increasing, although this may imply a greater public awareness rather than an actual increase in the incidence of abuse. It is likely that a significant minority of students will suffer some form of abuse during their time in compulsory education.

4   Schools form a natural focus for professional groups dealing with children. As the focus for this *inter-professional network*, schools – and thus their teachers – have an important role to play.

5   Child abuse is not constrained by social class, economic circumstance or geographical setting; child abuse is likely to occur in all communities and is not confined to deprived, inner-city areas. Awareness of the problems of child abuse should be the legitimate concern of all teachers.

Inter-professional teamwork

The importance of inter-professional teamwork cannot be over-emphasised. There are two major reasons why inter-professional teamwork is so important. First, the complexity of many child abuse cases may mean that a whole range of different agencies are involved in dealing with a child abuse case (see Chapter 8 by David Jones and John Pickett). A typical case conference may include representatives from social services, the GP, the Health Visitor, an NSPCC worker, police, teachers, educational psychologists, the educational welfare officer and so on. These professionals need to work carefully together in order to coordinate the help that is offered to the child and the family; they have a shared responsibility for the safety of the child. Second, the emotional stress experienced by workers in child abuse cases should not be underestimated. The team-work setting allows these case workers the opportunity to share their difficulties and find support from colleagues. Professional teamwork is increasingly accepted as the most appropriate method of working in this arena.

There are, however, a number of factors which limit the role of the teacher in this inter-professional setting. These factors need to be clearly stated, understood and remedied if teachers are to take their proper place in the network of supportive agencies.

1   Schools are large and complex organisations. Teachers need to be sensitive to the fact that other professional groups may have difficulty in deciding which teacher they should be talking to. It is worth considering ways in which schools might simplify the process of liaison between themselves and other professional groups. There certainly seems to be a case for limiting the initial contact to specific named teachers. Given the potential complexity, severity and sensitivity of such casework it seems to be advisable that those named individuals should come from the senior group of staff. This too would clarify formal links between schools and other professional groups.

2   Some teachers have a very simplistic view of the work of other professional groups. Teachers often look to the social worker or the educational psychologist, for example, to find 'solutions' to the often complex and difficult problems that some children pose. Such solutions, even if possible, are elusive. The attitudes of some teachers to these other professions is coloured by their perception that these professional groups are largely ineffective in dealing with the more difficult students. Teachers thus tend to be cynical about the very people with whom they need to work closely in child abuse cases.

3   Many of the issues which involve the inter-agency network are complex and sensitive ones. Rules of confidentiality are clearly understood, and acted upon, by other professional workers. Teachers, on the other hand, have a more complex problem in terms of maintaining confidentiality. If a child's circumstances affect their performance as a student in the classroom, then it is important that all teachers who might have had contact with that child are made aware of some of these difficulties, so that they can enable the child to make the most of their academic potential. As a group, teachers generally have not come to terms with the problems of confidentiality, of access to sensitive information, and of the need to maintain limits of the range of the disclosure of such facts. It only takes one or two cases of inappropriate use of such information, for the important bond of trust between teachers and other professional groups to be weakened.

4   In some inter-professional settings teachers are seen, by other professionals, as of only minor significance. There is a reciprocal cynicism and lack of trust, and doubts that teachers can be fully involved in sensitive issues. In fact this is not generally applicable; the

vast majority of teachers, particularly at the senior level where such cases may be dealt with, exercise the same high professional standards as other groups. Moreover such a stance undervalues the professional contribution that can be made by teachers; it minimises the role of teachers, denies the very considerable training and expertise they can offer and further damages the cause of proper inter-professional liaison.

Local authority guidelines on child abuse

Virtually every local authority has issued guidelines for teachers and others, outlining the procedures that should be followed in child abuse cases. But frequently there is a disturbing failure to ensure that these guidelines are passed on to every teacher in the school. Some headteachers limit the distribution of such material on the basis that it is relevant only to those senior staff who have a stated responsibility for the care of children. I suggest three reasons why such a judgement is not appropriate:

1 I have already indicated that it will be the child who selects the person for any disclosure of child abuse. The person chosen may not be, indeed often is not, a member of that senior group of staff. *All* teachers should be aware of, and familiar with, the local authority procedures.
2 Sensitivity to abnormal behaviour and the possible explanation of abuse as its cause is an important factor in the early detection of child abuse cases. Every teacher needs to be aware of different forms of abuse and their possible consequences for a child's behaviour. On this basis it is inappropriate to limit information about child abuse to a few teachers.
3 Generally speaking, child abuse, as a cause of abnormal development, is not part of the veritable armoury of explanations that teachers draw upon when faced with disturbance to normal development. There is an urgent need to put this firmly into the professional vocabulary. Limiting the number of teachers who are properly informed about child abuse further restricts this aim.

Further to the difficulties outlined above, three problems about local authority guidelines need to be urgently addressed. First, many local authority guidelines do not reflect changes in understanding and thinking about child abuse. Some guidelines have not been reviewed and updated in the light of developments in this field and offer a very poor explanation for teachers and others about the nature of child abuse. Second, some guidelines place the emphasis entirely upon non-accidental injury and failure to thrive, treating sexual abuse merely as a sub-set of physical abuse and ignoring the problems of emotional abuse altogether. Third, the information offered in some guidelines on recognition of the abused child is woefully inadequate and further supports the erroneous belief that teachers should be alert only to signs of physical injury.

Some specific guidance needs to be offered to different professional groups. The general comments contained in local authority guidelines cannot contain the detailed information that is needed in order to alert, for example, teachers to the problems of abuse. Such specific guidance for teachers might include:

1   Information about teachers' work with the families following confirmation of child abuse. What comments there are about 'on-going support' again stress the role of the teacher in the detection of further injury to the child and reporting this appropriately.
2   An emphasis on the importance of home/school liaison and the part that teachers can play in supporting families.
3   Consideration of curricular issues and the extent to which an indirect approach might contribute to a reduction of abuse in future generations by affecting attitudes towards child care, community and parenting.
4   Discussion of the question of how schools might organise themselves to be more sensitive to the needs of children in general, and to abused children in particular.
5   Examination of how schools should translate these issues into practice. Clearly schools need to establish internal procedures for dealing with child abuse cases, at present no information, no proposals are offered, as to how this might be done.
6   Information about the on-going role of the teacher and the need to keep the teacher informed of both developments in the case and of 'treatment' offered.

Specific recommendations for changes in local authority guidelines are offered at the end of this chapter. As a starting point for this discussion, I refer to local authority guidelines as they currently stand. The reader is asked to view these guidelines critically when referring to them. The information that is offered is sometimes inadequate; in some instances they do not give a sufficiently comprehensive view of child abuse and appropriate reactions to it.

In some cases professional help may be offered by one of the specialist centres dealing with child abuse, or by a local clinic. It is likely that this therapy treatment will last for some time and will probably involve the whole family. The key worker should keep the school informed about what is happening. While teachers may not be involved in the management of the case following the initial case conference, it is important to realise how crucial their role can be. It is generally accepted that the school should keep a close eye on the child with a view to spotting early signs of continuing or renewed abuse. In many ways this is easier than the initial task of identifying abuse for the first time; the teacher will be aware that abuse has taken place and will be alert to it. If there is something that gives rise to concern, now – as was not the case in the initial reporting situation – there is a named person, the key worker, that the teacher can go to for advice and support. Clearly, this is far less traumatic than bearing the responsibility for first time disclosure.

What is less well appreciated is the potential importance of the teacher/pupil relationship. Take for example the case where a child has selected a particular teacher, perhaps their form teacher, as the person to whom the initial disclosure was made; this says a lot about the relationship of trust that exists. The teacher has subsequently been involved in discussions about the case and in the case conference, is aware of the action plan that was developed in the case conference and of the sorts of experience that the child is now having as a result. The teacher will know the key worker well, a relationship that is common to the teacher and the abused child. It is highly likely that the child will want to further exploit the relationship with the teacher.

There is no doubt in my mind that the teacher should allow this to happen. First, if they refuse this approach from the child, the child will look for motives for this refusal and may well conclude that it is a sign of disapproval, that the teacher has concluded that they have done wrong. Second, it will be a lot easier for the teacher to keep in touch with what is happening if they have close contact with the child and can hear the child's version of events. The teacher is much more likely to pick up, at an early stage, any suggestion that things are going wrong if they are able to maintain this close relationship with the child. Third, the child may need the freedom to talk to someone outside the immediate family or group of professionals involved. In the same way that children often choose teachers to disclose to, because of their perception of the teacher as a trusted adult, they may also feel that they need this impartial support at this later period.

It is unlikely that this will do any harm, particularly if the teacher is careful and deals with the matter in a sensitive way. The teacher should discuss such a situation with the key worker so that it can be seen in the context of the action plan developed in the case conference. It is probable that the key worker will keep the teacher informed about the nature of any work being done by other professionals with the family and the child. This continuing relationship, of support, between the child and the teacher, can prove very valuable as part of the overall support being offered.

It must be appreciated, though, that there is the potential for tension here. Such tensions may arise for two main reasons: first, if the inter-professional teamwork is not operating properly, the teacher may be in the dark about what is happening with the family and about what therapy is being offered. Second, the child might, quite deliberately, feed the teacher misinformation, in the hope of gaining an ally in what they see as a continuing problem. It is a well-accepted and researched phenomenon that different professional workers, operating with individuals within the family, get drawn into the tensions within the family, taking sides or reflecting particular points of view. As a result, the therapy being offered is much less likely to be effective. The teacher needs to be alert to this so as not to allow it to happen in their relationship with the child.

I give one example of a case of incest where a teacher found herself isolated from the action plan and yet placed by the child in a situation where support was anticipated. In this case, which involved two girls from the same family who were attending the same secondary school, there had been an incestuous relationship with the father. Following investigation by the police, the father had been convicted and imprisoned and the two girls were given specialist help at a hospital clinic. There was no feedback to the school from this clinic either during the therapy or when the case was closed.

One of the girls sought out the teacher who had been involved with the family and with the key worker. There were two problems that the girl wanted to discuss. Her first anxiety was 'We were told that, because we were sexually abused, we might abuse our children when we grow up and have a family; I'm frightened by this. I don't ever want to get married or have children'. How was the teacher to respond to this? She was aware that some advice and counselling had been offered at the therapy sessions; she knew how she wanted to respond to the girl, but what if that advice ran counter to the advice offered during therapy?

The second concern that the girl expressed was also based on her recollections of what had been offered at the hospital clinic. 'We were told that we ought not to discuss what happened with anyone. They said that when we got married, we should not even tell our husbands about it. I shouldn't be talking to you now about it.' The teacher had no idea if this report was accurate, if she was really engaging in a discussion that was, in the view of the hospital clinic, not in the child's best interests. How was this teacher to respond?

This illustrates two points; first, that all professional groups need to appreciate the close relationship that exists in many cases between the teacher and the child. The teacher needs to be kept in close touch, by the key worker, with the action plan and how it is proceeding. Similarly the teacher should maintain close links with the key worker and discuss concerns that they have.

Second, that specialist clinics dealing with child abuse cases need to appreciate that the child has another 'incarnation' outside the therapy situation; they take away with them the advice and help that has been offered and have to try to put it into the context of their other life. It will make the work of other professionals, and particularly teachers, difficult if they are not made aware of the treatment that was offered. Serious thought should be given to the need to report back, in some way, to the other professional groups involved with the child and the family. The argument about 'the need to know' needs to be interpreted with a wider understanding, for example, of the potential role of the teacher in this post-therapy period.

Teachers tend to underestimate the importance of their role within the context of the professional network during this time. This arises partly from the perceptions of the teachers themselves as being inexpert in this area; teachers need to have their confidence boosted if they are to be expected to contribute effectively in this setting. It also comes from the assumptions of other professional groups in terms of what can be expected of teachers; we ought not to forget that teachers are highly trained not just in their role as subject specialists, but also in child development. At one case conference, all those present believed that the child under review was no longer at risk and could be taken off the register. It was the teacher, aware of the whole picture, of the relationships within the home, of the child's reactions and of some other special circumstances, who was able to persuade that group that the child was indeed at risk and should be kept on the register and under review. Teachers and others need to accept that they have an equal and important role to play in this multi-disciplinary setting.

Movement of families

One of the responsibilities that the key worker has is to keep track of the family. It is well understood that families involved in child abuse cases, do tend to uproot and move away from the area. The key worker has to be aware of this possibility and has to make every effort to trace the family when this happens.

Schools can play a key role here. It is a common experience for schools that families turn up at the school during the year, asking that their child be admitted. The presenting circumstances may not appear to raise any questions at all. In any event, the vast majority of schools will make contact with the child's previous school and ask for details of the child's records to be sent. The teacher concerned with such admissions needs to be alert to the potential that this family might be an 'abuse family' on the move. A telephone enquiry to the school may reveal more information than has been offered by the family in interview; many schools would make this contact as a matter of course. Even so, the school should instigate further enquiries, perhaps through the Education Welfare Officer, with the other professional groups in the area the family have moved from. A telephone call to the social services department and to the child guidance clinic will soon reveal if the family is known to these agencies. Most of these enquiries will draw a blank. However, if there appears to be a history of involvement with other agencies, the school should make immediate contact with the duty officer at their local social services office. That department will then take on the responsibility of tracking down the records of previous agency involvement.

Most existing guidelines, in their section on 'schools', begin with, 'Headteachers are required to bring this document to the notice of all teaching and ancillary staff'. My experience, in talking to groups of interested teachers around the country, is that this instruction is not carried out. In the audiences I have spoken to it is rare to find more than 20% of the teachers in the audience who are aware of the guidelines, let alone having been asked to read them. Moreover, these groups of teachers are the ones who have been sufficiently motivated to give of their own time to learn more about the subject; this would seem to suggest an even lower uptake within the profession as a whole.

The implications here for teachers, Headteachers and Local Authority Officers are clear.

a The Local Authority should establish, through its advisory or inspectorial staff, the extent to which this instruction has been carried out.

b Headteachers need to appreciate the potential harm that a decision not to circulate such guidelines may do to many children in their charge. The Headteacher alone is ultimately responsible for the welfare of the children in the school's charge; Heads lay themselves open to public criticism if they fail to act on this Local Authority instruction. In the few tragic cases where things do go dramatically wrong, all the professional groups concerned in the care of the child are open to public enquiry. Headteachers risk severe censure if they have failed in this important, though elementary, part of their task.

c Teachers have a responsibility to inform themselves properly about the local authority procedures in child abuse cases. Their repeated requests for information to the Headteacher and to the Local Authority can help to raise awareness of the need to prepare teachers properly in this area of work.

School organisation

Having read and understood the local authority guidelines, the individual school needs to decide how it is going to respond. For example, Blom-Cooper in the Jasmine Beckford Enquiry Report recommends that there be one teacher in the school who is responsible for the liaison work with other professional groups in the handling of child abuse cases. There are four points worth noting here;

1   The size of the school may determine how many of these 'specialist teachers' are needed. There is some evidence to suggest that in our larger schools one contact person would not be sufficient to cope with the caseload. It has to be remembered that these teachers have a range of responsibility of which child abuse cases will form only one small part.

2   The emotional burden of dealing with this particular type of case has led other professional groups to develop a teamwork approach. It would seem inappropriate, whatever the size of the school, to limit these specialist teachers to one per school. Teachers, like other professionals, need the opportunity to share their feelings, experiences and thoughts with colleagues.

3   We have to consider carefully the legal position of the teacher/expert. We have witnessed cases where key workers have been called to task for not having done their job effectively, and may even have been dismissed. The level of training that we would be able to offer teacher-experts would, almost certainly, be no higher than that offered to some social workers. The profession needs to clarify whether these teachers might be placed in a unique and difficult legal position, being held accountable following some tragedy and even dismissed from the service.

4   There is a tendency in schools to see the appointment of a specialist, whether it be, for example, in reading, mathematics, pastoral care or child abuse, as a signal to other teachers to abrogate their responsibility in this particular area. Hand-in-hand with the training of teachers to specialise in child abuse cases, we urgently need to consider ways of training all of our teaching force about the issues relating to child abuse. Each school needs to consider, especially in the light of new arrangements for the funding and provision of in-service training, what steps it will take to raise levels of awareness among the whole of its staff.

As in other forms of organisations, there is a propensity in schools for procedures to *decay*; this may happen because of changes in staff or through shifts in responsibility. The senior management in the school need to understand this tendency and to act accordingly. With the specialist teachers, the senior management team might review their school procedures following every case of child abuse. By posing the questions, 'How well did the school respond?', 'In what ways did our procedure fail in this case?' and 'What changes and improvements are called for in the light of this most recent experience?' the school will be able to keep its procedures under review and progressively improve the way they work.

Developing inter-professional links

When the school has come to terms with the problem of child abuse and knows how it is hoping to respond in terms of the detection and reporting of cases, the next vital stage is to develop proper inter-professional contacts. Having identified a possible case of abuse, the school needs to be confident that the request for help will be heeded.

If teacher-specialists are to be identified, then it will be primarily their responsibility to establish and maintain these links. However, as indicated earlier, many schools will need to work hard to establish their credibility in an inter-professional forum.

The starting point is to discuss with members of these other groups how the school hopes to deal with cases of child abuse. This emphasis on seeking help and guidance from other trained professionals, offers the best hope for productive discussion. It accepts that teachers are generally inexpert in this area and do need the help of colleagues. While it might be appropriate for the local authority to coordinate such an approach, the individual school needs to make its own contacts, identifying specific individuals within these other organisations with whom they will work. Thus a school approach to a range of professional groups seeking help and guidance, perhaps, initially through the forum of a formal meeting, might be the better way of proceeding.

When it comes to the point of seeking help in an individual case, the teacher needs to know the named person(s) whom they should contact, for example, staff at the local social services office. Equally importantly they need to be known to that person both in relation to their role in the school and in terms of their professional integrity.

It is only when the school has established how it will work, when all teachers in the school are alert to the problems of abuse and how they should act, when individual expert teachers have been identified and trained, and a proper inter-professional network has been set up, that we can begin to feel at all confident that we have given appropriate priority to the issue of child safety.

What becomes evident in discussions between groups of professionals, is that teachers are not the only group who need additional training. There are a range of other professional groups who would argue that their training is inadequate for their needs. Variations in levels of training are marked and it is not safe to assume that the professional network needed for dealing effectively with cases of child abuse, is complete and effective.

The question of teacher training brings in wider issues of training; since the effectiveness of the inter-professional network relies upon teamwork between a group of disparate professional workers, it would seem appropriate to consider training in an interdisciplinary setting. If these individuals are to work together effectively, they need to understand the different terms of reference under which they operate, they need to understand how their roles interrelate and, most importantly, they need to get to know and trust each other as professionals. This call for joint training comes from a range of professional groups.

If such inter-professional training is to be undertaken then it needs to be centrally coordinated. This implies that the local authority, its officers and its elected members, must be persuaded of the need for – and the urgency of – such a training programme. The funding for such training programmes runs counter to the separate funding arrangements for these groups. This might imply the need for national groups, for example the DES and the DHSS, to look for a coordinated approach on this issue.

When should teachers report?

Teachers are naturally anxious about reporting cases of suspected child abuse. They frequently ask 'suppose we make a mistake?' This anxiety is quite understandable, and arises from a number of tensions. Teachers suggest, 'If we are to maintain our credibility with other professional groups, then we cannot afford to be wrong too often'. If this were the case, they feel, then their professional credibility would be called into question. As in the fable of the boy who cried 'wolf!', their failure to accurately detect cases of abuse may lead to their request for help being ignored in the very case where their anxiety was justified.

Teachers devote a great deal of time and energy to promoting links between home and school. In many areas there has been an increasing effort to develop an educational system that forges a three-way partnership between school, parents and pupil. Particularly where the abuse is within the home, and this will be the case more often than not, what are the implications for the relationship between the teacher and the parent? Teachers express natural anxiety on this point.

The confidentiality of the relationship between teacher and pupil can inhibit a teacher from reporting alleged abuse. This is a question that the teaching profession needs to address. Unlike the relationship between lawyer and client, teachers do not enjoy any privileged confidential relationship with their pupils. Yet, when students seek out a teacher when they wish to discuss an issue which is crucial to them, they often begin with, 'Will you promise not to tell anyone if I tell you a secret?' Clearly some of these 'confidences' are more critical than others. 'I've broken up with my boyfriend' has to be seen as a different problem to 'I'm very worried about my dad; he's drinking too much'. A student may offer, 'I think I'm three months pregnant; don't tell my parents will you'; this creates the same tensions for the teacher as the child who begins, 'Can I share a secret with you; will you promise not to tell?', and then goes on to say 'I've had sex with my dad'.

Essentially a teacher has little freedom in such circumstances. Their role, *in loco parentis*, requires them to take charge of the child and to act in the way that a responsible parent would act. In the case of the suspected pregnancy, the teacher has no other option than to inform the parents; indeed, from experience, this is what the girl wants as well, though at first she may be unwilling to admit it, even to herself. In the case of alleged abuse, again the teacher has no option. The child is at risk of further abuse; by all criteria he or she should be on the formal, 'at risk register'. It is highly likely that they have chosen to disclose to the teacher after great emotional struggle and turmoil, because they know that the teacher cannot allow such a statement to go unreported.

The final constraining influence, linked with the question of confidentiality, is the teacher's fear that they will lose control. Once that phone call is made to the social services office, the teacher has little influence over the chain of events. This is a problem for the child as well; they see the teacher as an authority figure and are used to teachers controlling situations. In choosing to disclose to a teacher, they anticipate that the teacher can maintain an influence over the pace of events. The teacher and the student need to explore this together. Helen Kenward makes the point very strongly, in Chapter 7, that no promises should be made to the child that cannot be kept. The child needs to understand the chain of events that is likely to follow and that the teacher cannot determine the outcome.

From my experience of this situation I would suggest that maintaining the link between the teacher and the abused child is a very important factor and one that is not always appreciated by colleagues from other agencies. The teacher has to work with the child both during and after the investigation of the allegation. If the teacher makes promises which are subsequently broken, this can irreparably damage the relationship between the teacher and the child and can inhibit the level of support that can be offered to the child following disclosure. This situation can be eased if other professionals working with the child involve the teacher to whom the disclosure was made, through the subsequent events. So for example, it would help if the teacher were invited to be present during interviews with the child. Such a step would offer the child additional support during this difficult period and would confirm the bonds, that clearly must have existed, between teacher and child.

Given these constraining factors the temptation is for teachers to 'make sure' before reporting what they suspect. In so doing they may be placing the child at further risk or damaging the prospect of any subsequent investigation. For example in cases of suspected physical abuse a teacher may decide to 'wait and see'; the evidence of their own eyes may not be sufficient for them to feel confident about reporting. If the child sustains further unexplained injury then they would be more certain that their suspicions are well founded. Such a stance of course ignores the question of the child's safety. The child has to suffer a further period of torment while the teacher, 'makes sure'. In such circumstances it is much better to consult a social work colleague in order to establish whether or not they feel it is appropriate to refer the case.

A second example might be in the disclosure to the teacher of incest. The temptation, especially since the consequences for the child and the family are likely to be so awful, is to question the child, make them repeat the details of their allegations, trying to find some contradiction in their story which might give cause for doubt. As experience has taught us in such cases, the more often a child is required to 'tell', the less valid their account becomes. The facts become distorted through repetition, and this may even invalidate their evidence in law. In an ideal setting, a child would be required to describe their experiences only once; with the aid of a video, such a disclosure can be most valuable both in terms of assessing the likely truth behind the allegations and in terms of the treatment that the child is offered (see Chapter 3 by Dr Colin Stern). Teachers need to understand that their detective role here is minimal; they need only to suspect that abuse has taken place before they report.

The only advice that can be offered in answer to the question, 'When do we report?' is 'As soon as possible'. Our primary concern must be for the safety of the individual child. To delay places the child at further risk and is inexcusable. The anxiety about reporting cases of suspected abuse which in the event turn out to be unfounded is countered by the advice offered by all child care groups; they would rather investigate cases of this sort, in the knowledge that the net is cast wide enough to catch all abuse, than run the risk of cases going undetected or unreported.

Such a policy has important implications for the provision of resources. Since the Beckford enquiry, the number of reported cases of abuse of all forms has increased. Again, it needs to be emphasised that this is probably a matter of increased public awareness rather than an actual increase in levels of abuse. In the week following a talk I gave recently to the staff of one secondary school, eight cases of alleged child abuse were identified in that school alone; in each of these cases the allegations were subsequently substantiated. Raising the awareness of teachers is bound to massively increase the level of reporting. Implications for funding, both of Local Authorities and for independent groups, are considerable and urgent.

A number of teachers have described resistance they have met from their Headteacher in following up reports made by classroom teachers. It is not possible to say how widespread such resistance is, but it does imply the need to train the leaders of our educational institutions. Headteachers carry the ultimate responsibility for the children in the school's care and it is usually they who are mentioned in local authority guidelines as the person directly responsible for reporting cases of suspected or alleged abuse. This group needs to be more sensitive than most to the issues of child abuse.

In one reported case the headteacher refused to take the word of the teacher who had passed on information in a case of alleged sexual abuse. He insisted that he should interview the girl; in the interview that followed, the child withdrew her allegations. In a second case the headteacher insisted that the teacher should not 'make a fuss', suggesting that, 'the school governors would take a very dim view of it if we started reporting allegations like this'.

What is a teacher to do in such circumstances? When a similar example was raised in a panel discussion following one of my lectures, one panelist suggested that the teacher should exercise their rights as an ordinary citizen and should report their suspicions in that context, rather than as a teacher. Even so, this places the teacher in a very difficult situation, and has the potential to undermine the important and professionally dependent relationship between the headteacher and a member of staff.

In an environment where all staff have received training and named individuals act as coordinators of such work, a situation of this sort would be far less likely to occur. Examples of this type of behaviour by headteachers do, nonetheless, underline the need to offer in-service training to headteachers as a matter of some priority. I give other examples of these tensions for teachers later.

Record keeping

Teachers, and others, need to be meticulous over the records that they keep. Often, evidence which leads to the conclusion that a child is being abused is a collation of small pieces of evidence. On this basis alone it is important that exact details are kept by teachers of injuries, behaviour or conversations which lead them to be suspicious; included in these notes should be the dates when these records were made.

It is important to distinguish between fact and opinion. It is possible that the teacher may be called as a witness in court and their report must include only that evidence which would be admissible. The record should therefore include factual detail; it may also include opinion, though this would not be admissible in court. Where records, for example from schools, are referred to in court they are referred to as 'discoverable' that is, the other side can ask for a copy. Occasions when teachers are called to give evidence are relatively infrequent; often the matter is dealt with in some other way, or if a case is brought, then other professional groups have sufficient evidence and do not need to call upon teachers to act as witnesses.

Case conferences

Following the report of alleged abuse and after preliminary enquiries it is likely that a case conference will be called. The case conference forms a very important element of the child abuse procedure, and along with the teacher will include representatives from a range of other organisations. The case conference is likely to be convened by the Social Services Department and will probably be chaired by a senior member of that service. The conference chairperson is likely to have had specific training in case conference management and the proceedings will follow a set pattern (see chapter 8 by David Jones and John Pickett).

The initial case conference, having identified the individuals taking part, will trace the history of the case and the evidence that has led to the decision to convene the meeting. The teacher present will be asked to offer their evidence. It is at this point that accurate records are invaluable.

The case conference will try to reach consensus about the course of action that may be needed. A key worker will be identified and this person will take the responsibility for the case following the conference. From this point onwards, it is the key worker that the teacher should liaise with. The case key worker will want to be kept informed about the child's progress at school and will expect immediate notification if any further problems are experienced.

It is important that mutual confidence is developed between the key worker and the teacher. It is sometimes the case that the key worker will be hesitant about offering information to the teacher, especially if this is of a very sensitive nature. The teacher, on the other hand, may need such information if they are to deal with the child in a sympathetic and informed way whilst the child is in their care. Only through mutual respect and confidence can these problems be overcome.

The abused child in school

How does the child respond in school after abuse has been disclosed? The first possibility is that the child may well be feeling an overwhelming sense of relief. Their secret is out and for the first time, for probably a very long time, they are able to feel safe. This may be particularly obvious where the child's behaviour had changed dramatically; after disclosure I have known the child to revert, almost overnight, to their more normal behavioural pattern.

They may, of course, be living with the consequences of the discovery of their abuse. It is possible that the child has been taken into care and so their surroundings and life-style have altered. If the abuse took place within the family, there will almost certainly be some reaction there. The police may be involved in an investigation and the Social Services will be taking a keen interest in the family. If the abuse was outside the family, then coming to terms with what has happened may be a slow and painful experience.

Similarly, when a child leaves the school, there may sometimes be unusual circumstances. If the family has a record of involvement with other agencies the school should endeavour to pass on this information to the receiving school. Of course the family does not always tell the school that the child is leaving what new school the pupil will attend or even inform them of the area where they have moved to. In such circumstances, other pupils often know more than has been offered to the school, and can be a useful source of information. Again, the Education Welfare Officer may provide a useful resource in tracking down this family and in passing on important information.

Alerting children to danger

One of the most difficult areas of work is to know how far schools should go in terms of preparing children for potentially dangerous situations that they may encounter. We accept this as almost automatic in a whole range of situations. Road safety is a theme explored in both primary and secondary schools and many schools run cycling proficiency training and tests for their pupils. Thus we accept our role in preparing pupils for the danger that they meet on the roads, and a whole range of other safety themes run through the work done in schools: safety on water; safety in the home; safety from drug abuse; 'don't talk to strangers' and so on. Should we alert the children to the potential dangers that they face from abuse?

Child abuse is different from all these other examples; it is different because the nature of the danger is different, particularly where abuse is within the family. We cannot treat this subject in the same way as we do road safety. Neither can we expect the reactions of parents to be the same; there is probably not one parent in the country who would refute the value of a school covering road safety as a topic in schools, but the same is not true in child abuse programmes.

As yet there is no general agreement on this question. There are those who would say that we have a responsibility to prepare children in this area. Programmes which focus on this aspect of child safety have been developed in the United States, Canada and Australia and are increasingly common in the UK. The rationale behind such projects is that we need to develop a greater awareness in children of their control of their own bodies. Such programmes develop a self-assertiveness in children which means that they are more likely to question the situation where an older person tries to impose their will on the child. The child is also more likely to refuse such approaches and to seek help if necessary.

The argument that runs counter to this seems to be just as valid. It suggests that the vast majority of children will never meet a situation where they are likely to be abused. In most cases, relationships within the family function perfectly normally and the children are able to maintain that innocence that is such an important element of being a child. If we are going to warn children about the dangers of abuse that do exist for some, particularly within the family, we are inevitably going to be talking to children for whom this situation will never arise. Might we be affecting what otherwise might be a perfectly normal family environment? Might we sow seeds of doubt in children that make them cautious of normal contact from members of their family?

Many of those involved in such programmes refute this possibility, and suggest that the matter is dealt with in such a way and with such sensitivity that there are no ill-effects. I am sure they speak with the utmost sincerity, but this does ignore the fact that as such programmes become more and more common, there will be less control on which people will be using them and how they will be used. Neither does this argument accept that some of the materials that have been produced, particularly those from overseas, are inappropriate for use in schools in the UK. How do we establish a common agreement as to which materials are useful and which are not?

There is clearly a role for the Department of Education and Science here. Through the Inspectorate, they are aware of practice in this field across the country and are in a position to evaluate the effectiveness of such programmes of work. I would recommend that the DES set up a standing committee, The Standing Committee on Educational Responses to Child Abuse, to investigate this area of work in schools and to make recommendations for DES guidelines on, amongst other things, the use of material of this sort in schools. This must be an urgent priority for two reasons; first, our assertion is that children do need some preparation of this sort and the longer the delay, the more children may suffer unnecessarily from abuse; second, practice in schools gives cause for concern and guidelines on which materials are appropriate are urgently needed. Such a committee might address the question as to whether school teachers are the appropriate group to do work of this sort, and schools the appropriate forum for it to be carried out.

Summary

Teachers have an important role to play in child abuse cases. They have a role to play in the detection and reporting of abuse; in working within a multi-agency teamwork environment; in contributing to the ongoing support and monitoring of the abused child; in preparing children to cope with potentially abusing environments. This role can only be properly developed if the following recommendations are carried through.

1   Joint training sessions for all professional groups, including teachers, should be set up by each local authority.
2   There should be three levels of training for teachers:
   a All headteachers should undergo awareness training in child abuse and should be thoroughly briefed in local authority procedures. This should include sessions on establishing efficient school strategies for dealing with child abuse cases and on setting up review procedures so that schools can maintain the effectiveness of those strategies.
   b All teachers should undergo awareness training in child abuse issues.
   c Specialist teachers, at least two from each school, should receive such training as is needed to allow them effectively to act as the link between the school and other professional groups. Much of this training should be done in an inter-professional environment. This training should be validated and certificated and no teacher should be given this specialist role until they have undergone the appropriate training.
3   Local authorities and teachers' unions should establish the precise legal position of specialist teachers in their role as link-person.
4   *Local authority guidelines* Local authorities should carry out frequent and regular reviews of their guidelines and should ensure that:
   a the guidelines reflect current thinking and understanding of child abuse issues and procedures. They should offer information about all forms of abuse and about what behaviours or signs might indicate a child is being abused.
   b the guidelines should set out in detail the reporting procedures and the roles of each of the agency workers likely to be involved.
5   *Specialist professional guidelines* In addition to general guidelines there should be specific guidelines for particular professional groups; there should, for example, be a set of guidelines designed for teachers and containing advice relating to that profession. The guidelines should properly reflect the extent of the teacher's role,

including guidance on curricular issues, and make recommendations in terms of school organisation and practice.

6 Schools should be required to keep accurate records of all incidents of child abuse reported through the school. These should be factual reports stating the circumstances leading to the report and should be updated to include a record of actions subsequently taken.

7 Schools should be required to make enquiries, where children are transferred to their school, of the social services department and Schools' Psychological Service in the area from which the family have moved.

8 The local authority should require reports from schools on child abuse cases and should keep statistics on the number and nature of such cases involving initial reporting of the case through schools and their teachers.

9 Education Welfare Officers should work closely with schools to establish the background of students moving into their area.

10 Schools should be required, where an abused child moves from their care, to make every effort to pass on records to the receiving school and the receiving social services department.

11 The local authority should ensure that the standing instructions to Headteachers have been effectively carried out.

12 Case conferences involving children of school age should always include a teacher from each school attended by a child in the family.

13 Teachers should be acknowledged as an important element in the supportive network and should be kept thoroughly informed of the progress of the action plan.

14 Specialist units offering support and therapy for abused children and their families should keep the child's school informed as to the nature and progress of that therapy.

15 The Department of Education and Science should set up a Standing Committee on Educational Responses to Child Abuse. This standing committee should make recommendations on:

 a appropriate forms of training programmes for teachers on child abuse issues;

 b terms of reference of teacher specialists in child abuse procedures;

 c organisational implications for schools;

 d suitability of curricular materials in safety projects.

Chapter 11

The school's proactive role in reducing levels of child abuse

Peter Maher

As a society, we would want to see child abuse eradicated. Such an ambition clearly presents a difficult and complex task. It is not a thing that any one group can accomplish. Neither is there any single factor which we could change that would lead to this ideal state. Nonetheless, we do need to look for ways of reducing levels of abuse and to tease out the role that teachers and schools might play in this process.

A number of factors are common to a great many child abuse cases. These factors are largely cultural and attitudinal and as such capable of change. By changing at least some of these factors, we may be in a position to reduce the levels of abuse in future generations.

In this chapter, I have tried to outline some of these factors and, for those who do not see their relevance to child abuse, describe the ways in which they contribute to the likelihood of abuse of children; I then offers ways in which schools and teachers might help to change them. The factors I have included are:

- attitudes towards women;
- attitudes towards violence;
- attitudes towards parenthood;
- attitudes towards relationships;
- coping with money (or the lack of it);
- effects of unemployment and enforced 'leisure';
- attitudes within the community.

Schools are one of the social agencies that can affect change in society. We need to consider ways in which schools and teachers can be involved in such a programme. Teachers are persistently exhorted to include more and more within the school curriculum. With this in mind, the recommendations of this section focus on changes in style and emphasis rather than on content.

Attitudes towards women

There has been growing awareness of the ways in which women are perceived in our society and the extent to which these perceptions can influence the performance of students, particularly girls, in schools.

Similarly, attitudes towards women, particularly the view of women as sex-objects, influence the way that women are treated. Our historical and cultural norms have traditionally placed women and children as 'second class citizens', subordinate to men. Where such norms apply within a relationship the woman is often treated as a possession by the man; this question of ownership often contributes to a perception that violence towards women (and to children) is of little more significance than violence directed at inanimate possessions. For those who argue the relevance of these views to current social values sexual dominance is sometimes seen as a further expression of man's power over women and an extension of physical violence.

A range of factors influence these attitudes towards women and towards sexuality. Although hard pornography is, in theory at least, not available to minors, the experience of many teachers who confiscate such material when it is brought into school, would suggest that it is readily available to children. Increasingly, soft pornography appears as a matter of routine in daily newspapers and magazines. The home video has made such material much more readily available, and parental controls on what children watch are not as strict as we might like or the law would require.

Children are seldom offered a range of role models on which to base appropriate attitudes towards women. In schools, from the age of four or five, the child is likely to come into contact with a female class teacher. Yet the appointment of headteachers of junior and infant schools does not reflect the number of women involved in this sector of education; a disproportionately high number of Headteachers are men. This imbalance in the numbers of men and women in senior posts in schools becomes even more marked when the child moves into secondary school.

Many of the resources in schools reflect these distorted role models. In reading material found in many classrooms the female figure is more likely to be involved in domestic work while the male figure goes to work, builds and repairs in the home or works on the family car. Similar models are reflected in the roles played by the children in reading materials. The male child will build, help daddy repair or wash the car, play with 'masculine' toys; the girl helps mother with the domestic chores, plays with dolls (rehearsing for her mothering role) and is generally seen as more fragile.

Given that many children of both sexes are, from infancy, offered this form of role model in the home, that it continues in their experience at school – reinforced by the experiences and aspirations of their peers – and is imbedded in the materials that they use throughout their educational experience, it is little wonder that attitudes are so thoroughly hardened, on both sides, before the child is very old. Girls are often committed to success at school but their career aspirations are limited to seeing such a step as being merely a stop-gap measure until they marry and become mothers. Boys on the other hand develop an increasingly macho-image. Not for them the parenting role, except as super-stud; they are less often committed to school work but have very real aspirations in terms of employment and career.

Attitudes to women are ingrained at an early age. This can be seen in the playground where the activities are divided by the children themselves, into those which are and are not appropriate for boys. Such an artificial sense of supremacy and superiority is at the root of the attitudes which lead to the abusing situation. It is only by affecting these attitudes that we can begin to alter the situation where women and children are seen as a legitimate object for sexual and aggressive frustration. I am reminded in this context of the real-life story Helen Kenward tells in her chapter of Jenny, who was systematically abused by her father, with threats against the life of her and her mother unless she accepted his treatment of her.

We have to ask what schools can do to alter such attitudes and to begin to counter the propaganda that our children face about the inferior status of women and children. There seem to be a number of possible starting points. The first must be for the school to accept that this is an important issue. Having taken this important first step, teachers need to look closely at the way that they operate and the range of experiences they offer to the students. Schools need to develop a whole-school policy towards equal opportunity and to ensure that this is reflected, not just in the experiences of the children, but also in the experiences of the staff.

The importance of looking at staffing policy cannot be overestimated. It is not that women have not got the ability to take on additional responsibility or that they lack the motivation to do so. Schools, and indeed local authorities, need to confront the question of gender bias in the appointment of staff and need to offer training opportunities to all those involved in the appointment of staff, to enable them to overcome this prejudice.

The school may decide, in addition, to look at the way that its posts of responsibility are allocated. The usual hierarchical pattern of management in schools is increasingly being shown to be inappropriate for such a professional setting. Alternative managerial structures might well allow a greater range of staff to experience responsibility and demonstrate ability outside their classroom work. If a wider range of staff were prepared to take and accept responsibility, a greater number would accordingly be prepared to seek and gain promotion. The variety of role models that we should then be able to offer children would reflect the abilities and expertise of both sexes.

The second step might be for the school to look carefully at the materials which are offered to children in the learning experience. I do not here suggest that we prohibit materials which offer a 'standard' viewpoint but rather that we ensure that students are offered a range of possible models. One strategy might be to use material which shows a sitation where the woman and the man within a relationship are seen to share equally the responsibility for different parts of their joint life. It is not that uncommon an experience for a man, within a family setting, to accept at least a share of the parenting responsibility; washing, cooking and feeding, playing, reading and so on. Neither is it unknown for the woman to decorate, undertake home repairs or wash or repair the family car. Materials offering such a balance are available and should become increasingly common in schools.

It is more difficult to counter the media propaganda that affects children's perceptions of male and female roles. One way that it can be done is to raise levels of awareness among the students so that at least they develop a critical facility. This can be done quite simply, for example, through a project where the students study the ways in which men and women are presented in the media, the press, in magazines, advertising and so on. It is a fascinating study for pupils, for example, to look at the ways the two sexes are portrayed in advertisements. What are the images projected for men? In what ways are women used in advertising campaigns?

This raising of awareness can have a marked effect on the attitudes of children. It not only points out to the boys that the images that are projected of women are distorted, that they are often presented as sex-objects and that their appearance in advertising material often has little to do with the product; there is also the effect that such realisation has upon the girls; they become more critical and assertive and far less prone to adopt stereotyped roles. A final part of such a project for both sexes might be to draw up mock-advertising materials – some which first offer a proper view of the roles of both sexes, and others which present the male in an inferior and exploited position. The potential for creative work here in English, art and drama is almost limitless.

In other curricular areas too, there is scope to look at the ways in which these stereotyped models are projected. In history, for example, how many of the historic figures studied are women? It is not that women have not figured significantly in our history, simply that our selection of that history tends to focus upon the male. Perhaps by redressing this balance and deliberately projecting some of the important female figures in history we may help to change attitudes.

There is scope too, to offer students a greater variety and balance of role models in the people that are invited into school to talk to them. Assembly might be an opportunity for guests to address students about, for example, 'my working life'. There will be women from a whole range of different employment situations who could talk about such experience. Women are engineers, scientists doctors, nurses, social workers, business-people. We need to work hard to ensure that the models we offer our students are not male-dominated and do not reinforce traditional stereotyping.

There is an increasing literature on developing an equal opportunities programme in schools. I do not pretend in this short section to have done more than raise the issue, and almost certainly I will not have dealt with it to the satisfaction of those better qualified than I. It is, nonetheless, an issue which needs to be addressed. The subordination of women and children is an issue at the root of much abuse that takes place in our society, and it must therefore be given greater priority.

Attitudes towards violence

Violence is an everyday part of our lives and those of our children. They see violence on the television screen every day of their lives, through news broadcasts, in plays, films and series which are a regular part of their viewing habits. Children act out these violent scenes in the play situation and, increasingly, in their relationships when disputes arise.

Until recently, such violence was reinforced by the way that schools treated children. The vote in the House of Commons, on 22 July, 1986, to abolish corporal punishment in schools and to bring us into line with other European countries, might well have marked a changing point in the history of schools. But while society's acceptance of violence, embodied in our right, as teachers, to physically punish children, might have been curtailed by this decision, physical punishment is not the only form of behaviour modification used by teachers that verges on abuse. Not until we have thoroughly considered all the ways in which we treat our children will we be in a position to have genuinely eradicated institutional violence, in all its forms, from our schools.

Coming to terms with the importance of this issue in schools is the first step. Acceptance of violence forms attitudes in our children, influences their adult lives and their treatment of their own families. The abusing parent often sees violence towards the child as a form of socially acceptable behaviour. These social norms are laid down in many ways; schools must accept part responsibility for this and see the way that our schools' treatment of the young reinforces these attitudes towards violence.

The school needs to reevaluate its approach towards violence and develop, in teachers and students, a belief that violence, of any sort, is not acceptable. Such an attitude will determine our approach when, for example, dealing with disputes between young people. It is no use simply *telling* children that recourse to violence is not acceptable, we have to provide them with alternative strategies for resolving disputes.

Such an approach needs to pervade the whole of the child's school experience, and not be confined simply to the child's playground experiences. This suggests that the skills of arbitration, negotiation and compromise need to take an important place in the ways in which children work. We need to develop in our students not just the skills of argument and advocacy, but also the skills of listening; to encourage in them an ability to listen to other people's points of view and adjust their own views or ambitions to take proper account of others' viewpoint would be a major step forward. There are examples, both in the primary and the secondary sector, where such an approach has been developed even to the point of the students playing a part in the negotiation of their own curriculum. We need to learn from these experiences and develop them.

The question of how a school counters the formidable influence of the media, which so colours our attitudes and those of our students, is a difficult one. In order to sell newspapers and magazines, or to attract greater viewing figures than the rival TV company, the emphasis is usually placed upon the outrageous, the violent or the sensational. The positive achievements of our society have to compete for the minimal coverage that they receive in the media.

One way of countering such media bias is to focus, in school, upon the benefits of positive achievement. Such an approach applies, in microcosm, to the achievements of individuals in the classroom, broadens to include students' achievements in extra-curricular activity and might then legitimately focus upon the broader achievements within the community served by the school. Such a focus may actually encourage greater motivation within students to see their positive achievements rather than to morbidly concentrate on their perceived limitations. Much of the work currently being undertaken in the area of records of achievement and student profiles addresses these issues.

Here, as in the project on sex-bias in the media described above, students might valuably analyse the range of topics covered in their daily newspapers or in news broadcasts. It might be a useful basis for a mathematical project for children to analyse a video-recording of a 30-minute TV news broadcast, to time the content under certain headings and then to represent these subjects in graphical form. Children of all abilities could contribute to such a piece of work. Such an analysis demonstrates the morbid emphasis of a lot of news material and clearly shows the bias towards sensationalism and violence.

Inevitably, such a project would focus attention on the need to give space for positive achievement. It might prompt students to produce their own positive newscast or newspaper. Again, we need to raise levels of awareness among the students as to the negative input that we are continually being offered and to develop in those students a more critical frame of reference.

As a society the image that we present is that violence is an accepted way to resolve problems or to release frustration. When our young people grow up and are faced with, say, a domestic situation where they feel enormous personal anger and frustration, to resort to violence is not just socially acceptable but is the norm. There are other ways of resolving such frustrations and anger, but these skills need to be taught and practised. When a child is violently beaten or abused in some other way, the perpetrator of that violence is often of the view that what they are doing is both normal and acceptable. By changing such attitudes, we could have a very significant effect on levels of violence in all situations, and violence towards children in particular.

Attitudes towards parenthood

Our working definition of parenthood in schools seems to be based on the assumption that all children, when adult, will procreate. Evidence demonstrates that such a theory is not proved in practice. The assumption about young women commonly held by schoolgirls, is that their role in life is to marry and have children; in fact many women choose to do neither.

It is certainly the case that when domestic circumstances are such that tensions exist, these tensions can be exacerbated by the number of children in the family. I am careful here not to imply that large families are unhappy places; indeed the experience of many of us who come from a large family background suggests that the benefits of living and learning in such an environment far outweigh the disadvantages that sheer numbers inevitably bring in terms of the limitations that are imposed on personal freedom and liberty. Nevertheless, in a tense family environment, even one child in that family can further develop those tensions and create a situation which might result in volence.

Professor Richard Whitfield, both in chapter 9 and in his other work, notes that the family, as we know it, has undergone some radical changes. This is not simply a matter of the breakdown of the extended family, but also of the increasing experience of separation and divorce. He argues that we should be putting forward the view of parenthood as an option to be consciously chosen or refused, rather than an obligation.

Given that many of our students, when they reach adulthood, will have close familial contact with children, we pay scant attention to this issue. There is little curricular input to this important area; where it does appear it is often at secondary school level. Such courses as 'childcare', are often available only to older children, usually girls and usually those perceived as being of lower academic ability. While it may be important to consider providing such courses in some form, this particular arrangement merely serves to emphasise our prejudice, that ' "childcare" is not an appropriate area of study for boys or bright girls', and, 'if a girl is not able to demonstrate academic competence, then the only proper role for her in adulthood is as wife and mother'.

Schools are in fact uniquely placed to offer genuine opportunities for students to develop and practise childcare skills. Older students taking a caring responsibility for younger members of the school community is one obvious area, but there are others. Some of our secondary schools, usually in connection with a childcare course, run an on-site playgroup facility. An extension of this principle could offer a range of benefits. The question as to how this might be used as a service to the community and to support young families, though important, I leave to later in this discussion. It certainly could provide a structured opportunity for all students to work with the very young, to develop 'parenting skills' and to learn about growing children's needs.

I am always struck by the contradiction between our anxiety to attract mature and experienced women back to the teaching profession and our awareness that they return to work at the expense of their own children. This dilemma could be much more readily resolved if we were, as a matter of course, to provide creche and playgroup facilities in every school. The benefits to be gained by the profession would be mirrored by the benefits offered to the school's students in enabling them to develop skills that many of them will need in adulthood, whether or not they become parents themselves.

What certainly seems to be the case in many abusing environments, is that the parents simply lack the skills that go to make an effective environment in which children can grow and develop. Furthermore, they often have no alternative models of better practice to copy. This group of parents do not understand that they should be offering a stimulating and changing environment as their child develops. They do not recognise that the needs of the child change as the child grows towards adulthood; that the child as infant needs more than to be kept clean and fed, and that the child's intellectual development begins at birth (if not before) so that the infant begins to develop important concepts from the moment it leaves the womb.

Early environmental factors have a marked influence on learning. The extent to which structured play situations can affect a child's eventual performance at school cannot be too greatly emphasised. Even after the child has started school, the active involvement of the parents in the child's learning programme can significantly improve the child's attainment. The Coventry Reading Scheme demonstrated quite clearly how parental involvement of this type could improve the child's reading skills.

Of course, it would be a mistake to assume that the responsibility for such work rests with the parents; the educational establishment has to take the initiative in generating schemes of this sort. We still tend to deal with parental involvement in a very unsatisfactory way; we give the impression that parents are a necessary evil and that their involvement is of only minor significance and importance. All the evidence shows that the reverse is actually the case and we need to actively pursue means of involving parents.

There may, I suppose, have been a time when parenting skills were instinctive to all human primates; in some instances this may still be the case. However I would argue that the majority of the skills associated with good parenting, especially those that we develop through a greater understanding of the child's learning needs, are not instinctive and should and need to be taught.

Where are our parents of the future generation to learn such skills? If we accept Professor Whitfield's proposition that the quality of family life is deteriorating, that for an increasing proportion of children, instability, crisis and separation are becoming the norm, it seems unlikely that many of those children, though not necessarily all, will learn appropriate skills based on the models that they see in the home. Neither may it be safe to assume that all of the apparently stable family situations are necessarily providing good parenting models. If this is the case, then the only other place where all children could be encouraged to learn the necessary insights into child development and the skills of parenting, is the school.

Is this yet another call for more subject material in the formal curriculum of schools? How do we measure this demand against, for example, the assertion that all children should learn at least one science subject and a foreign language until they leave compulsory education? I have said at the outset that it was not my intention to seek remedies that called for an increased curricular input; this is one prime example.

Schools generally accept a responsibility to develop caring attitudes among their students; yet they are often at a loss to know how to put this into action. A school might adopt, for example, a programme of mutual support for learning; that is, groups of students helping with the learning and play environment of young children within their school. If such a programme were undertaken within the context of an understanding of child development and what constituted a stimulating learning environment, these older students would begin to learn the skills associated with good parenting.

Encouraging an increasing number of infant and very young children into school by providing creche and nursery facilities, could provide an extended opportunity for this type of work, as well as supplying a valuable community service. Not only are we providing our young students with the opportunity to develop the skills of working with children, we are offering them the opportunity to take responsibility for others, an aptitude we look for in our students, but rarely provide the environment for them to practise.

Attitudes towards relationships

The vast majority of our students will form at least one long-term relationship within marriage or otherwise, during their adult life. How do schools prepare students for these, most important, choices that they will have to make? Apart from the model of cohabitation that they may learn from home, what other models are offered to them? In a large proportion of abusing environments, abuse takes place when there is a failure in the relationship between the adults in the family. If we can help young people to understand the importance of the choice of partner to their future lives, and so, arguably, help them to make a better-informed choice, we may be able to reduce the number of such relationships that go wrong. We also need to explain the stresses that occur wthin a relationship and to try to develop strategies that might be used to resolve these stresses in a more rational way. In so doing we may well be reducing, as well, the number of situations in which abuse is one possible outcome.

Probably one of the most important aspects of such an informed choice is self-awareness. Until a person knows themselves, it is difficult for them to make a choice as to what sort of person will best suit their temperament and personality. If we were to develop in our students an ability to say, 'I don't think I'm ready or mature enough for this experience', we would have done them, and society, a great service.

This area of personal and social education is one that is too often neglected in schools. If 'life is a journey of self-discovery' then, at an early stage in the pupils' development, some emphasis needs to be placed upon acquiring self-knowledge. Some areas of work currently being developed by schools for the personal and social development of their pupils attempt to tackle these very difficult issues. Such work merits further exploration and development and needs, in some schools, to be given a greater priority.

Some argue that our cultural norms have actually changed and that long-term relationships and marriages are no longer the pattern adopted in society. Whether or not this is the case, it follows that we need perhaps to give some thought to the way that relationships are ended, as well as the ways in which they are begun. Further, the role of step-parent perhaps needs to be considered. An increasing number of people are placed in this role and such circumstances dictate that adapted parenting skills are required. It is no coincidence that a disproportionate number of abuse cases occur where there is one natural and one substitute parent figure (see chapter 2 by Susan Creighton). Strife within the family at a time of matrimonial breakdown is a common experience and has, at times, very damaging effects on children. Whatever the nature of the changed circumstances after a breakdown of this sort, the need for parenting skills still continues. The father and mother maintain these roles even though they may no longer be living within the family home.

Children have first-hand experience of strife in relationships. It is a most unusual child who does not meet with situations of conflict in the playground, between siblings, or in the family setting. This might be an appropriate starting point for a school to explore, with the student, the area of work dealing with stress within a family environment and how to cope with it. How do we resolve difficulties within a relationship? How do we approach contradiction and conflict within a shared habitat? When is it appropriate to end or change the nature of a relationship? Again these are skills that the students can learn in a variety of situations in a school. Thus prepared, they might then be able to cope with such situations more readily and equitably when confronted with them in the home as children and later as adults.

Coping with money (or the lack of it)

Many of the stresses in family life revolve around the family's inability to cope adequately with their finances. Financial inadequacy or poverty is another common thread in abusing situations. We need to develop a society of adults who know how to cope with money and where to go to seek help when things don't work out properly.

While there have been interesting developments in some schools in 'social mathematics', we tend only to deal with 'money matters' at a very simplistic level, relating much of this work to computational skills. As with child care, what further work is done, tends to be limited to the less able, and to be treated in a very unrealistic way. Average and above average ability students don't usually come into contact with this area of work. Yet on leaving school this is the very first experience that most students will have. After their first week at work they will be given a wage packet and they will be expected to cope. Students will have to cope and manage on an appallingly low grant. For those not lucky enough to find work or a college place, the problems of coping on Social Security payments are even more severe. The arguments raised over the question of parenting models in the home also apply here; if, as the evidence suggests, many families do not cope well, what skills will they pass on to their children?

There are a range of ways that schools can help their students to develop the habits that they will need in order to cope adequately in the adult world. Some of these teaching strategies, like savings schemes run in conjunction with a bank, building society or post office, can be fun as well as educative. Allowing students very real responsibility for, say, costing, budgeting and organising a class trip can provide valuable experience in a real-life situation.

In mathematics classes, similar real-life situations can be found. With one low-ability group of 14 and 15-year-olds, I recently ran a term's project on, 'funding the family'. In groups, they selected the family grouping that they wanted to consider; these varied from a mother, father and four children, to a young married mother living alone and on the dole, to two young men sharing a flat together. They decided the range of weekly purchases they would need in order to keep a grouping of this sort for a week and the weekly income that they might expect. They then set about the task of meeting these needs within the financial constraints that they had set. This involved them visiting local shops on a number of occasions, assessing the extent to which prices fluctuated and deciding where they could cut corners in order to make ends meet. The resulting work and reports-back to the class provided more than simple experience of money management; their learning raised a range of other issues which may well help them to cope with real-life responsibility when it comes.

There is wide scope here for a whole range of subject-based and creative experience. A history project might compare, 'then and now', in terms of family income and budgeting. A geography or social studies project might explore the extent to which prices are affected by locality or local availability of produce. Students might be encouraged, with the help of their parents, to come to terms with the way their own family budget is managed. If we could develop an understanding in children that 'money does not grow on trees' what a boon it might be for many families!

All these approaches aim to develop a greater awareness in our young of the skills that they will need to make their budget stretch to meet their needs. The ready availability of 'easy terms', of credit cards and of companies prepared to offer loans with little reference to their client's ability to repay, forms a trap for the poor or those in our society who lack basic financial management skills. The tensions that are created by debt and by inability to cope with financial limitations can lead to family breakdown, to personal violence and to the abuse of children.

Unemployment and enforced 'leisure'

It may not be immediately apparent why schools should offer some response to unemployment and in what ways this is related to child abuse. The profile of an abusing environment is usually such that there are a number of contributory factors which create a climate in which children can be ill-treated in this way. Stress is one important common-denominator and stress caused by unemployment is no exception to this. Since there is a direct correlation between unemployment, stress and child abuse, we might hypothesise that abuse is statistically more likely at a time of high unemployment. That is not to say that all unemployed parents abuse their children. However, if schools could contribute by developing strategies to help the unemployed, there might be a reduction in stress which could in turn lead to a reduction in child abuse.

Unemployment or redundancy often brings with it the problems associated with financial hardship and poverty. As important are the effects which strike to the heart of the self-respect of the individual. A feeling of desperation, of worthlessness, can have a devastating effect on a person at any age or at any stage of their career. For someone to seek work and to be continually rejected has a cumulative effect. An individual can only be told so many times that he or she is not needed before beginning to believe that the problem is something within themselves. These associated problems of financial hardship, stress and low self-esteem can often give rise to violence in the home.

In some areas of the country, unemployment levels have reached frightening proportions. In inner cities, in some of the areas of East London where I have worked, in the North East and North West of England, and in Northern Ireland (as just some examples) it is not an uncommon experience to teach children from families of the long-term unemployed. There might be two, three, four or even more potential wage earners in a family; if all, or many, of these potential wage earners have been unemployed for a substantial period of time the effect on the family can be devastating.

We often see the effects of unemployment in schools; at a simplistic level the children may be poorly clothed; they may be undernourished and in no fit state to learn; they may be suffering from illness and disease associated with poverty; they may well demonstrate signs of real anxiety and find it hard to participate in school work. It is difficult to motivate such a child. The education system still assumes a full-time employment situation; the child knows better than we what the real prospects of work are. Further or higher education is often out of the question; if a student is lucky enough to find an employer prepared to take them on as soon as they are able to leave school, they will go. The needs of the individual are subjugated to the wider needs of the family. What can schools do and how should they respond?

There are two ways in which schools might address this problem: the first is to look critically at the preparation that is offered students, through their school experience, for the adult world. Second, we need to look at what schools might do for the unemployed through using the school for further education and training or as a recreational or support centre. This latter area is explained more fully later in the chapter in the section 'Attitudes within the community'.

Probably the most difficult area to consider is the extent to which we adequately prepare children for an adult life where they will experience several changes in their employment pattern, if not, indeed, some periods of unemployment and enforced leisure. Schools need to ask themselves how well adapted their students are to such a lifestyle in adulthood. How general and transferable are the skills that students learn?

For those students who find little motivation in an educational system which seems irrelevant to their perceived needs, we need to focus attention on the demands that will be made of them. A broad, general education, with an emphasis on adaptability, will serve them better than a narrow skills-based education where those skills, probably acquired at the expense of a general education, may be considered redundant in a short period of time.

There are implications here for assessment procedures; formal examinations are limited in their ability to make valid assessments in all the areas of learning identified in the Hargreaves Report. Employers are just as concerned with qualities like reliability, punctuality, and social skills as they are with narrow academic achievement. There is some excellent work going on in terms of pupil profiling and records of achievement which are looking at ways of valuing these qualities in addition to any success in subject examination. We need to widen the range of success criteria that will enable a greater proportion of our students to demonstrate positive achievement.

Among the important aspects that we might consider offering through our formal curriculum are: computer literacy, keyboard skills, self-employment, how to use leisure time, either voluntary or enforced, and inter-personal skills. We need, too, to try to emphasise to students that their ability to demonstrate achievement through the educational system, whilst it might, to some, seem redundant and irrelevant at a time of high unemployment, will nonetheless determine their employability in the longer term. Employers will be looking for an educated and adaptable workforce.

We need to widen the opportunity that students have to sample the real-life work situation. Such an approach can start in the junior school with visits to work environments, so that, at an early stage, students gain an understanding of the types of employment available and the skills and qualifications required. In the secondary school, this 'visit' pattern can gradually be replaced by work-shadowing and work-experience, where, over a period of time, students have actual experience of a working environment. Not only does this serve a useful educative role in helping to clarify students' ideas about different types of work environment, it offers them a range of goals which will help to motivate their other work in school and provide relevance to their learning.

In general, schools need to be more responsive to the demands made by students, parents and employers. An education that is seen to be more relevant, that values skills in all areas rather than a limited range of academic performance, that develops versatility rather than conformity, might motivate students more successfully and prepare them more adequately for the harsh realities of adult life.

Attitudes within the community

Probably the most significant thing that a school can do to help relieve the problems of child abuse, is to change the way that it works within the community. There are a number of strands to this argument. Abuse is conducted in isolation within the community; schools can contribute in bringing the community closer together, reducing isolationism and developing mutual responsibility.

Abuse is a result of stress; a supportive community can be alert to the stress problems of its members and can intervene to offer support. This could start with the school accepting its responsibility to community members; by being aware, by offering help and by being involved in the community, the school sets an example for other individuals and groups.

Any potential benefit that may develop from a closer relationship between school and community is two-way. The potential for enrichment of the school's environment, learning, variety of input, and ethos is very great. There is a real possibility here to positively influence the motivation of students and to affect their achievement.

Overcoming isolation

Abuse takes place within the context of a community; it is likely that in virtually every street in the country, there is a child who is suffering in some way or another, some form of abuse. It could be the house next to yours or the house after that. How does a community respond to such a possibility?

The loss of the extended family has meant that many households are isolated within the walls of the place they call home. It is perfectly possible for a family to have no contact with anyone outside their immediate family or those that the adults and children meet in a work or school environment. Child abuse is not the only tragedy taking place in our communities; it is just one symptom of the failure of our society to properly care for its members. There is also the neglect of the elderly; winter after winter, the old suffer and die in isolation, neglected by their families and ignored by the community in which they live. Isolation, within an apparently uncaring community, creates the environment in which these human tragedies occur.

It is difficult to know how to begin to change the isolationist attitudes which exist in our communities. Clearly schools have a part to play in this process, though I would not pretend that the responsibility is either solely or largely theirs. Some schools have been very active in developing in their students an awareness of community responsibility. All concerned hope, or even expect, that such work will have a long-term effect on those students when they grow up to take their place in adult society, but there may also be a shorter term effect on their parents, families and the communities in which they live.

An example of a community-related programme is the Harvest Festival collection. As well as playing an important part in the development of at least one religious culture, the distribution of these gifts to the elderly in the school's local area, serves a useful and worthwhile community function. The very positive feedback from the elderly as young children visit them in their homes to deliver these harvest gifts, is enough to demonstrate the extent to which this is filling a very real need. The contact between the young and the old is a worthwhile side-product, developing, as it often does, mutual understanding and tolerance.

A more systematic approach is seen in some schools where students each 'adopt' an elderly person from the community. Students help their elderly friend with shopping, housework or gardening, or just offer conversation and companionship. A range of purposes are served by such an exercise; apart from the obvious community service that is offered, children can actually learn from their contact with the elderly. It is strategies like these which will begin to create a responsible and responsive community not just for the elderly, but for all groups.

Helping young families

We need to look for ways of offering support to other groups in the community. If we turn to the needs of young families, the suggestion made earlier that creche and playgroup facilities could be provided in schools can be seen to come into its own. Many young families, where one or both parents are at home all day, need to find contact and enrichment for their lives. Various schemes have demonstrated that schools can help to meet these needs, perhaps by providing an environment and setting where young families from the community can come together and share mutual experiences and interests or, more elaborately, by enabling them to use the school to further their educational requirements.

This 'second chance' style of work in schools that can lead to qualifications, can offer invaluable experience for people who wish to extend, or perhaps even begin, the process of acquiring necessary certificates. There are many examples of such opportunities leading to 'O' and 'A' level qualifications, and then on to further and higher education for people, who, at school, were not considered to be of an appropriate intellectual abiltity to cope with such activity. I have seen examples of womens' groups, whose members have given up a couple of mornings a week, using the facilities of the school, to study first 'O' and then 'A' levels and then gone on to find a new career. Individually, these women were more surprised than anyone that they actually had the ability to do this. It has transformed their lives and given them a valuable alternative to the routine of housework and repetitive jobs in local factories and offices. We have a duty as well as a responsibility to release the untapped talent that resides in these undervalued and suppressed groups.

One of the areas that might be covered when, for example, young mothers are attracted to the school by its creche and playgroup facilities and its recreational provision, is to offer help in developing parenting skills. I do not suggest that this work be done by teachers, indeed this is one area where a multi-agency approach would be most valuable – classes in childcare might be run by the Health Visitor. Not only might such sessions help to educate the present generation of young parents in effective parenting techniques, they might also serve to help identify promptly those young families that are 'at risk'. In conjunction with social services and other professional groups, help could then be offered at an early stage, before abuse actually takes place, or at the worst, before it reaches a point where the child's life is in real danger.

Helping the unemployed

'Second chance' courses don't have to be academically orientated; courses of general interest, photography, art, local history, sport and so on, can provide an interest for other isolated groups – the elderly, young parents and the unemployed. The unemployed, many of whom will not have done well at school, are perhaps one of the most significant target groups. Schools need to change their attitudes towards such young people, to learn to understand their disaffection and offer to help rather than to criticise. Schools tend to view 'failure' at school as final and definitive. They conclude too, that a youngster who, as a student, was difficult to motivate and perhaps presented control problems for some teachers, has sacrificed the goodwill of teachers and cannot expect to be welcomed back. There are many examples where schools and pupils have managed to adapt successfully to the changed circumstances and where real achievement has been gained the second time around. The school has to understand, though, the way that it will need to change, and will be changed, when groups like these, the unemployed and mature adults become part of the school scene.

The unemployed are an important group. As outlined in an earlier section, unemployment, along with the associated poverty and low self-esteem, is a breeding ground for abuse. By working with the unemployed we may begin to resolve a range of problems, not least the one of child abuse.

Work with the unemployed, using the school as a focus, could usefully bring in professional careers staff. They could help the young to find work or training opportunities, identify areas of skill that individuals lack, and may now be able to make up for earlier lost ground, and even offer guidance in the establishment of self-help and self-employment groups. It might be possible to see the school acting as a part-time jobcentre. My vision of schools as the focus for a multi-agency approach to the community would certainly include this possibility. Using the school as a local resource would certainly make the task of attracting members of the community into the school a lot easier. Schools, particularly the vast majority which have undergone a fall in their roll, now have the facilities and the space to make such a project a viable possibility.

There is also a possibility that the young unemployed might use the school as a focus for community service projects. Funding for such projects does exist and this might provide the opportunity for further development in the role of the school, within the community setting. Teachers do not have the resources to offer such a programme and my argument again would be to draw in other professional groups, youth workers, community workers and social workers, to operate in partnership with the school. The work habit, the growing self-esteem and the work-experience that such schemes offer (all valuable indicators to a future employer of a candidate's ability and motivation) are only some of the benefits to be gained through such a project. The ability to use their enforced leisure time in some constructive way can have a very real effect on young people's attitudes and their ability to seek positive ways of moving forward.

Minority ethnic groups and the community

As well as the groups already mentioned, members of ethnic minorities need to be given access to opportunities of this sort. For a whole range of reasons, these groups suffer from disadvantage and prejudice. Language often accentuates the isolation that I have referred to earlier; therefore ethnic minority social work teams and women's groups working with these members of our community should form a part of this multi-disciplinary team. The ethnic minorities need special consideration when the school contemplates such a community orientated approach.

This global concept of community schools, is being adopted by a range of local authorities in a variety of social settings. While it provides a challenge for teachers, it offers tremendous potential for community development. This development of community awareness, of mutual responsibility and of supportive activity can offer a chance of reducing levels of child abuse. Child abuse is one of the examples of poor practice within communities which can be overcome with concerted effort.

This broad approach towards community development cannot be implemented by teachers and by schools alone; the responsibility rests with a whole range of social and voluntary agencies. Nevertheless schools, whether they are following an official LEA policy or not, can take some very major steps towards establishing such a programme. We need to see child abuse within the context of broader social and moral issues if we are to understand the effects that such a programme can have.

I emphasise, yet again, the need for inter-professional cooperation on these issues. The responsibility rests both with schools and with other professional groups, to work together to establish greater mutual understanding and cooperation. Working in such a multi-agency setting may provide some solutions to issues of child abuse as well as other problems which we see reflected in the needs of our school students day-to-day.

Conclusion

It is possible to draw up a series of actions that could be taken, in terms of what schools do and how they operate within the community, that might have a significant effect in reducing levels of abuse. Such a reduction in violence against children might have immediate effects where the school, as a focus for a multi-disciplinary team, was able to identify at-risk groups among present students, and offer appropriate support. Of greater significance is the fact that, by changing attitudes in children, and in the communities that are served by schools, it may be possible to alter some of the more negative influences current in our communities and in so doing have a marked effect upon the levels of violence in future generations.

Violence towards children is a result of a range of factors, but of these, two are particularly significant. The first is the extent to which violence is used in a whole range of situations to resolve problems and is seen as culturally acceptable. Schools can have an important role to play in dispelling this myth and in developing alternative strategies in their students. The second is the extent to which individual communities accept responsibility for their members. Whilst communities remain non-supportive and individuals and groups within those communities are abandoned and isolated, the crisis situations, that will inevitably develop for a few, will go unnoticed or unheeded. Child abuse, which is only one of the inevitable consequences of such isolationism, will continue to occur and to shock us. Communities which accept responsibility for all their members, which are prepared to intervene and to offer help and support, communities that value all of their members, which are self-sufficient and meet the social, personal and intellectual needs of all their disparate groups will provide a healthy and constructive environment in which children can grow to adulthood. This will enable these children, in turn, to perpetuate a social pattern and order in which further generations of children may be raised in safety.

These conclusions clearly relate to the problems of our willingness to accept child abuse as a significant and disturbing social phenomenon. Unless reduction of child abuse is firmly on our agenda and we make a concerted and coordinated effort to counter violence towards the most defenceless in our society, it will continue.

1 Funding

Reduction of child abuse must be taken as a national priority. It requires funding from local and national government, from commerce and industry, from trade unions and other groups and bodies. Such funding should be used to offer training for the various groups directly involved in child care, and to raise levels of awareness of the severity of the problem. Funding is required for various programmes and community projects which will contribute to a long-term reduction in levels of abuse.

2 Coordination

The effort of a range of separately managed social agencies needs to be coordinated. In particular, the Department of Education and Science needs to establish reduction in child abuse as a national educational priority. Such a policy needs to be more thoroughly coordinated with the work of the Department of Health and Social Security. Governing bodies, professional associations, voluntary bodies and trade unions representing the different social agencies involved in child care should work together, represented on a *National Council on Child Abuse*, for greater inter-professional cooperation and understanding.

3   Training

Accepting that some training is offered, it must be appreciated that this is only selectively available. Training in the recognition of the abused child, in procedures for detecting, reporting and supporting the abused child, is urgently required for many professional groups. Particular emphasis should be placed on inter-disciplinary training, both to stress the importance of cooperative work in this field and to foster greater inter-agency understanding. Such training needs to be *general* to raise levels of awareness about the problem, and *specific*, for those who will have direct responsibility for working, in an inter-agency environment, with abused children.

Groups which should be included in such a training programme are teachers, social workers, health visitors, police, educational psychologists, youth and community workers, general practitioners, paediatricians, and a range of voluntary groups currently working in the field, victim support groups, crisis lines, community groups and so on.

The remaining conclusions relate directly to schools. Taken individually these may seem of little value, but as part of a coordinated approach their effects could be far reaching. These recommendations are not so much to do with content as they are about focus and emphasis.

4   Schools

In order to develop such a coherent, coordinated approach a school should:

- establish training on child abuse issues as a priority in its institutional plan for in-service training.
- evaluate its curriculum in terms of the preparation that it offers students for adult life as balanced and productive members of society, and for home and family life – employment, unemployment and leisure.
- develop an equal opportunities policy and carry this through in terms of the way that it deals with students, staff and community. As part of this equal opportunities programme, schools should

look carefully at the role models they offer to students through staffing, materials used, the selection of curricular content and other experiences.

- reject violence as a legitimate way of resolving problems and offer students experience of other ways of coping with difficulties. As a starting point the school will need to study its own methods of social control and behaviour modification. It should counter the violence that is selectively offered through the media by focusing upon the positive achievements of students, of staff, of community members and more generally in our society.
- offer to its students, as part of an explicit personal, social and moral education programme, an understanding of human relationships and human development through the life cycle. As part of a self-awareness programme, this should be designed to help them make considered judgements in relation to long-term relationships. Through their work on relationships, students should be offered the opportunity to understand and learn to cope effectively with situations of stress that develop in long-term relationships;
- offer all its students the opportunity to learn about child development and child care in terms of how this relates to good parenting. Students should be given the opportunity, in practical situations, to develop good parenting skills.
- accept the definition of parenthood as an option, and teach about different methods of contraception which allow that option to be exercised.
- include, in the curriculum of all students, practical and relevant experience of money management.
- provide, as a routine part of their education, opportunities for pupils to experience the working environment through visits, work shadowing and work experience.
- develop a community orientation and provide a focus for community activity. The school should encourage in its students and those outside the school, a greater community responsibility by:

1   fostering in students an understanding of the importance of community support, and an active approach to it through work with the elderly, and other at-risk groups
2   establishing creche and playgroup facilities in schools in conjunction with the local authority
3   working as part of a multi-disciplinary team, to offer support to families at risk
4   undertaking, in conjunction with other professional groups, to run child care and child development courses for adults
5   in conjunction with other professional groups, offering careers

and employment advice to students and to other members of the community

6   in conjunction with other professional groups, providing work-related skills training to members of the community

7   working with other professional groups to develop community projects both for students and for unemployed members of the community

8   providing leisure and academic courses – both day-time and evening – for the community

9   allowing individuals and groups within the community to use school premises and encouraging their use.

With such a comprehensive programme of strategies, taken in conjunction with the recommendations following Chapter 10, we may see a significant improvement in the actual levels of abuse against young people in our society.

Appendix

Report of Stoke Rochford seminar on child abuse

Peter Maher and Rick Rogers

In the spring of 1986, a seminar held at Stoke Rochford marked the climax of a period of work undertaken by the editor for the National Association For Pastoral Care in Education.

It had been clear for some time that child abuse was an important issue for schools and teachers. Other professional groups had addressed the issue, but the level of thought given to the educational implications was very poor. What work had been done was largely focused on the teacher's role in detecting and reporting abuse; little thought had been given to the curricular implications.

The NAPCE Child Abuse project set out to achieve two aims: first, to provide material for a text book for teachers on child abuse; second, to address the issue of what were the appropriate educational responses to child abuse. To achieve this latter objective, the seminar brought together a range of experts in the field with a group of people closely concerned with education – teachers, advisors, administrators, inspectors and so on. It was hoped that, by focusing on the issues, the group might establish what were the appropriate educational responses.

The seminar would not have taken place without the four bodies who provided funding: the NSPCC, Save the Children Fund, Dr Barnardo's and The Education and Social Research Council. The resources of NAPCE and advance royalties from Basil Blackwell (Publisher) contributed to its success.

People attending the Stoke Rochford Seminar

Olive Abbey	Deputy headteacher, Essex comprehensive school
Alan Bedford	NSPCC Training Officer
Arnon Bentovim	Consultant child and family psychiatrist
David Blight	Dr Barnardo's social worker for foster families
Loise Bottomly	Principal Officer, Save the Children Fund

Dr Kevin Browne	Lecturer in medical psychology
Rosina Burslem	Headteacher, first school in Shropshire
John Butler	HMI
Richard Buller	Detective Chief Inspector, Northamptonshire Police
Bernard Clarke	Vice-Principal, Community College, Leicestershire
David Collins	Social Work Education Advisor for CETSW
Susan J Creighton	Research Officer for NSPCC
Professor D'Aeth	Member, Professional Advisory Committee, NSPCC
Michelle Elliott	Founder of Child Abuse Prevention Programme
Margaret Field	Parent Governor
Eleanor Frost	Education Welfare Officer (Training), ILEA
Merlys Howells	Education Advisor
Bernadette Jackson	Deputy Headteacher, Liverpool Comprehensive School
David N. Jones	General Secretary, BASW
Helen Kenward	Professional Staff Officer, Northampton Social Services
Keith Kirby	Principal Profession Officer, SCDC
Dennis Lampard	Education Advisor, Dr Barnardo's
Don Lane	Senior Social Worker, Calderdale
Joan Lestor	Chair, Defence of Children International
Susan Leyden	Educational psychologist
Keith R Livie	Assistant Divisional Director, Dr Barnardo's
Andrew Lockhart	Chief Education Officer, London Borough of Newham
Jenny Lund	Education Welfare Officer
Margaret Lynch	Senior Lecturer in Community Paediatrics
Peter Maher	Deputy Headteacher, comprehensive school, Newham
Michael Marland	Headteacher, comprehensive school, ILEA
Marge Mayes	Senior Teacher, Essex comprehensive school
Fiona McFarland	Teacher, comprehensive school, Milton Keynes
Ian Milner	Inspector, Social Services Inspectorate
Alysoun Moon	Senior Research Fellow, Helath Education Council project
Jo Mortimer	Research and Policy Advisor, Save the Children Fund
Marcia Newsom	Deputy Principal, community home
Carolyn Okell-Jones	Supervisor/Senior Social Worker, Tavistock Clinic
John Pickett	Regional Child Care Officer, NSPCC

Jacquie Roberts — Social Worker in Adoption and Fostering, Lambeth

Anne Rodgers — Research Officer, Save the Children Fund

Rick Rogers — Freelance journalist

'Dick' Searle — Principal, Dr Barnardo's residential home

Jill Sherman — Freelance journalist

Jessica Skippon — Skippon Videos

Colin Smart — Director of Social Services

Dr Colin Stern — Consultant Paediatrician

Ian Storey — Head of year, comprehensive school, ILEA

Rolene Szur — Principal child psychotherapist

Kate Talkington — Representative, Community Education Development Committee

Victoria Taylor — Principal Officer, Save the Children Fund

Eileen Vizard — Senior Registrar in child psychiatry

Noreen Wetton — Senior Research Fellow, Health Education Council Project

Richard Whitfield — Reader in Advanced Studies, Gloucestershire College

Jackie Yeomans — Representative National Confederation of PTAs

The seminar was informed by papers that were written and circulated well in advance of the event, by a number of those present. In each of the first six sessions, one or two papers were considered and the discussion was introduced by a respondent who offered their personal reactions to the paper and said which were the educational issues that they thought were raised. In the final two sessions, the membership split into groups to consider various issues that had been raised and reported back to a final plenary session with an outline of their group's discussion and recommendations for further actions.

Throughout the eight sessions, a freelance journalist, Rick Rogers, made notes and tape recorded the discussion and it was he who produced the account and summary of those discussions that follow.

Two of the papers included in the Stoke Rochford Seminar are not reprinted in this book. Further, some of the papers which *are* included have been revised in the light of that event. As a result, the notes which follow may refer to source material not contained here. However, the inclusion of an account of the discussion was felt to be helpful because it demonstrates the range of agreement about the problem, and shows the ways in which some of the conclusions and recommendations in this book were reached.

Discussion on introductory paper
CHILD ABUSE – AN EDUCATIONAL OVERVIEW
by Peter Maher

The discussion endorsed the approach taken in the paper of seeing the issue of the school's role in terms of proactive and reactive. Pastoral care has hitherto been coping with problems when they happen instead of helping young people for the future. Such proactive work was becoming an important theme.

Colin Smart, South Tyneside director of social services, made the point that teachers should not be too pessimistic about the lack of awareness of their preventive role in child abuse. Many people in social services have not yet begun to see themselves as having such a role. So much of the work and the literature is about reacting to situations and picking up the pieces. Few people have looked at the question of what professionals and the community are going to do to stop child abuse.

Teachers are well placed to identify cases of abuse – by a child's behaviour, or a child (or parent) confiding in the teacher; they are also faced with a problem of confidentiality. A plea for confidentiality may well be a plea for someone to provide help. But teachers may often feel they cannot control a situation once it goes beyond the school. Some may not refer a case on to outside agencies – or, at least, will agonise over doing so. Teachers are faced with a conflict between their caring brief and the need for that of control. It is a conflict that affects other professions too.

All this raises one of the critical issues that needs to be addressed – the development of an inter-agency perspective on the supportive infrastructure that already exists. Not only should teachers understand that structure and the way it works, the other agencies must also have an awareness of teachers as professional partners and the role they have to play.

In turn, this leads to the need for initial and in-service training that is inter-professional.

A further issue – taken up in later sessions – was the need for the way schools organise themselves (the 'school structure') to be sufficiently flexible to allow a child to choose in whom to confide or make a disclosure; rather than for him or her to be faced with just one avenue of help which – or rather, who – may be unacceptable to the child or just too difficult for them to cope with.

Two other linked issues were highlighted as areas to be debated: first, fears of creating a generation of suspicious and isolated adults because of discouraging them as children from seeing touching and so on as a positive activity; second, the need to consider how to work with and relate to those children in a class who are not the victims of abuse.

Discussion on paper one:
THE HISTORICAL AND CULTURAL CONTEXT OF CHILD ABUSE
by Dr Eileen Vizard

As respondent to the paper, Fiona McFarlane focused initially on sexual role divisions and their profound effects on families and social relationships. Secondary schools are substantially masculine institutions and they play a major part in shaping male and female identities, implicitly and explicitly. Most schools merely instil or reinforce the traditional male/female stereotypic roles.

It is a rare secondary school that develops and makes more time for a core curriculum on relationships and preparation for parenthood as topics relevant to all pupils. If schools did pay more attention to this, pupils would not only acquire greater knowledge but would pick up a new message about what sort of institution the school is. However, although schools can implement social change up to a point, they are not the driving force in such change. It will take major political action and change within society in general to make inroads into the pattern and extent of child abuse.

In schools, many teachers need convincing that abuse is widespread and that it affects the pupils they teach. They also need to change their own assumptions about the kind of institution a school is – or perhaps should be. Thus, the statement in Dr Vizard's paper that: 'History has shown us that knowledge and perception are not synonymous – seeing is not necessarily believing' and the quoted experience of Jeffrey Masson in his Freud researches ('wilful blindness') are particularly important in attempts to change a school's work and influence.

A related point is how far teachers are going to be able to accept a greater focus on children's civil liberties. If schools are to teach children to be assertive in relation to their own bodies, it seems essential to extend that ability to be assertive into other areas of children's lives.

Eileen Vizard picked up the question of religions and their effect on child abuse and attitudes to abuse. This was not covered in the paper, but Dr Vizard considers this to be 'tremendously important'. Religions have often held ambivalent views about children. On the one hand there is the concept of childhood innocence, and on the other the notion that children possess the potential for evil and the need for this to be controlled. Those attitudes towards children which have their roots in religious thought have been, and often remain, confusing.

Discussion

Four main themes emerge in debating this paper: cultural differences in attitudes to bringing up children and to notions of abuse; differences in definitions of abuse and types of abuse; professionals' ability and readiness to understand the problems of abuse; and issues of treatment and prevention.

An underlying issue was the need to see child abuse as a cultural phenomenon and not a deviant psychiatric problem – hence the value of being able to set abuse in an historical context (even though very little has been written on it). But this, in turn, highlights the difficulty of defining what *is* child abuse – and what is generally accepted as abuse within society. An ambivalence exists in our society towards abuse. Everyone responds to what Jill Korbin terms 'idiosyncratic' abuse or neglect (a departure from normally tolerated cultural behaviours). But that is the only one of the three types described that creates general concern. The other types relate to cultural and political perceptions.

This raises the question of the tactics of prevention and legislation. In the USA and here, conscious decisions have been taken not to generalise the nature of the problem of child abuse into broader cultural issues. The most frequently quoted example here of 'dissonance' in the abuse issue is the widespread social and political acceptance of corporal punishment of children.

This may well just be a question of *real-politik*; by broadening the abuse issue, will you alienate the majority of parents who either punish their own children by hitting or threaten to do so? In the 1960s, legislative change in the USA was achieved and more resources gained by *not* broadening the issue.

However, there is also some evidence that when people acknowledge that some form of extreme and socially unacceptable behaviour is present to a degree in everyone, then the issue becomes easier to handle and people are more willing to discuss and act on it. The dilemma is in deciding just *what* you then set out to prevent. Some, therefore, see society's general attitude to the exploitation of children to be an integral part of the problem and maintain that the wider cultural issues cannot be ignored. Tactically, goes the argument, highlighting these wider issues may make life more difficult, but for long-term permanent change they cannot be pushed aside.

There is considerable debate on different cultural attitudes – of both class and race – to bringing up children and ways of disciplining children. There is, for example, the dilemma of ensuring the proper development of children and their ability to understand limits without slipping into physical or emotional violence – the stated need to ensure a balance. Children have rights but only up to a point – that point being to ensure their proper development as children.

The debate over alleged attitudes to and behaviour towards children by different ethnic and social groups brought references to conflicting research and elicited personal statements on the strictness or otherwise of different groups.

Colin Stern quoted the experience of his own paediatric practice that one can look at groups with apparently different parenting practices, both of which lead to some level of child abuse or aggressiveness by adults. (He used his observation of West Indian and Arab families.) Research was quoted from a Surrey study that the level of abusing families from different ethnic groups matched their population proportion. The Newsoms' research was also quoted as showing that working-class groups use corporal punishment more than other groups – and the preponderance of West Indian families defined as working class merely compounds the problems of accurate comparisons. The weight of comment was that one cannot make general statements about the childrearing habits of different groups and a major problem was the persistence of stereotypic attitudes towards different groups' ways of bringing up their children.

Overall, though, different social and ethnic groups are left to their own beliefs and misconceptions about childrearing. The issue was widened by focusing on what schools can do to improve parenting skills generally. Educating young people in such skills – linked to a proactive rather than reactive pastoral care policy and to an anti-sexist policy within a school – was seen as a major step in helping the next generation of parents. Boys can be encouraged – by learning about touching, tenderness and sensitivity and also that these are legitimate responses for males – to avoid taking on sexual-stereotypic roles. Reference was made to research which suggested that one reason men may abuse is in part due to a lack of 'socialisation' when they themselves were children.

Related to this was the lack of male teachers in nursery schools. Attempts to change this imbalance have met with unfortunate results. For example, in the USA as more men took up posts in elementary schools, they took over the principals' posts, leaving women in subordinate roles. In the USA, too, women tend to be given traditional posts as heads of department – especially in pastoral care. In short, men are seen still as commanding, women as caring.

A brief exchange took place over whether the sexist aspect of perceived underlying causes of abuse should be separated from the cultural aspects. On the one hand, if you concentrate on the sexism you may miss the cultural implications involved in the perceived causes; on the other, sexism is an inescapable part of the cultural aspects.

A more significant discussion focused on the problems of the abuse of children within institutions, especially children in care. (The incidents at Kingcora and Leaways were quoted.) Dr Vizard referred to the experience of the Great Ormond Street treatment team, reporting that in the last 18 months or so they had increasingly consulted with institutions over incidents of sexual abuse of children by staff. Such incidents often left an institution 'in shreds of guilt and anger' and the

Tavistock Clinic was doing useful work in helping to 'rehabilitate' an institution after an incident.

Colin Smart suggested that some people were attracted to working in such institutions because of their own background problems and were seeking some kind of help or healing by working there. So there were vulnerable adults interacting with vulnerable children. Both wanted affection and attention – and in such situations abuse can arise, even though the intention may not be of any destructive abuse of a child. He argued that the number of adults seeking power over children in this context were small. Several people said that such abuse can go on in schools too.

Such incidents were taken as examples of how abuse is a problem that spans all social classes and circumstances. There was also a need to avoid 'sex-stereotyping' offenders, because of the risk of overlooking non-reported abuse by women. The different nature of abuse by men and women was raised elsewhere in seminar discussions.

Dr Vizard summed up with the point – raised several times – about both abuser and abused being victims. There is a circular pattern in child abuse because perpetrators are labelled as offenders when they too are victims. While it seems pointless to be judgmental, professionals must remember that what is done to children is illegal – 'criminal and wrong'. So while not wishing to pass judgment, one has to be clear that the responsibility for abuse never lies with the child. It obviously has to belong to somebody – and that is the adult who abuses – but without detracting from the vulnerability of that adult. This is an important issue in both treatment and prevention of abuse.

Discussion on paper two:
QUANTITATIVE ASSESSMENT OF CHILD ABUSE
by Susan Creighton

Susan Leyden, as respondent to the paper, raised three general statistical issues and highlighted several educational ones that emerged from what the paper reported.

The figures used for the incidence of child abuse are based on incidents reported and the number of children put on an abuse register. It is difficult to generalise – or extrapolate – on the actual incidence of abuse. For example, the NSPCC figures show that between 1977 and 1984 there was a steady rise in abuse reported. Are we seeing an actual rise in abuse or rather improved methods of collection, greater awareness of the problem, better detection and greater willingness to report cases of abuse?

The ratio of types of abuse has also changed, according to the statistics. For example, 95% of cases in 1980 related to physical abuse whereas in 1984 this had become 78%. Again, is this a 'real' change or rather an enlarging of the types of abuse included? Are we able to conclude that cases of sexual abuse have increased or is there just greater willingness to report incidents?

The figures also provide information on who abuses, and women are shown to be as involved as men, albeit with differences in types of abuse carried out. This suggests that abuse is a human as opposed to a gender problem. A further worrying aspect highlighted is the rate of abuse by step-parents – of concern because of the continuing increase in the number of reconstituted families.

The educational issues raised by these findings focus on the recognition and identification of abuse and on the response schools should make to the problem of abuse and its causes.

There is important information about the ages at which children are most vulnerable to abuse. This has implications for teachers. For example, children are most vulnerable between 0 and 9 – so primary school teachers should be particularly concerned about acquiring expertise in recognition and observation of abuse and in how to cope with abused children. Too often, teachers do not link unusual behaviour in children with the possibility of abuse.

The average age for sexual abuse is 11.7 years and the greatest reported incidence is between 10 and 14 (52% of children). This is the period during which children change schools and move from an environment where teachers know them well – and behaviour changes can be recognised – to a setting where for a time they will not be well known.

Finally, in the figures, girls at 15 plus are shown to be more abused than boys. This seems a worrying reflection of what happens to women through society.

What are the implications of all this for schools? First there is an important role for schools in helping children to develop human relationships properly. Girls can be taught to be more assertive and to have the self-esteem to defend themselves from abuse. Boys can be encouraged to avoid or eradicate an abusing approach in relationships. Schools should set better educational models. Indeed, many teachers do not realise that schools themselves – especially comprehensive schools – are not safe places for children and young people. Vulnerable children are often further damaged by the schools they attend.

Schools can be more creative in their community response to some of the causes of abuse – inadequate families, the problems of unemployment, the inability of some parents to cope with normal child behaviour or to respond to the maturational needs of their children. Schools can provide support by encouraging parents to share and discuss difficulties and by offering their services and resources to help parents, not just in the parenting role, but to develop personal interests and so build up their sense of worth and ability to contribute.

Preparing young people for parenthood is a valuable role for schools. But it may be of limited value. Adolescents are often absorbed with themselves ('their own personal life angst'). It is difficult for them to see the care of others, particularly young children, as a priority. Schools could well be of greater value in parent education involving the parents themselves. Infant, nursery and junior teachers can be of enormous help in giving parents support and guidance with children at the time they need it – for example, with behaviour management, language development. Secondary teachers can help with adolescent crises. There is too little such support and partnership between education and parenting.

Susan Creighton confirmed that all our knowledge is based on *reported* cases from all those agencies concerned with children. We can be more confident in drawing out patterns on the incidence of physical abuse because figures have been collected since 1973. These show a rise in reported cases in the early seventies followed by a stable period to 1979, since when the figures have steadily risen again. Collecting figures on 'newer' types of abuse, such as sexual abuse, has been going on only since 1981. A different picture is now beginning to emerge and it is clear the abuse profile is going to change – particularly on sexual abuse.

Finally, Susan Creighton pointed to the 'size of the problem' as reported. For 'idiosyncratic' cases (see the reference to Jill Korbin in Eileen Vizard's paper) the rate of reported cases is 0.73 cases per thousand children. This means that the average teacher in the average school will come across an abused child once every 30 years. So it is understandable why some teachers might not be as aware of the problem as we might wish them to be.

Discussion

The debate focused on how far child abuse statistics obscured, unintentionally, key facts about incidence and the age at which children are vulnerable to different forms of abuse; on how teachers should respond to cases of abuse and how they acquire the expertise to act effectively and in the interests of a child; and on what structures a school should develop to cope with identification of and action on abuse.

It was argued that since child abuse is associated with unemployment and poor housing (both of which are increasing) and with the level of social support (which is being cut down, in terms of social services and health visiting) it seems a reasonable hypothesis that physical abuse of children is increasing. It was pointed out that spending on health and social services had gone up in real terms – the real issue was whether that increase matches the growing demand for services.

There was a call for caution with definitions of abuse – the notion of abuse can range from a fractured skull to someone not liking the way a parent was bringing up a child.

The suggestion of teachers encountering an abused child once every 30 years was queried – it was based, as Susan Creighton had pointed out, on *reported* cases only and some schools would obviously have to cope with a much higher rate of abused children than others. The general assumption was that the actual level of abuse much exceeds reported abuse.

The onset of sexual abuse was likely to occur many years before any disclosure of it. Children can be sexually abused at an early age. Eileen Vizard reported that some very young children in primary schools were being sexually abused and that disclosure is coming quicker than it seems to do with adolescents.

Another key issue raised concerned social class and child abuse: is there under-reporting of abuse within middle-class families because those families reported for abuse are less skilled at concealing what is happening to a child? There are, again, problems of reporting here. One indicator which has prompted such questions is that on the register-samples, abuse in employed families shows a slight class jump compared with unemployed families. However, there is also some research evidence that professionals interpret injuries to children differently according to the social class of the parent presenting those injuries. This does suggest under-reporting among middle-class families.

There was a tendency to talk about the teacher rather than the school. For a proper and effective response to abuse, there had to be a team approach. A whole team of people in school ought to be aware of the range of problems facing children. Child abuse should be placed within a general context of children's problems and not isolated as some kind of extraordinary phenomenon.

Views on the Blom-Cooper enquiry recommendation for a key worker in schools seemed, largely, to be that it was not a good idea to have just one 'expert' staff member concentrating on abuse. This took us back to the need for both a team and a multi-disciplinary approach.

Concern was expressed that many multi-disciplinary systems were not working properly. Often there was little knowledge of the training and preparation other professionals had gone through. There was mutual frustration among professionals that they did not live up to each other's expectations. Contact between professionals was frequently poor. Each seemed to blame the other for having to pass on or deal with disclosures at the end of a day.

Some argued that the main issue was not the need for teachers to be more sensitive, but rather for all professionals to improve sensitivity. Training should be multi-disciplinary with the emphasis more on appropriate responses than on a body of knowledge. There should be more training for managers as a way to get things moving and effect greater commitment across the whole system.

Some teachers voiced concern at the lack of control over what happens after a disclosure. They may find themselves acting as a form of control, rather than as carers, by getting a child on to an abuse register and thus labelled – which might have harmful as well as beneficial effects. Teachers fear they will switch from being partners with parents to having to make judgments about them and the future of their child. It is about such practical management decisions that teachers are concerned. What guarantees can a teacher give a child in such circumstances? Helen Kenward previewed her paper by arguing that if a teacher cannot be sure about future developments, they should not make promises to the child or give spurious guarantees of confidentiality.

Schools should have strict guidelines initiated by LEAs, with teachers able to be open with the head and to talk about problems. There was criticism at the inability of many schools to pass on basic information about children.

There was a warning that if teachers did take on a more responsible role with greater control over what happens to a child after disclosure, they would also become more accountable – perhaps even in a statutory way. Social workers can be – and are – sacked for mishandling child abuse situations. If teachers do want to become key workers in the process, are they also prepared to be sacked for mishandling a case?

Discussion on paper three:
THE IDENTIFICATION OF CHILD ABUSE
by Dr Colin Stern

Respondent Margaret Field raised two key issues about teachers and their role in identifying child abuse. First, that it is essential to provide expert training and experience in order to inspire others with confidence; second, the dilemma of whether to train all teachers or rely on specialist teachers for each school – running the risk of a specialist teacher not being trusted by a child.

Colin Stern emphasised that general paediatricians do not normally have any specialism in child abuse. Their role in cases of abuse is more restricted than many people realise. They have little impact on a family in such cases and are expected to decide only if an explanation of an injury is valid or not.

Discussion

The debate centred specifically on issues – practical and moral – related to processes of identification and of questioning and talking with abused children. For example, the issue of videotaping disclosures was raised – in particular, the advantage that a child did not have to repeat a disclosure perhaps several times; and the concern about whether people were in a position to make a rational decision on whether to be taped or not, given the traumatic circumstances. This discussion was not pursued in detail.

The role of the police in disclosure was discussed. Eileen Vizard emphasised the importance of working closely with the police – especially over sexual abuse. The police were seen to be anxious to develop their skills in sensitive examination and questioning. Although mistakes are still made, the police are becoming more sensitive in matters of disclosure and questioning to identify the circumstances of abuse. Detective Chief Inspector Richard Buller highlighted new police developments with, for example, abuse victims being offered a choice of venue for disclosure (not just a police station). He also referred to the complexity of the evidence required in court to substantiate abuse or rape so as to give the maximum chance of a conviction. 'The constraints are so onerous in terms of proof.'

The rest of the discussion dealt mainly with how teachers and schools can respond to the need to identify and to handle disclosure.

Colin Stern spoke of how to improve interviewing techniques. All doctors – and by implication, teachers – should be good hypocrites in the classical Greek sense of being good actors. Interviews should be participatory affairs and interviewers should take on the colour of the interview and, to provide support and illustrate key points, should use and discuss parts of their own life that best fit with what the other adult is trying to talk about. Interviewers cannot be mere cyphers – they will not only learn less but also give less. A risk in this approach is that the interviewer may burden the person being interviewed with her or his own problems without realising it.

Interviewers should also be prepared to pass parents on to others for help if their relationship with them is not working well.

Focusing on schools' responses, it was pointed out that while schools are frequently urged to work more with and support the local community, many people still see the school as a threatening environment. The development of community education and community schools may even have set back the general movement to better school/community involvement.

While there is great potential in this area, teachers are not trained to interact with adults. There is almost nothing in the literature of educational training to do with how teachers should work with adults. The evidence is that many teachers are very uncomfortable about talking with adults in their teacherly role.

For example, Colin Stern writes in his paper: 'It is not necessarily a good thing to be impassive in discussing unpleasant events. Although calm should prevail, anguish, distress and solace may be all-important.' However, teachers are rarely if ever advised on such interviewing techniques and how much they can or should 'give' with parents.

Primary schools are better at involving parents in the life of the school. What happens to that relationship further on in the educational system? Is it that in the early stages, parents consider education to be a matter of commonsense; and only later do they feel threatened by educational processes?

The need for training and for proper organisation and structures in schools was again emphasised. Many teachers are young and inexperienced and are not given the right kind of back-up by schools – especially when they have to handle distressing situations. Counselling should be available, as should training in interviewing skills, strategies in extracting information and guidance on how to cope with the information received from parent or child.

The point was made again that teachers should be taught to see abuse not as a specialism, requiring expert key workers, but as part of their whole concept of dealing with children. However, the assumption is too often made that all teachers know how to talk with children. Many may find it hard to discuss or accept a child's disclosure of abuse. There is also the requirement to be able to signal to a child that it is acceptable to reveal incidents of abuse. Two questions were raised here:

1 Is the teacher necessarily the right person to be prompting disclosure – or can they be adequately trained to handle disclosure competently?
2 How far is it possible to avoid the situation where a child has to recount many times the nature of the experience?

This led into a further discussion on the key worker idea from the aspect of a child possibly rejecting any designated 'key worker' and confiding in the person in the school with whom he or she feels most comfortable – ie the child will seek out her/his own 'key worker'.

A series of issues were raised but not discussed in detail:

- Questioning the cliché that abused children grow up to be abusing parents; those who grow up and are non-abusing parents are not known about. Is this chance or the result of intervention?
- While guidelines for handling sexual abuse are generally to be welcomed, there is a risk that they are made too complex or rigid and are thus less valuable to teachers and others.
- The anxieties felt by many professionals over setting themselves up as a judge in abuse disclosure could be eased if mandatory reporting was introduced.
- The problems of having to deal with a suspicion of abuse over a

long period rather than the quick, unanticipated disclosure.
- The question of whether a teacher is obliged in law to report any disclosure of abuse.
- Again, the point about it being acceptable to tell a child one does not know how to deal with aspects of a disclosure and that further help will be sought on the child's behalf.

Discussion on paper four:
BREAKDOWN OF PARENTING FUNCTION IN
ABUSING FAMILIES
by Dr Arnon Bentovim

Responding to the paper, Jackie Yeomans drew on her work with an MSC project on parent education. She stressed that most families need 'caring time'. The workload of those in the caring professions often allows too little time to talk with parents and help them develop better ways of dealing with family difficulties.

Some parents feel guilty for having failed their children if difficulties arise, especially outside the family circle. Reaction to such feelings takes different forms – from over-indulging a child to resentment at personal inadequacies which may turn into aggression towards a child. Removing the child from the home to save it from possible or actual abuse can make a parent feel even more inadequate and less able to achieve success in parenting in the future. This can be 'a very real and cruel dilemma'.

The legal status of statutory agencies can lead to an authoritarian approach which instils fear in families rather than creating a caring attitude. Parents who fear their children will be taken into care often go to great lengths to avoid this by not cooperating with statutory agencies. Such non-cooperation can often be prejudicial to all concerned.

A final issue raised but not pursued was how far there could be a link between inappropriate schooling and unsuccessful parenting.

Arnon Bentovim focused on the kind of relationships that develop not only between professionals and the family but also among professionals themselves. He referred to the 'mirroring phemomenon' where the way one looks at, observes and assesses families can just as readily be applied to professionals (the hopeful-doubtful-hopeless prognoses). The network of professionals often reflects what goes on in the family – for example, scapegoating, chaotic and fragmented communication, boundaries that are blurred, complex and ill-defined, and no control functioning. This can be seen in case conferences, and in other circumstances where professionals try to work together. They display stereotyped attitudes to each other's roles.

Discussion

Four main issues were raised: the problems of professionals working together; the role of schools in helping families; the myth of motherhood and the inhibiting nature of the idealised parent; and the problems of 'labelling' children and parents, especially over the assumption that the abused child becomes an abusing parent.

Dr Bentovim argued that the concepts in his paper were relatively simple ones in that they apply to a wide range of people, including teachers, at various stages of their professional development. There should be better 'ways of looking'. One professional difficulty is being unable to see patterns through focusing only on an individual in isolation. Better training is needed to ensure that not just the individual but also the context in which an individual must operate is understood. Ways had to be found to intervene in the whole rather than just a part and to work together rather than sticking to an individual framework.

Professionals too are compartmentalised – defining their own boundaries about what they are prepared to accept. A major issue here is the boundary between what professionals, like Bentovim, are trying to do and what teachers are trying to do in an educational framework. It is a question of what can be done that best produces change. For example, children may welcome a response in school that is different and separate from the response they receive from other professionals in, say, therapeutic work. This enables them to be seen in their own right without pre-conditions or labelling. One concern about this approach is that schools need to understand when and why a child is going through a difficult time – otherwise appropriate help may not be given by a school.

School is often the first place where a child gets a more appropriate response to her or his needs – often just being talked with. A child can freeze up when being abused and be unable to communicate because they dare not. Meeting someone warmer and more caring can encourage disclosure. A major issue for schools is for them to be a place where a child can develop an ordinary (not therapeutic or special) relationship with other people. It was also pointed out, though, that a bad relationship with parents can affect a child's relationships with all adults – so the school may not be able to help in that way.

There was considerable criticism of the idealisation of parenthood in our society – and particularly the expectation of maternal instinct in all mothers. Many mothers cannot admit they often need help to acquire parenting skills and develop a secure attachment with their child. A vicious circle of disappointed expectations between mother and child can be created. People's perceptions of motherhood and fatherhood had to change with an acceptance that not being an adequate parent is a normal situation. In that way more people would be prepared to ask for help.

A question raised was whether there is any evidence of attitudinal difference in parents which makes some less able to cope than others in achieving parental skills. Carol Dweck's theory of intelligence (entity and incremental) might apply here, too, in that some parents may merely accept their existing ability while others believe they can build on what they currently possess ('I may not be so good today, but I can always improve tomorrow').

Labelling was a frequent theme of this session. Do we put too much emphasis on the notion of the abused child growing into an abusing parent? We have little or no statistical evidence for this. We do not hear of those abused children who do not become abusing parents. Abuse is caused by a wide range of factors. There was a call for studies which follow children who have been through a bad time and survived. Often a child can be 'saved' by contact with a significant adult – teacher, relative, spouse – who provides a contrasting model, enabling change to take place.

The characteristics that might lead to breakdown in parenting were discussed, as was the need for various forms of educational support for families in distress. Here the form of the relationship between school and family was highlighted. In short, can schools do more than offer some kind of counselling?

Because of current views about education, schools are being asked to help children with a far greater range of difficulties. Do schools have the resources to cope with additional problems? How best can teachers work with families? How do schools work effectively with the wide range of agencies dealing with disabilities: paediatric services, psychiatric teams and social services departments? The general feeling was that schools should be encouraged and be able to provide support – the question was how? This was particularly pertinent given the problems that professionals have in working together. Bentovim concluded: 'We are dealing with very complex systems and simplistic notions of what we should be doing probably make matters worse.'

Discussion on paper five:
EMOTIONAL ABUSE AND NEGLECT
by Rolene Szur

Respondent Olive Abbey pointed out how difficult an area is emotional abuse and neglect – it is intangible, complex and intertwined with so many other matters. Rolene Szur's paper provides not answers but a pattern with which to move forward. It pinpoints aspects of the issue of which all teachers should be aware. Solutions to emotional abuse are probably as complex as their causes.

The danger of emotional abuse is that abusers often hide the fact from themselves, which creates a very real problem for teachers and support agencies. There also has to be a special quality of closeness if a child is to be weaned away from an abuser. A child will often cling to an abusing parent because of a delicate love/hate relationship. This produces difficulties of helping children bond to another adult. Teachers must look at the whole family situation and be aware of the problems of what happens when a child has to go back to a stressful family situation.

Rolene Szur confirmed the intangibility of such abuse and the difficulty of identifying signs of abuse, because of there often being no obvious signs of distress. There are multiple reasons for emotional abuse. What the teacher can do is try to pick up and encourage something positive in a child, thereby starting a different sort of cycle.

Discussion

Three main issues were developed: that of emotional abuse being a continuum and the point at which such abuse becomes unacceptable; that children often lack the language to put their feelings into words; and that while both abused and abusing are victims, decisions must be taken which are detrimental to the abuser, victim or no.

It can be argued that all children do not get the emotional and mental stimulation they might. How then do you decide on the cut-off point – when is the abuse too much? There was a comparison with gifted children in that one should not try to assess if a child can be labelled as gifted but rather assess what each child's needs are.

One problem is that families often behave idiosyncratically and such idiosyncracies must be accepted. People have different models of how families are and how they should behave. Research shows – Becher at Sussex, Johnson at Brunel – that schools know very little about how families behave at home. The worry is how to decide at what point idiosyncratic behaviour goes over into emotional abuse and deprivation.

This leads into issues of culpability. There is the beyond-reasonable-doubt level, where the act was deliberate. But another level is concerned instead with establishing an avoidable impairment in a child's development, where the cause is not as important as stopping the impairment. This can put the professional into the uncomfortable position of making a judgment. While both children and parents have rights, in such a situation parents retain their rights only if certain activities and behaviours are followed.

Where abuse is an unintended consequence, one can consider the act unacceptable but still accept the perpetrator. Yet decisions must be made which affect one victim more than the other – the abuser more than the abused. There are even situations where matters cannot be retrieved – a case is hopeless with no reconciliation feasible. In such cases, one must consider not a 'solution' but the least harmful and detrimental alternative form of care.

Children often do not have the language to describe their feelings in words – simple words are used for a whole range of emotions which adults would define more specifically and with different words.

Other issues raised included:

- teachers are often inadequate to the task; children sometimes have to be counselled to cope with teachers' inadequacies; so how do you create institutional environments that are more caring and generate more caring attitudes?
- when children become scapegoats in a family, the pattern can often be repeated in school; teachers should be aware of this and try to break the pattern.
- children sometimes feel a lack of concern by the school, for example, if no-one checks up on them when they are absent.
- the view that issues of power and control underlie emotional abuse; the educational challenge is to teach how to handle power and control effectively and compassionately; schools also have to look at themselves and ask if they are truly providing a proper context for treating children's needs.

Discussion on paper six:
CHILD SEXUAL ABUSE
by Helen Kenward

Marge Mayes, in her response to the paper, expressed worries about too great an emphasis now being put on sexual abuse at the expense of concern for other forms of abuse. Her own experience was of teacher colleagues not wanting to know about sexual abuse. While people could relate to emotional and physical abuse – appreciating why and how it can happen, sexual abuse was beyond the scope of most people's comprehension. They would rather not know about it.

Questions of defining abnormal sexual behaviour were raised – if it was taught that a sexual relationship was the extension of a normal loving relationship, who decides – and how – when a relationship is abnormal?

How do teachers cope with a child who has been sexually abused? If the abuser is a member of the family, the child is unlikely to talk to other members of the family. If it is a close family friend, the family will tend not to hear, nor want to hear, of any attempted disclosure. Children often lack the vocabulary and the courage to reveal what has happened to them. Parents can be of little help to a child in this situation. The teacher may be the next line of defence for a child. But teachers who receive disclosures often find they have no back-up. If an infra-structure for support is there, it may be difficult to link in with it.

A final issue is how to help a child when he or she returns to school after the experience – how do schools cope with the child's fears and the abusing relationship's effect on the child?

Helen Kenward argued that children who are sexually abused are subjected to adult power. If teachers open their minds and senses to sexual abuse, they will see many examples of it around them. They can start in school by showing children they are willing to listen to them – they will, says Helen Kenward, be overwhelmed by the response and the revelations. She emphasised how important it was to have a professional network but that it takes time to build one up; teachers should be confident such a network exists before embarking on encouraging revelations.

Discussion

The session focused particularly on who abuses and how to handle disclosure, with the main area of concern being to set up an effective and comprehensive professional network of support.

Arnon Bentovim explained how boys who have been abused can become abusers of young children as a response to their own abuse – acting against being a 'victim'. While frightened of their own feelings, they also enact them. Helen Kenward's Northampton study looked at all people known to have been sexually abused outside the family and at the abusers. Of 225 offenders, 30% were under 18, assaulting other children under 16. Here, says Helen Kenward, is a very real problem of what young people are doing in acting out their feelings. Social services know very few of them. They know about abuse within the family, but not much about it outside the family. An additional problem is that families can refuse help and counsellng for a child who has been abused.

A child can sometimes be abused within the family and then proceed to be abused by someone outside it.

The question was raised that if there is a correlation between being abused as a child and becoming an abusing adult, and as most abusers are men – where are all the abused boys? This was not discussed in detail, except that it was agreed abuse of boys was under-reported. Cultural norms of the macho male can inhibit boys in making disclosures.

The impulse to abuse can be realised – if not acted on – as early as 13 or 14. This has implications for what schools can do if they are to pick up such a development in a child. This could be a major preventative measure. But schools have crucial dilemmas to solve. For example, how do teachers cope with a sexually abused child, especially in relation to coping with the abused child and other children in, say, a tutor group context?

Schools have to relate to outside agencies, and this raises questions of sharing knowledge and disclosures, about which there is much confusion. Professional networks often exclude teachers because they have no statutory responsibility in this area. So a teacher can be isolated and unable to share knowledge. Other professionals also feel teachers may become confused about what they are trying to do in working with the whole family in a child-abuse case – the teacher may feel the priority is the abused child and this may seem to be lost sight of in working with the family as a whole. There is also the issue of a child's right to privacy and how much professionals *can* reveal to others given confidentiality rules within professions.

Yet it is also seen to be difficult to help a family without operating within an open system of communication. One of the first therapeutic steps is to encourage openness in the family about what has happened.

While it may be suitable to be open within the professional network, it becomes problematic within a school with all the other children. A linked problem is the effect of disclosure on any siblings of an abused child. Much taunting goes on in schools; in addition there is the impact of disclosure through the media and on the local neighbourhood.

Finally, reference was made to the ability and sensitivity of police stations and police surgeons in dealing with sexual abuse cases. This varies greatly between areas. Ensuring the police can operate sensitively is a key element in the success of any professional network.

Discussion on paper seven:
PREDICTING AND PREDISPOSING FACTORS OF ABUSE
by Jacquie Roberts

The respondent Bernadette Jackson made the point that when children arrive at secondary school, some will have already been abused. It is therefore important for secondary schools to have close links with primary schools. Identifying and dealing with abuse has important consequences for a school's pastoral system. She described the situation in Croxteth – high unemployment, large numbers of so-called problem families, a high proportion of single-parent families, some drug abuse among young people – and what Croxteth Comprehensive was doing to help abused children through setting up effective procedures for identifying and handling abuse, and through the curriculum. Jacquie Roberts emphasised the need for professionals – social services and teachers – to work together.

Discussion

The key issue was the value and morality of predicting in which families abuse might take place and the quality of existing procedures for doing this. Checklists are often used with little real thought or discrimination. Equal weight is given to a range of family characteristics and the level of false alarms is described as phenomenal. Families are labelled high-risk in terms of potential child abuse when no real danger exists. Screening systems are neither adequate nor refined enough to provide a proper indication of risk.

There was some support for seeing a high number of false alarms as a useful safety net – better a false alarm than an abused child. Lists of characteristics could also be used as a basis for designing a system that would help to prevent child abuse.

But the main thrust of the argument in the session was that one cannot predict accurately that someone is going to abuse a child. There is 'a delusion of more knowledge than really exists' about families who abuse. One problem is an attitudinal one – expecting a family with one set of problems to develop additional ones. The term 'vulnerable' might be better used here. A further point is that not all children in a family are abused – suggesting the subtlety of causes in terms of the family environment and the problematic nature of prediction.

It was argued that preventative structures have to be general. This throws up a wide range of problems. The ethical issue for professionals, including teachers, is whether to target preventative measures on the large number of children (25/30%) usually picked up in this 'blunderbuss' method as 'at risk'. How far should families be 'pursued' if nothing happens? At what stage is it appropriate to intervene, given our lack of understanding of the reasons for abuse? Should we rather be saying that prevention is to do with the way we all look at all children and what is important is that schools develop an understanding of relationships in children and teachers?

How far can the attempt to predict become a self-fulfilling prophecy? Practitioners are often asked to assess the likelihood of a child being exposed to the risk of abuse. The question becomes how to make the best use of the data available. This self-fulfilling argument can also be used in the 'prediction' of the abused child growing into the abusing adult.

There may, though, be a danger in confusing two issues. One is the risk of oversimplifying the significance of the knowledge we have in terms of prediction; the other is whether to move away from trying to predict altogether. Is it wrong to try to predict? Must we rather be more careful and analytical about the information we have, its limitations, and how we use that information? Moreover, while there is an ethical dubiousness surrounding prediction, what of culpability in inactivity?

What is the position of people who use a checklist but don't act and abuse takes place?

The issue may rest on a simple statement: we should predict if we know how to prevent.

One preventative approach is to let families come to the professionals for help at various levels – such as the GP's surgery or local health centre. The professional network has to become sensitive enough to understand and handle this approach.

Other specific points put forward included:

- schools should develop strategies to interact more with the community.
- unemployment is not regarded as having a causal relationship with sexual abuse. Abuse among unemployed families is related more to additional stress factors.
- it is not so much a question of providing more resources but rather adjusting what you are doing already and changing attitudes and responses to the families with whom professionals are working.

Session five/paper 8
DEVELOPMENTAL PROBLEMS FOLLOWING ABUSE
by Dr Margaret Lynch

Rosina Burslem defined neglect as failing to provide adequate care for a child. Inadequacies in child rearing will develop further behavioural and developmental difficulties in a child which can be identified as the child attends school. Her school deals with three basic issues relating to the school's role in helping these families by

1 trying to influence future parenting in young people through the curriculum, integrating children from middle and upper schools into the pre-school unit as part of their life skills project.
2 influencing present parenting through home-school link units or similar set-ups, so abuse can possibly be prevented.
3 being able to identify problems that may point to abuse early on, initiating assessment, and meeting the special needs of these children.

Attached to the school is a home-school link unit which on the one hand prepares pre-school children for their entry into school and on the other provides an area that families and the community feel is their place to come to chat, work, relax and play in a supportive atmosphere.

As pregnant mums attend, work can begin at the beginning of the child-rearing chain. The unit tries to influence mothers to look after themselves in pregnancy by eating well, and not smoking so the child will be healthy. Dads are also encouraged to share the child-rearing process. In her paper, Dr Lynch suggests that ill health in parents and children is a contributory factor to child abuse. This applies especially to premature babies and babies with growth retardation.

When parents bring their babies into the centre they are encouraged to provide verbal stimulation right from the beginning. Dr Lynch states that promoting language development in children from abusive and neglectful homes should be a priority. The support and friendship of the home-school link is on a day-to-day basis so trust and confidence can be built up between teacher, parents and children before they enter school. It is important to try to show the parents we value them. Often parents have talents they can share in the unit which raises their own confidence and self-esteem. If they feel better about themselves they may be able to value their own children more. If abuse is occurring, the daily contact may enable the parent to unburden, so damage and conflict intervention can happen.

If parents and children attend regularly, the tendency for unrealistic child-rearing expectations, intolerance and rigidity so often found in abusing parents should diminish as they see that children getting messy is acceptable. They also see that it is normal for children to want to communicate verbally. Interaction between adults and children is encouraged so they can support one another.

As these activities take place in a supportive and secure atmosphere, their failure is minimised. The hope is that similar activities and communication will take place at home. Other early developmental problems can be identified in the home-school link, such as hearing difficulties, speech and sight problems, language delay and physical handicap. The failure to thrive syndrome can also be watched closely on a daily basis. Though attendance for pre-school children cannot be enforced, it is encouraged and teachers make home visits to ask about absent parents and children. This can only be done because of the trusting relationships between teachers and parents in general.

Bringing the medical services into the family unit in an informal way allows assessments to be carried out in a known environment. Speech therapists, audiologists, and health visitors are frequent visitors to the link to talk about problems and show films. In this way they build up a trusting relationship with the parents.

Dr Lynch states that abusing parents frequently make inadequate use of the medical services and do not follow up appointments. If teachers and parents and medical staff are working cooperatively, this can be carefully monitored. It is vital that parents should not feel isolated, especially if they are one-parent families.

When children come into school the underachievement and behavioural problems prevalent in abused children become noticeable. It is easy to identify children with physical scars. But children suffering from emotional or sexual abuse or neglect can also reveal themselves in behaviour that is identifiable. At one extreme, they may be aggressive, hyperactive or provocative; at the other, compliant and highly vigilant. Anti-social behaviour is most easily identified. Dr Lynch states that abused children give high rates of mental retardation at time of identification and follow-up; thus underachievement, language delay and developmental delay must be watched carefully. The lack of self-esteem and fear of failure may also be contributory factors. Showing children that they are valued can also raise their self-esteem. Displaying children's work, offering praise and giving encouragement all help to this end.

Staff should be alert to possible identifying factors; and know what procedures will take place after identification. An open climate should exist where staff can talk to other teachers about possible worries – and this policy should extend to parents who need to feel the school's head and staff are approachable so they can unburden themselves. If parents and children are to be helped and explosive situations defused, there must be an atmosphere of mutual trust between home and school and between social and other agencies.

In responding Dr Margaret Lynch said that Rosina Burslem had shown practical ways in which some of the long-term problems identified can be tackled in school, and how much people can be brought together to solve problems. It is important to look at long-term consequences of abuse on children and not just focus on the drama of disclosure and initial procedures. After things have quietened down, the children are either still in their own homes with parents who may not be physically abusing them any more but with other continuing child-rearing problems – or they may be in foster or adopted homes. These children are still at high risk for a number of different reasons: hearing and sight problems, development problems and difficulties stemming from the abuse, particularly language delay. Often the parents cannot communicate well either. There is work to be done with very small children – such as talking in groups so that they may be able to verbalise what is bothering them rather than having to act it out. People's expectations of abused children's academic achievements are too low. There is thus an urgent need to ensure that the appropriate help is given.

Discussion

The role of the community paediatrician can be very important. This professional seems to be the ideal person for making the links between home and professionals/services, partly because as a medical role, it is seen as a neutral or benign one. The community paediatrician's presence in a school is not seen as odd or inappropriate. (An example was given of community paediatricians in Leeds.)

Some thought is needed about the school health service. This is changing from the provision of routine medicals in schools to the setting up of a base in the school, responding to crises and a constant factor in the school services, able to follow children up and give advice to teachers.

Two problems highlighted were: first, lack of experience and training of community staff in paediatrics; second, the division between hospital and community and the need for a single agency offering medical care for children, whether in hospital or outside. It is important that an abused child is looked after by the same team of people – part community-based, part child development based.

There is a need for schools to give special scrutiny to some children who have passed out of the paediatric or other specialist help as years go by. Examples are those children who fail to thrive, then get a bit better, then re-emerge with educational problems around the age of five or six. Often, it is hard to ensure that their progress is reviewed once they are out of specialist medical hands.

A key point was made about the role of the school nurse. The service seems very variable. However, the Southampton Health Education Council project maintained that a lot of work was going on to improve that role and involvement.

The suggestion was made that child psychiatric clinics should be held in school, working with individual children, groups, and families. One possible effect of this might be to counter what was regarded as a strong anti-psychiatrist feeling which still exists. One teacher summed this up as teachers seeing youngsters going off to 'the psychiatrist' and coming back apparently worse.

In relation to greater on-the-spot involvement of schools, an example was given of the Newham SPS team with an emerging strategy of responsibility to work with teachers and in institutions; advising teachers in a proactive way; and doing casework in a school setting not in a clinic.

The majority of pastoral care is seen as reactive. Individual casework, for example, usually responds to crisis. We tend not to routinely go through a child's file, with the child and tutor, and look forward to the future – except perhaps at critical times like option selection. In such an environment, a child under stress but not showing symptoms of crisis, can pass quietly through the school. There were numerous calls for a 'multidisciplinary approach'.

Arnon Bentovim argued that it would be interesting if we were to do an exercise: If there were child psychotherapists in every secondary school and networks of consultation and so on, what would be the implications for staffing and costs? Add in too the extra teaching hours and secretarial and other administrative back-up and infra-structure –

much of which schools do not have. Add too the problems of fitting something like that into the timetable.

This raises the issue of being prepared to see schools as a resource for the community on a year-round basis as is happening in family centres and other types of provision. If schools close down for 13 weeks of the year, the community understandably takes the view that school is the place where you go for cognitive learning, passing exams and that sort of thing.

The medical profession does need to share more with teachers. We must hope for more co-operation in getting children to the medical services they need. A lot of time and resources can be saved if everyone is pulling in the same direction, with teachers helping to get children to medical resources.

The lack of appropriate training in pastoral care was highlighted – nine out of ten teachers had not received a day's training in this area.

Session five/paper 9
CASE MANAGEMENT AND INTER-PROFESSIONAL LIAISON
by David N Jones and John Pickett

Respondent Bernard Clarke explained that a primary aim of his school – Burleigh Community College (1450 students) – is to create a caring ethos. There is a core experience in social and personal education for everybody. But more important than that is an attempt to match what the staff say about relationships with what the relationships within the college are like. The ethos seems to work.

This paper discusses issues that are somewhat outside the ambit of the school and the experience of teachers. He felt that Peter Maher's proactive concept is a bit remote in an upper school, where it feels as though the die is cast by the time students arrive at 14 plus. It is all a bit late. The college therefore has to concentrate on the reactive. But there are a number of obstacles preventing the teachers from reacting in an appropriate and adequate way.

There seems to be a lot of ignorance in each profession about everyone else's profession. We make all sorts of assumptions about what happens in schools or about what the psychiatrists or social workers ought to be doing. For example, the paper says: 'Teachers are qualified by training and experience to identify normal and abnormal behaviour and development in children.' That is a myth. In surveys, 80% or more of teachers said they had insufficient training for their pastoral role as a tutor – let alone being able to identify children who have been abused.

The county review procedures for Bernard Clarke's area list what teachers should look out for in children in relation to abuse: lethargy, withdrawn wariness, passivity, frozen awareness. All these seem a fairly *normal* set of responses from adolescents. Teachers are told to look for similar features over drug taking and exam stress. Add to that the difficulty of working with adolescents that adults encounter – the fantasy, exaggeration and anxiety that adolescent children confront adults with. It all seems a bit unrealistic.

Another point mentioned is how teachers react when not in their own 'patch'. Some seize up, partly because they realise in a case conference that they don't know a pupil as well as they thought they did. No-one actually knows the whole child in a secondary school in anything like the way a primary teacher might. Moreover at such a conference teachers are surrounded by other professionals with a particular aura. There are problems of case conference jargon.

Another important area is how to manage the feelings aroused by the issues of abuse. Teachers receive very little preparation for dealing with other people's and their own feelings. Many teachers do not see this as a part of their role. They need emotional support, but they need a lot more before that. A related question is that of confidentiality. Teachers are probably the only professionals involved to have difficulty with this, because for them it is scarcely an issue – unlike the doctor or social worker. Teachers are only on the edge of the confidentiality dilemma and manage it in a different way. There are problems of the young, inexperienced teacher receiving a disclosure and finding the confidentiality of it a great burden.

Two further issues were raised. First, in identifying a 'key worker' in school, the implications for the school should not be overlooked. Creating key workers and specialists can reinforce the divisions between academic and pastoral and damage the notion that every teacher is responsible in these areas. All teachers in a school are eligible for being a key worker – according to the choice of the child. Finally, there is a reiteration of the need for more training.

David Jones accepted that there is a lot of unreality in what we expect of teachers. School structures are immensely complex; it isn't just a question of talking to one teacher but several about a child's behaviour – plus a pastoral care tutor and year tutor and so on. In practical terms, it is often difficult for schools to manage laid-down procedures for handling abused children.

There had been much discussion about the response to the initial crisis and the difficulties encountered by teachers, but little about 'other structures'. There is the Dutch structure – a medical model with a confidential doctor reporting; or the American model – a specialist child abuse response team responding to all cases. But David Jones had grave reservations about those. In big cities like Manchester, there are up to 10 000 professionals from different groups who might come across child abuse. Each of them cannot be allowed to pursue their own idiosyncratic response. That would be very damaging and even less predictable. On the other hand, we know that the response structures we have set up can be inhibiting and do at times cause damage to the families who are the 'victims' of the system. The challenge is to ensure our complex welfare systems cause no more damage to families than is absolutely necessary in this process. Both at Government level and among professional bodies there is an awareness of this need and progress towards this end is being made.

In one way, it boils down to a question of trust; we are untrusting people and in many ways we have good reason to be. On the positive side, there are examples of professionals working together with considerable developments in understanding and co-ordination between professionals.

Discussion

No teacher would refer a child to an outside education unit without ensuring proper knowledge of the aims and objectives of that unit. But many teachers do not fully understand the aims and objectives or recognise what help is available to them outside the school and how to use the system. So children don't get referred to the help they need.

Schools are often very complex and difficult places for people other than teachers. Social workers and psychiatrists often don't know who to talk to in a school.

Michael Marland expressed concern about assumptions that large secondary schools create major problems of communication and involvement and, by the same token, that the small primary school does not. Smallness does not automatically mean ease. Two issues underlie all this – one is managerial and the other structural. Examples were given of tutors in large schools not getting appropriate professional support – but that could as easily happen in a small school. It is also important to identify who should deal with these cases. Do we go the American way and have trained professionals as sub-specialists within the schools, or do we equip everyone with the expertise? At the moment we are fudging the issue between the two. The Blom-Cooper concept of the key worker is highly dangerous because it means the expertise will be left in the hands of just one person. It should permeate everyone's work with a team leader to whom we look for advice, instruction, support and appraisal. (The point was made that in all the current discussion about teacher appraisal there has not been one word from NUT or Sir Keith Joseph about appraisal in pastoral care.)

In relation to the vulnerability of teachers in the case conference, with unfamiliar jargon and 'strange' professionals to contend with, there is a need for someone in the school to know how to work the system.

Concern was expressed that the personal and social education element of initial teacher training courses is tending to be squeezed out – a fact that runs counter to the stance taken in this seminar.

Richard Whitfield argued that we all have been socialised in our different social and professional groups and we have a different notion or model of 'person'. The only way to tackle the problems we are discussing, in terms of providing the right services, is to ensure from the outset that there is much more commonality in the training and socialisation of professionals. It is unclear how far the different professionals will have to find new ways of working together or do actually share any of the fundamental assumptions about the nature of human potential. We have a common experience of having gone through the same education system; however, we may well have had a wide range of different experiences in going through that system.

An additional problem is that of accepting that it is proper for there to be a different professional stance from a different person. For example, teachers criticise EWOs for not being teachers – because their stances are close but not the same. The medical profession seems better able to handle this and to argue out differences without denigrating the other's stance. Teachers seem more inclined to want everyone to have the same stance. The list of professionals and their work in the Jones/Pickett chapter, does remind us that people have different powers and tasks – and therefore different stances.

John Pickett highlighted the importance of acknowledging 'sameness and difference' that exists in and between people's work, role and tasks. Many examples were given during the seminar sessions of the failure to construct a system of multi-disciplinary work which enables people to operate effectively both in areas of sameness and of difference. Teachers should ask why they are not being helped to operate effectively with families and a multi-disciplinary network of professionals. So a major issue is why these systems disable rather than enable us.

David Jones summed up by saying that the theme that has run through the session is the work with children and with families. But there is also the work with the professional network. We have to accept that such matters are complex; it requires effort and work to make the system operate. There are models around for constantly oiling the wheels of the network – reminding people of the procedures, offering personal consultation opportunities, watching to see where problems are developing, working at policy level and on individual case management. Such effort does need to be put in; to launch procedures without following them up with that sort of supportive network is to disable people significantly.

We must accept there will be tension between professionals because of statutory duties that might be in conflict – say between police and social work. That creates an appropriate tension and one must learn to live with it and not pretend it is not there.

The challenge is for teachers to work out how they feel schools can better gear themselves to the needs of children. It is not a matter of the needs of the abused child but rather the needs of children in schools. We must be sensitive to that and in the process help these very needy children who are desperately seeking our help, even if not articulating it very clearly.

Session six/paper 10
STRATEGIES FOR PREVENTION:
EDUCATION FOR
GOOD CHILD CARE PRACTICE IN OUR SCHOOLS
by Professor Richard Whitfield

Responding, Merlys Howells observed that this paper tries to focus on a school's response to not just child abuse but child abuse in a broader perspective including child development and perhaps family involvement as well. It focuses on the needs of the children and a lack of self-understanding and self-control under stress among those who have key responsibilities to provide the care.

Six points in the paper appeared particularly important:

1 the focus on good child care practice; the definition is blindingly simple – it is 'non-possessive warmth and willingness and ability to take and go on taking trouble'. But it requires great effort – day-to-day parenting and teaching and learning.

2 providing a clear framework to think about curriculum. Professor Whitfield quotes from his Aston project of evidence of the exclusion of controversial topics about personal life from the curriculum because of the dilemmas which they present to teachers. That is worrying and significant. The list provided by Whitfield seems to offer a great potential for teachers to use it in a cognitive rather than affective way which enables one to work through the series of topics without giving children an affective experience at all. The implication of that is contained in the comment that interactive teaching styles must be dominant and emphasis has to be placed on group discussion methods, role play, stimulation, and interactive assignments.

3 similarly in training colleges, by inclination tutors, along with teachers, concentrate on cognitive rather than affective learning. Training is too restricted, as much for students as for trainers.

4 even if we offer children the affective experience we think they need, (Richard Whitfield talks about adequate space being provided for participants to perceive insights at their own pace and in their own manner in relation to their unique experience at home in family life) is the school setting the most effective place for that to happen? What

about the space for those trying to encourage children to have that space?

5   the suggestion that suitably equipped personnel be available to take on leadership roles. This should not be entirely colonised by professionals – suitable lay-people should not be excluded. We should be concerned with opening access rather than restriction and exclusion. This would be an exciting development, especially for those in voluntary organisations – bringing into schools lay experience.

6   there should be a commitment to proper resourcing – the paper expressed disappointment that the DHSS and the Court impetus had been lost and had not triggered response educationally. Is this lack of will, inertia? Do parents under stress give low priority to the needs of children? Do agencies under stress give low priority also to the development of affective programmes and those demanding cooperation to make them effective? Thus, is it not so much a lack of will or inertia, but rather too much pressure on agencies and families?

Finally what is significant about this seminar is its educational focus and initiative – and the paper highlights the point that there is room for educational initiative in this area.

Richard Whitfield drew a striking analogy – that if we look at trends in our social care system, we have a bucket that is full of holes and the spillage from the holes is faster than we are able to tip in the resources and methods in order to cope and provide enough safety nets for children and others. The pressure on social services, police, teachers and voluntary agencies to care is enormous. Even if we can provide twice as much money, we know that would be insufficient. So he would emphasise proactive, primary prevention for everybody rather than looking at child abuse as a minority problem.

We suffer far too much by examining single issues but single-issue problems lie in the psycho-social wellbeing of those labelled as deviant on those single-issue problems be it delinquency, drug abuse or child abuse.

The fundamental issue is to raise the cultural status of childcare, and human care more generally and to increase the knowledge and skills we now have about these areas. As a follow up, we would thus raise its curricular priority in formal and informal educational networks.

We should provide a programme of teaching and learning in which all young people have serious opportunities to consider the parenthood option and what it might mean to them, with serious ongoing, lifelong programmes of parent and family development where the further issues of human development for themselves and their offspring can be examined and contained in a safe environment.

While most of us can nod at the notion of a caring society, our children go to school for eleven years with very little in the formal curriculum which could be said to promote their abilities to care for each other and themselves. A curriculum for caring seems a concept to be taken seriously. In the development of technological, social and built-environmental change, the concept of neighbourliness has become very tenuous. We must learn again, in ways appropriate for our society's development, some of the basic capacities that all have to care for ourselves and others.

The Aston study on preparing for parenthood funded by the DES shows no room for complacency. Urgent educational action is needed. There are serious questions and problems of mental and psycho-social health in the community which relate intimately to the ingredients we give in the formal experience of young people.

One key problem in terms of action is that child care agencies collectively give a set of incoherent messages to Government about children. Perhaps a conference like this can help to reduce that incoherence.

What we put on the menu for young people is crucial. That menu, or curriculum, does change things; the way we are, the environmental circumstances and so on. Thus, both curricular content and teaching styles are of key concern. Many of the topics listed raise deep questions in the agenda of us all, and those we teach or work with. We are at an important stage in the evolution of our social ecology; how can we ensure that a sufficient proportion of our population develop a secure, worthwhile and comfortable identity within the complexity of this ravaged and painful world.

Discussion

The paper outlines that behind personal guidance and growth, there has to be knowledge, skills and content. Exhortations on relationships are not sufficient. If you do not have knowledge, you normally fill the vacuum with false knowledge. The issue for schools is how to get this knowledge into the curriculum. The paper's section on location is particularly important and could do with extension. What is fascinating is the effect different locations have – for example, a tutor in a pastoral care situation covering some of the content compared with an economics teacher. This is a crucial question to be addressed.

How much this is a question of the actual content of the curriculum has something to do with the relationships established between teachers and young children. This relationship conveys to the child the capacity to relate to others, and to be aware of other people. We need to foster in teachers the capacity to empathise with the children – and not to resort to labelling.

Problems for professionals of lack of time, being overstretched, coping with cuts, developing frenetic styles of management, were all discussed. A request was made to take the label, 'preparation for parenthood' out of the curriculum for schools and keep using the term personal and social education. This was proposed partly on the basis that if children and young people are helped to get their current situation right, then that augurs well for future situations and relationships. However, Richard Whitfield goes only part of the way on this as the parenthood option needs to be flagged in some way. Personal and social education should at some point give serious attention to that issue and the understanding of a child in their own family environment; from here they can begin to understand their own needs and ways of relating to new significant other people outside the family. Implicit in the paper is the fact that many of the activities in the curriculum will not have the tag of parenthood when young people come to deal with them. It is a convenient label for planning purposes only.

What Richard Whitfield is talking about is the successful nurturing of children into adults; one then sees disordered children against that background. Two points are raised: the paper is essentially interventionist, and the starting point of that intervention is still fairly fluid (eg will we get compulsory nursery education and can we build programmes into that; what about under-twos who are at risk?). Is training in planning and management rather than education in life processes important for those who are trying to design curricula?

Richard Whitfield's answer is a qualified yes; but in planning and management he would not want to lose sight of intrinsic aims of what the plans are, and there is a risk in that. We need to keep in mind the five aims listed in his paper (see pages 169-189).

In all this, however, it is important to take account of current conditions of teachers and the difficulty of introducing new developments into schools.

If we are going to make progress on these kinds of issues, it will involve a reworking of the contract in schools with parents. The ideas put forward cannot operate without negotiation with parents – they cannot be imposed. There must be a reworking of the relationship in terms of who is responsible for what in the upbringing of children and questions of who is going to provide the care – and when. For parents too are under pressure, and it is worth remembering that parents and other carers around the home are a child's first and most important and continuing educators. Their efforts make teachers' tasks in school more easy or more difficult.

There are often feelings among parents that professionals have all the answers and they do not. Some feel that professionals are too remote and would not understand parents' problems and feelings. Both views raise barriers between the two.

How can people in the community be more effective in carrying out the work described in the paper? One answer might be to allow more people into school to help curricular planning and provision. This can only enrich the teacher's role, and of all the things discussed here it is the easiest and requires least money.

Some parenthood courses are not well planned and tend to 'turn some children off'. Adolescents have various concerns and emotions not always compatible with caring for young children (a point raised in the previous session). They are more concerned with creating new identities for themselves. Are there more creative and motivating ways in which children can be enabled to experiment with caring for themselves without putting them off other forms of caring?

Richard Whitfield does not accept, necessarily, that you cannot get adolescent boys interested in the care of babies and young children. One of the developmental stages of adolescence we do next to nothing about is preparing young people to leave home – a crucial step in terms of development of adult relationships and marriage. The question of timing and interest is perhaps the least of our problems when you think of the other things we try to teach them. Young people do find this subject interesting if it is not treated like a first-year sociology or psychology course – it can be spellbinding material for youngsters.

Should there be a more family-based approach here? There is a danger of developing what was described as a front-end model. Young people should have a matching experience in their own family in order to reinforce what is going on in schools. This relates to Merlys Howells' fourth point. Is there indeed a case for starting with the current parents rather than the children?

Richard Whitfield believed that it is a case of not only . . . but also. Work is going on in family centres and elsewhere to try to make non-threatening links with family situations. If there were more encouragement for parents to come into schools and have a legitimate say, the invitation might start to flow both ways. There will then be a more relaxed parent-teaching relationship in which the problems of development and learning that arise in the home will not be shut behind the front door in a claustrophobic privacy which sooner or later bursts out in some form of difficult behaviour of the parents or the children. We are a long way from having that kind of 'permeation' – and it must begin by teachers recognising that the home environment is the foremost educator, which formal external school systems encourage and develop from.

Whitfield gave an example of work in Nuffield maths where it was found that in performance in maths and other school-based subjects, the variation in achievement loads in British society depends about 20 times as much on home variables as on school variables. Even looking at it from very narrow educational perspectives, if we want to raise reading levels and maths scores and so on we will not be able to do much about that until we can give children basic motivation and a sense of wellbeing about the future. Then other questions of child abuse will begin to be seen in a better and more central perspective. If such issues are seen as marginal, deviant problems, then we undermine the whole policy question – which is crucial. We cannot make many changes unless we tackle the policy question and encourage politicians to take seriously the White Papers and reports and take action on them.

Discussion with Carolyn Okell Jones and Michelle Elliott

Carolyn Okell Jones: If, like us, you are exposed to the short-term and long-term psychological damage to both boys and girls in terms of child sexual abuse, partly for one's own sanity one has to get into thinking about prevention. And to give oneself a sense of hope because this kind of work is so depressing. I am thinking of the concept of prevention in two different ways – in the sense of trying to empower children and to provide them with accurate information and skills to protect themselves from ever being abused; and also in the sense of facilitating disclosures of abuse and ensuring it does not re-occur.

Sexually abused children experience great guilt and confusion, together with the burden of secrecy and silence that they carry – for example, through fear of breaking up their families, of getting people they know and love into trouble, of not being believed or of being blamed, and also not having the language and the words to explain and describe what has actually happened. All these things are, in my view, as damaging as the actual sex acts themselves. It is the context, not only the sexual act, that matters.

There is no doubt in my mind that the introduction of prevention programmes in schools comprising a range of materials – and I underline that – is vital. The video *Kids can say no* is just one modest attempt, just one tool, as part of a prevention programme. Certainly, I think its effective use with children is very contingent, of course, on how ready and well-prepared adults are to deal with the emotive subject of child sexual abuse, the kinds of issues the video raises, and the inevitable disclosures of past or current abuse that it provokes.

A video is a quick way of getting to a lot of people. It is the most effective way of having people well trained and getting in to see kids. But a video is a tool, not a substitute for well-trained people.

There are limitations to the preventative approach. Nor must we leave the burden of protection or prevention on the children themselves. That is an objection some people raise to some of our work. We should not put the full responsibility on to the kids. I think we will ultimately try to provide preventative strategies to stop potential child molesters – to figure out who they are and get them to come forward for help.

A lot has happened in the child abuse prevention area since we sought support for the first British video in this field in 1984. Public and professional awareness that child sexual abuse does represent a major public mental health problem have increased enormously – even in the past two years. It is reflected in the exponential rise in referrals to all kinds of professionals; and the much more open debate about the subject and media coverage of the problem.

As a result some people have criticised us recently and said that our approach in *Kids can say no* is perhaps a rather cautious approach to the subject. The video perhaps is not explicit enough. This is in marked contrast to the shocked reaction from a lot of people in 1984 about even making a video for kids. We did come up against an awful lot of ambivalence and official resistance – mainly from public and official agencies and professional groups – rather than from parents, on the whole.

We experienced real and prolonged reluctance to fund such a venture and to be publicly associated with it. We were never allowed to acknowledge the source of funding for our video. This is a kind of mirror image – in which people who work in the field feel dirty in the same way that victims and perpetrators do.

There is also a deep concern that the child care system will be overloaded if prevention programmes do lead to more and earlier disclosures, plus the issue of staff not being sufficiently prepared and of cuts in resources. Then there is the outrage, or at the very least extreme concerned reactions, that such programmes will disturb children, march them out of innocence and make them unduly anxious, suspicious or frightened of their parents and people close to them.

I hope we have achieved what we set out to do – which was to make the second in a series of child safety programmmes (the first one is on water safety) and that we haven't frightened children unnecessarily. And here is a very important point – American colleagues have fully acknowledged to me that there are some very negative side-effects of some of the prevention programmes in the States at the moment. Many of them are laudable but some are injecting such fear and hysteria into adults, parents and children that I worry about destroying kids' basic trust and also their future mental health. Compounding this dilemma in the States is an ever-increasing commercialism and investment in child abuse prevention which is virtually creating a new growth industry, and which I very much hope we will avoid in this country.

Finally, a very quick report on the progress of *Kids can say no*. We launched it in October; we put it out as a pack. We didn't get any backing from the DES or DHSS; we didn't know how to distribute it – so the first thing we did was to put Michelle (Elliott)'s book and teaching notes in with it. This was to make sure that people didn't think you just put the video on to keep a class quiet during a wet afternoon. We have sold over 500 copies since October and on the whole the reviews of the video have been very favourable. We reckon about 20 000 adults have seen it. It has also been used very creatively with parent-teacher associations, preparing foster and adoptive parents for taking in sexually abused children, residential care workers and so on. The people who haven't seen it are kids. While clearly there is a need for time to prepare before showing the video, we are worried there is such fear and reluctance about showing it. This has to do with the question of people's own biographies – you do get an enormous amount of disclosures of past abuse that people are still hurting from. That is also impeding people's ability to use the material because they haven't come to terms with the subject themselves.

Another issue I would like to raise is where male teachers come into this. Do they feel comfortable about using material like the video since the majority of perpetrators are men?

One of the things we have done is to raise more money from our original source to make a short training film to try to guide and support teachers. We also have a modest evaluation programme on the use of *Kids can say no*. Richard Whitfield emphasised the difficulty of this kind of evaluation. At its simplest what we are interested in is; will careful presentation of things like the video, plus ongoing discussion in the classroom, really help children resist adolescent or adult perpetrators? How long will they retain the message – especially young children – and how often do the messages need to be reinforced? Have we even got the message right in the film?

We didn't use explicit sexual language in the film – not because of being cautious – but rather because we felt there was such a variation in the language children (and adults) use for private parts and activities that it would be better to keep explicit language out. Moreover, there would have been an uproar in making the film if we had used such language.

Finally, although we have a lot of procedures, there is still a need to try to co-ordinate services and make sure that sexually abused children who disclose are heard and believed, and that they and their families get all the help they need.

Michelle Elliott: The difference in Peter Maher's educational overview – between an informed statement based on factual experience which is intended to provoke discussion as opposed to a misinterpreted statement which fosters misunderstanding – is exactly what we are trying to get away from in what we are doing. And I would like to talk with you about some of the statements that were made in that. I have spent 12 years working with children in the classroom on the prevention of abuse – although this has not gone as far as talking about people that they knew. The last two years of intensive work led to the launch of *Kidscape*.

Two years of research has been going on in schools, at their invitation. We based this on several premises – the first being that affection is absolutely vital for all children; and in school programmes it must always be remembered that up to 80 or 90% of the children we are talking to have never had a sexually abusive experience – and probably won't. If you do not link what you are doing with children to the vast common ground of children who have not had this experience, then you will lose what you are doing.

We also said that under no circumstances should any child ever be made distrustful of adults. And I feel/fear that we [collective 'we'] have been doing that for years by warning them about 'strangers'. After the first 2000 children I started to ask children what they thought a stranger was. They think strangers are ugly, have beards, wear glasses, look like Captain Hook. I am not a stranger because I am nice. Go and ask children what a stranger is and then decide what we have to warn them about.

Personal safety is the key element we are working with not 'sexual abuse'. Safety is a whole concept and for that reason I have a little trouble handling child assault prevention programmes on their own. I think they are very much a school curricular package. I can understand why they are there – for discussion purposes – but I do think it is very much a personal safety issue.

Parental involvement and response is absolutely vital and must be built into any kind of programme based on safety. No materials for implementing any programme with children should be produced or used until parents, teachers, EWOs, school doctors and nurses, social workers and health visitors are involved and consulted.

It is vital that children's concerns should be included – hence questions about people like strangers and what they are actually worried about.

Schools have to be aware of the existing procedures – if there are any – and I can tell you, having been in many schools all over the country, there is a great deal of confusion about that. Where there are no existing procedures schools need to be given a form to help set up a line of communication. Teachers must have discussion with regard to their role in disclosure. There is no substitute at all for talking with children.

The programme must not be imported and imposed on people. I share Carolyn's concern for what is happening in the USA. What we do is to evolve with and involve key people in agencies, as we go along, discussing what will happen in the programme. We talked with 4000 children and 9000 adults; we had over 3000 adult responses to workshops and we had all the children's feedback. We were only doing this at the invitation of schools – we never sought anyone to ask us in. We said to one or two parents, we are here, we are available – and it grew from there.

Every parent and child must be given the option of not being involved. In the pilot project, out of 4000 children, 6 parents decided not to allow their children to be involved. No child ever decided not to participate or to leave any workshop – and to our knowledge no-one was upset by the lesson. (I say to our knowledge because we asked teachers and parents to come back to us if any child showed signs of distress.) That was important. We were very conservative. We wanted to teach about children's right to be safe, not about bits of their body. We did ask teachers if they wanted to be involved. And out of over 200 teachers, only one declined.

As I said, we erred on the side of being conservative. It is essential to realise that you cannot go out and clone individuals to come from outside the system. In America there are 177 prevention programmes – including some with people dressed up as bears coming in and talking, along with a lot of other very strange happenings.

We decided it was absolutely essential to work within the existing structures and authorities and to provide training for people to decide, within their own communities, how they wanted to implement programmes. We have now developed materials based on those two years' experience of 4000 children in 14 schools, one large play association, and a lot of scout troops.

Plenary session:
WORKING GROUPS REPORT BACK

Group one/two Susan Leyden

We became aware that throughout the conference there had been confusion among ourselves over terminology about the agencies and structures we were talking about. For example, some people in our group did not know what area review committees were; some were unclear about what was meant by pastoral care and how secondary and primary schools organised it.

As a group we felt that what had to be done to raise awareness is to inform schools and teachers about the structures that exist within their own authority, what responsibilities the various organisations have and what are the means of accessing resources. That was a fundamental body of knowledge that should go into schools.

Second, we talked briefly about questions of identification and reporting. We did feel there should be a clear structure for people to follow and this should be known within schools. But beyond that, there needs to be a climate within which teachers feel willing and able to report, and feel supported in their reporting.

This led on to a discussion about supervision and support, picking up the issue of whether we need key people with more knowledge, experience, expertise and skills to provide mutual staff support. We looked at models of support that exist outside the teaching profession, where people who work with others are supervised in this way and have chances of discussing how they do it, how they manage it, the ways they go about things and whether modifications are needed. There is a great lack in schools of this kind of professional supervision and consultation, on a clinical model that exists in other agencies.

On the issue of key people, there was no clear agreement about whether we thought key people – in terms of responsibilities for child abuse – were necessary. The consensus was that it was *not* right. But we did feel there should be named or key people who at least had a body of knowledge and experience, to act as staff consultants.

We looked at the process of dissemination and on this it was felt essential to have the co-operation and commitment of the head and senior management. It is extremely hard work evolving any kind of professional development without the consent and support of the head.

All agreed that it is very difficult to get parents involved, willing and confident to join in any of these activities in school. We recognise this to be a problem.

We looked at dissemination across agencies and how an effective exchange of information and training could be set up. It is sometimes difficult to be effective in sharing experience and expertise in a multidisciplinary team – and there may be other models we could look at, such as different agencies, different experts coming into school to answer teachers' specific questions about an area of experience – eg paediatricians holding workshops.

NAPCE may well have a role in dissemination through its information base. For example, we recognise that area review committees have different procedures across the country and it would be valuable to have an inventory of national procedures – collating them to look at differences and enabling people in various districts to see how others operated. (Many people here did not know what NAPCE was! – so a publicity campaign in schools might be appropriate.)

On training we need to think about who is going to do this and how. The sheer statistical reality is that we cannot reach every teacher if we take an outside agency model for training. We considered the cascade model of training the trainers in order to get that into schools. It was recognised that whatever training does take place it has to do so within school, thus responding to the particular dynamics of each school. So we are looking at the need to build up the expertise of some people in school.

People are now building up materials, resources, activities and inventories for use in workshops, one-day courses and seminars – and perhaps we need to bring these together and make them more widely available.

Group three Kate Torkington

We took a very different line from group one in that we concentrated much more on the proactive idea rather than the reactive. As a group we were wholly committed to the notion of inter-professional training. While child abuse was seen as a possible area for this, we felt it was only part of a wider area of common concern that might be labelled something like *Parenthood education* or *Family life education*.

Such inter-professional training should take place at both initial and in-service level. At initial training level we recognised with some dismay that there is no initial training for teachers in their pastoral role. If we accept that the key person in the pastoral role is the form teacher – and most teachers are form teachers – this seems extraordinary, to say the least. And if the esssence of pastoral care is the recognition of the whole child and not merely the cognitive dimension, then this part of the teacher training could combine with the work of other professionals on shared issues, insights and sensitivity. Other professionals – social workers, health workers, EWOs, educational psychologists, and so on – have specifics in their training which are held in common, such as human growth and development, study of the family, group work training and so on. All seem to be part of what could be a common core course at initial training level.

We feel that initial training is a desirable focus but it is going to be a great deal harder than the development of inter-professional *in-service* training. However, we can see a number of developments already occurring in in-service training and there is room for many more.

The way teachers were trained was an important issue for us. Teacher training concentrates considerably on didactic methods, and this is mostly the case for other professional training too. The developments in in-service teacher training which emphasise the affective dimension – experiential and active learning – such as active tutorial work programmes and the Open University health education/family life education in schools programme, seem a good starting point for bringing professionals together. This has already started with the OU project.

Another of our ideas is to encourage more involvement by other professionals in the planning and development of social education programmes rather than their one-off appearance at points in the programme. From such involvement inter-professional training courses might emerge.

An essential part of training is the development of a continuous support system. Other professionals, especially social workers, were amazed that there was so little support in schools for teachers, not only on child abuse issues but for the whole of the stressful part of their role.

Discussion:
A point raised by Michael Marland was that if there is a curriculum it has to be planned, and there is no training for the planners. This is interesting because apart from £73 million spent on the supporters in schools, there is the very low level of advisory and inspectorial support. There is a pastoral care element in some initial training. But the NAPCE survey shows that 87% of teachers said they had no coverage of pastoral care at all in their initial training. It was pointed out that the education welfare services can do a lot in this area of support for teachers.

Southampton initial teacher training project was given as an example of how things are changing. The project focuses on health education and is working with teacher training institutions all over the country. Already some have health education awareness days and are establishing health education as part of the core curriculum. An example was given of form tutors visiting homes and talking with parents there to see what sort of set-up the children come from.

A useful model of supervision, familiar with social workers, is the timetabled surgery whereby your colleague meets with you as supervisor for a regular session, not just when the need arises – and this works right through the school hierarchy.

There were queries about the role of deputy heads in support provision; and the potential danger of teachers having to report problems to senior member of staff who may also have to evaluate the teacher, write references and so on.

Group four Andrew Lockhart

We had a wide-ranging discussion on policy. We looked first at the school itself – in two directions: curriculum and structure. On curriculum the group felt we should have a broad-brush approach with a cluster of social, personal and health education. We did not want to engage in picking out narrow points to focus on – specifics such as child abuse, drug abuse, parenting and so on. On structure, following the broad brush approach, we could not identify any one organisational pattern. We took the flexible approach, that it is best to develop structural change according to the needs of school and community.

We looked also at policy at LEA level. Education authorities should offer a broad policy framework. We sidestepped the discussion of what the relative powers should be of LEAs, governors, headteachers and DES. We noted there is an Education Bill going through parliament by which every LEA must publish policy guidelines on the curriculum. It is important for this conference and NAPCE to put forward what pressure they can to ensure that such policy statements cover not just the academic but also the pastoral curriculum.

Another element of policy at LEA level is the business of networking or multi-agency working. One model is the agreed syllabus on religious education enshrined in the 1944 Act. This requires LEAs to set up a standing conference which is multi-agency – or, in the case of religion, multi-faith – representing community, professionals and so on. This may be a useful model to follow in a multi-agency procedure.

Third, we looked at the DES. We felt it would be helpful if the DES ensure, through administrative memoranda and so on, that LEAs, in submitting their curriculum guidelines, did include statements and policies on the pastoral curriculum. With the new funding arrangements for the in-service education of teachers – and this may apply to other professionals in the education field – the LEA will be charged with submitting a plan for in-service training for all its staff in education. It may be possible to extend that to inter-disciplinary training. But here again is a new and unique opportunity – LEAs being required by the DES to submit training programmes which will be specifically funded. This is an excellent chance to try to persuade the DES to ensure the categories that go to the Department are not narrowly vocational and concern significantly personal development. The DES could use its planning powers of in-service training to offer a co-ordinated and broad inter-disciplinary in-service programme.

The fourth area is inter-agency co-operation. We talked of structural problems, boundary problems between health, education, social services, voluntary agencies and so on, the divisions that exist between and within these organisations – with the need to come to terms with those divisions. Two possibilities were put up – at national level, perhaps NAPCE could try to engage in some political lobbying for a parliamentary committee or a minister charged with responsibility for the family, child or whatever to focus thought and resources at national level; second, LEAs could set up committees to look at the welfare of families and children, or inter-disciplinary groups where people with access to resources and staffing can try to develop effective local networks for support.

Discussion:
Pastoral care, counselling and tutorial work are integral to CPVE courses, according to their guidelines, but these courses are very vocationally-orientated and aspects like parenting or human relationships are not an essential part of some of the specific vocational courses. If we are not careful, pupils can go on a CPVE course at 16 plus and not experience pastoral care with their peers. Thus parenting for A-level students will be dealt with separately from non-parenting for vocation-

ally specific CPVE courses. The effect of the MSC may be to make even worse the already low level of the pastoral provision for the group tutorial work preparing people for this.

A further point was the relationship of guidelines to individual teachers. Even where LEAs have policy guidelines about the way teachers should deal with child abuse, these are not generally known nor understood by the teaching profession. There is a lack of dissemination and that is a matter of concern. We should put down a marker that this seems to be a problem in some areas.

Nottinghamshire, said Susan Leyden, is trying to address this situation by getting together a multi-professional team to draw up a process and resources for schools – so schools can handle their own examination of the procedures. The LEA has made a statement that it sees this as part of every teacher's professional development, and is building it into their own extensive in-service training programme.

Richard Whitfield commented that if there were some overall minister who was able to oil the relations between government departments, that could have the effect at local level of having a more unified management structure which had health, social services and education people interlocked much more tightly within a management framework. In addition, the geographical distance between health districts and education authority areas and social service sub-patches also militate against co-operative working.

Colin Smart expressed a word of caution about seeing a minister for the family or for children as any kind of solution. For example, health and social services colleagues in the DHSS hardly ever meet and liaise. Michael Marland pointed out that of his three school sites, two are in one health district, the third in a different one. Colin Stern pointed out that the DHSS now has a separate 'region' which is responsible solely for training and is prepared to fund initiatives for all sorts of things.

Group five

We chose not to report back because ours was an exploratory and wide-ranging discussion. However, several points did repeatedly surface and we thought it worth summarising those for people's interest.

First, everyone saw the value of personal safety programmes both throughout the school system (viewed as a continuum across the whole age-range) and in work outside the school system. It was important to arrive at some closer definition or analysis of the skills needed to promote and support personal safety work and in planning training. Introducing such programmes would also raise a lot of issues beyond the immediate scope of the programme, to do with the whole philosophy of children's rights and self-determination. This would change very dramatically the teacher/parent/child set of relationships.

That has to be borne in mind from the start, because it would have a lot of implications for training and about how people would feel about being asked to take on this work and being trained for it.

Specifically in respect of training, a support system for the trainers needs to be identified and developed before introducing the work, and training given in the task of presenting these materials for children. The trainers need to be able to cope with their own feelings and with the aftermath from children and families who experience the materials. This would be quite a difficult task because, for example, few schools appear to have an effective in-school tutorial system that might provide a basic system within which to introduce this work.

One important aspect is that teachers actually using the material would have to have developed a fair amount of self-knowledge and to be able to explore feelings in their own development as people and parents. This has a lot of implications for the style of support and training they receive – a complete rethink of traditional teacher training – its approach and method – was vital.

The introduction of personal safety programmes could start with very young children – perhaps as young as three, when children are beginning to talk and communicate easily about this area. There are indications that parents are willing for this to happen, but there is still considerable resistance from institutions and professionals who would be responsible for developing the work. Work could be done with young parents outside the school setting. More thought would have to be given on how you work through play and the skills needed for this. Lots of material is available to start this off but it needs to be drawn together.

Discussion

Now getting many referrals from day nurseries and family centres of children under five. These units are easier about dealing with children's sexuality. This is a point where you may reach young parents who are more willing to talk about their own experiences.

Group six

The group's discussion was divided into two. Our brief was the curriculum input. We talked about the curriculum as it is – everything that happens in a school is the curriculum. And if one is in a residential establishment everything that goes on is part of its curriculum. All areas of that curriculum must be planned. New staff coming in must know what the curriculum is and how they play their part in it. We talked about the fragmented role of the teacher – a form tutor, a subject specialist, an administrator, a parent counsellor. Then we talked about the personal and social education input to the curriculum – which should cover a very wide range of areas to include parentcraft, life skills, personal relationships, in addition to everyday matters such as making choices, self-esteem, personal care. This should extend right through the education system, even beyond further education. Whatever programme is set up needs constant appraisal and attention.

We then discussed the potential for a programme of child safety curriculum development work in schools. There should be a development of work in an inner city area and a shire county, using a post-curriculum package in schools as a two-year project. A funded group could spend one year developing and trying out material in schools; in the second year evaluating material with a view to wider dissemination. This would work with teachers, educational psychologists, social workers, parents and voluntary agencies. There would be cooperation, discussion and counselling across the board. This would be an enormous development project with wide-ranging effects, should it take off. It would have a tremendous impact on inter-professional relationships.

We discussed whether this was now the right time to put in motion a formal process to form an advisory group to focus on further curriculum development and INSET – particularly in the area of child safety.

Discussion

We did talk about the potential for funding training for teachers and saw this as a key element which mirrors concern about the new arrangements from April 1987 in terms of the way in-service training will be funded. There are two possible courses of action – one is to persuade local authorities that this area of work ought to form part of their in-service programme for teachers, focusing on those LEAs where this is carried out in detail. Second, and perhaps more influential potentially, 10% of that budget can be earmarked by the DES for particular types of work. In order to qualify for that money LEAs have to submit in-service training programmes in, for example, maths education. If we could persuade the DES that *this* area of work is also a priority this could have an influence on all LEAs, rather than just a handful.

General summing-up discussion:

How far did teachers find the work presented here too theoretical to apply at ground level and how far did they find it useful and usable in the classroom environment?

- One view was that some of the discussion was far removed from the classroom situation – although much was gained nevertheless.
- One came with very little knowledge but acquired a lot of ideas about how to raise awareness and how more links with other professionals might be established.
- Spending time here with different groups of professionals was of great value although perhaps there were too few teachers especially from primary and infant sectors.

The nature of this event was not that we should all come here to gain professional expertise, which we would go away and use on Monday morning. Rather, it aimed to draw together representatives of different groups and to strike a balance. There were some gaps (*eg* health visitors) but it was a group of people with wide experience in education – and what we were trying to do was to tease out the very difficult area of the educational implications.

NOTES ON CONTRIBUTORS

Peter Maher is Principal of Harold Hill Community School in the London Borough of Havering. His previous posts have included Deputy Headships in Newham and Essex, Head of Mathematics Department, Head of House and Head of 6th Form. NAPCE was founded in 1981 and Peter was elected onto its first National Executive Committee. Since 1983 he has been the Association's Honorary National Secretary.

Dr Eileen Vizard was Senior Registrar in Child Psychiatry at The Hospital for Sick Children, Great Ormond Street before taking up a post recently in the Schools Psychological Service in Newham. Eileen has worked for 12 years as a psychologist and in her 4 years at Great Ormond Street specialised in child abuse within the Child Sexual Abuse Treatment Project and the Child Care Consultation Team.

Susan Creighton is Research Officer for the NSPCC and author of *Trends in Child Abuse* which offers a statistical analysis of data from the NSPCC child abuse registers. After a period in teaching and a Masters degree in Child Development, Susan worked in New York at the Albert Einstein College of Medicine and then at Surrey University doing research.

Dr Colin Stern is a Consultant Paediatrician at St Thomas' Hospital in London where he treats abused children as a routine part of his work. He has published papers on paediatrics, immunology and neonatology, as well as the biology of genetics of reproduction. Colin is a member of the action group for London as support for parents of children with disabilities.

Dr Arnon Bentovim is Consultant Child and Family Psychiatrist to the Hospital for Sick Children, Great Ormond Street, and the Tavistock Clinic, London. He also practises at the Institute of Family Therapy (London) and from 1986 has been Chair of the Institute. His international reputation and his extensive work in this area make him one of the most authoritative figures in the field.

Dr Kevin Browne is Lecturer in Medical Psychology at the Department of Psychology at the University of Leicester and an Honorary Research Fellow at Surrey University. He has researched and published extensively, particularly in the area of mother/infant interactions in abusing families.

Dr Sara Saqi was Research Fellow at Surrey University on an MRC funded research project into interactions within abusing families before embarking on a two-year clinical psychology training course at the Institute of Psychiatry, London.

Rolene Szur   began work as a child psychotherapist at Hounslow and then at the Hospital for Sick Children, Great Ormond Street, later combining this with work at the Tavistock Clinic, London and in Rome. Rolene is an internationally known figure in this area of work and has a range of publications on the subject.

Helen Kenward   is a Professional Staff Officer with Northampton Social Services and her responsibility is for staff training and consultation in child sexual abuse training. Helen started life as a teacher and then moved to residential work including two years running an adolescent girls' reception unit. She has also worked as a manager of a family centre, specialising in working with high-risk families and sexual abuse.

Detective Chief Inspector Richard Buller is a member of the Northamptonshire Police Force and is the Police Child Abuse Liaison Officer for Northampton.

David N Jones   is General Secretary of the British Association of Social Workers, a post he took up after working for the NSPCC between 1974-1985. Prior to that he was with Nottinghamshire Social Services Department with a special interest in child care.

John Pickett   is Regional Child Care Officer (North) for the NSPCC in northern England and Northern Ireland. John has been General Secretary since 1978 of the British Association for the Study and Prevention of Child Abuse and Neglect (BASPCAN) and has been a member of several committees of enquiry into child abuse fatalities. He is an author of considerable note in this field.

Professor Richard Whitfield is Reader in Advanced Studies at the Gloucestershire College of Arts and Technology, a post he took up after being Director of Child Care with Save The Children Fund. His distinguished academic career includes posts at Leeds University, Cheltenham College, Cambridge University and Faculty of Education. While he was Professor of Education and Head of Department of Educational Enquiry at Aston University he directed the *Preparation for Parenthood in the Secondary School Curriculum* project which was a four year project funded by the DES. He was elected Emeritus Professor at Aston in 1983, is Visiting Professor of Education at Moorhead State University, Minnesota, USA and in the Management Centre of Aston University.

Rick Rogers   is a freelance journalist and editor and was reporter at the Seminar. As well as being author of books and articles Rick regularly contributes to the *Guardian*, the *TES*, *Arts Express* and *Design Magazine* and is Education Consultant to Thames Television News. He was Education Correspondent for *The New Statesman* for 5 years.

Index